Praise for *Case Studies in Multicultural Counseling and Therapy*

Translating theory into practice is a challenge for every school of clinical orientation. This casebook has succeeded by focusing upon elements of process in multicultural counseling and therapy to give us a rich resource of conceptual and practical aids to assist the teacher, trainee, and practitioner in making a stepwise transition from cultural knowledge to practice competencies.

> Anderson J. Franklin, Ph.D., Honorable David S.
> Nelson Professor of Psychology and Education, Boston College
> Lynch School of Education

Anchored in our latest knowledge and research regarding cross-cultural counseling and spanning the whole spectrum of diversity, this collection of multicultural case studies serves as a wonderful companion to Sue and Sue's *Counseling the Culturally Diverse* and fills a gap for rich and contextualized cases illustrating the complex tapestry of our clients' lives.

> Frederick T.L. Leong, Ph.D., Professor of Psychology
> and Psychiatry; Director of the Consortium for
> Multicultural Psychology Research

Case Studies in Multicultural Counseling and Therapy offers a rich narrative of therapeutic engagement with diverse clients highlighting the complexities of intersecting dimensions of culture. Such emotionally-gripping cases facilitate a soul penetrating capacity for expanding cultural schema and increasing cultural empathy among mental health professionals and trainees.

> Michael Mobley, Ph.D., Associate Professor,
> Salem State University

Having taught Multicultural Counseling for more than 10 years, Derald Wing Sue, Miguel Gallardo, and Helen Neville have finally answered students' most oft-repeated question, *"How do I apply this knowledge to my clinical practice?"* Based on real life cases, contributors offer a practical guide for students and instructors alike who are committed to enhancing multicultural competence. This is a must-have resource for every current and future mental health professional!

> Lisa B. Spanierman, Ph.D., Associate Professor,
> McGill University

Case Studies in Multicultural Counseling and Therapy

Case Studies in Multicultural Counseling and Therapy

Edited by

Derald Wing Sue
Miguel E. Gallardo
Helen A. Neville

Library of Congress Cataloging-in-Publication Data

Case studies in multicultural counseling and therapy / edited by Derald Wing Sue, Miguel E. Gallardo, Helen A. Neville.

    pages cm
   Includes bibliographical references and index.
   ISBN 978-1-118-48755-6 (pbk.)
   ISBN 978-1-118-71583-3 (ebk.)
   ISBN 978-1-118-52852-5 (ebk.)

   1. Cultural psychiatry--Case studies. 2. Cross-cultural counseling—Case studies. 3. Ethnopsychology—Case studies. 4. Clinical competence—Case studies. I. Sue, Derald Wing, editor of compilation. II. Gallardo, Miguel E., editor of compilation. III. Neville, Helen A., editor of compilation.

   RC455.4.E8C378 2013
   616.89—dc23

                                 2013011558

Printed in the United States of America

10 9 8 7 6 5 4 3 2 1

Contents

Foreword

The challenge of achieving congruence between the conceptual templates theorists develop and the practical strategies that result from the application of those constructs and principles to counseling and therapy, is a difficult one indeed. Yet, it is precisely this challenge that must be mastered if clinicians hope to find a broader utility for the ideas they develop that extend beyond the traditional or virtual library bookshelves. Derald Wing Sue, Miguel Gallardo and Helen Neville have mastered this challenging task, and their latest contribution, as a free standing text or an accompaniment to the hugely successful *Counseling The Culturally Diverse: Theory and Practice* (Sue & Sue, 2013), is a magnificent resource that will help create a greater bridge of understanding between the academic, research, and applied domains of the mental health professions.

What this text does so beautifully is bridge the gap between aspiration and actualization; between what a clinician strives to do and what he or she is able to deliver within the midst of a therapeutic encounter. And, it does so with a cultural flavor that is easy to follow, interpret, and understand, taking into account the complexities that reside where various elements of culture (race, ethnicity, age, gender, physical ability, sexual orientation, and religion) intersect and sometimes collide. For in my mind, that is the essence of congruence and that is what this text at its core represents.

These case studies provide a window into the heart of a challenging circumstance. Unlike raw theory, case studies provide a context for situations clinicians confront. Using elements like history, personal background, elements of culture that must be attended to, and an outline of other strategies that might have been employed prior to the pending intervention, they help to inform and shape the narratives of theoretical relevance. That is the space that is so critical, where clinicians decide what measure of convergence and divergence to employ when anchoring their intervention in the core principles of a theory and/or research.

Upon first glance, creating bridges of understanding between theory and practice seems like a simple enough task, and yet, if it were that routine, I suspect that the profession would be ripe with clinicians who were all masters at their craft. We would have no concern about misdiagnosis or mistreatment. There would be less talk about cultural competence and incompetence. And more importantly, the broader public who rely on professional counselors, psychologists, psychiatrists, clinical social workers, and therapists would be better served by those who desire to render quality care, but for whatever reason, fall short of their own as well as client expectations.

Decades ago, as a young graduate student, I recall studying the works and theories of those who were considered the "giants" in the field, including Freud, Jung, Adler, Skinner, Horney, Perls, Ellis, and Rogers. As each theorist outlined their set of constructs and principles, they helped to create a conceptual template that informed each of our practice with an intellectual roadmap that detailed elements of counseling and therapy, like the nature of humanity, the etiology of client distress, how and why people changed as a function of interventions from that theory's perspective, and in most cases, the role of the clinician/therapist in addressing whatever debilitation a client was struggling with. For many clinicians, however, the intellectual understanding of the theory was less of a challenge than the ability to operationalize that set of constructs into therapeutic practice. This was analogous to what Carl Rogers described as the difference between the "real" self and the "ideal" self, and it was that gap that created the most profound sense of incongruence clinicians and lay public alike struggled with.

Compounding the dilemma of achieving maximum congruence was the fact that so many of the theories were anchored in assumptions that were conspicuous by their degree of cultural sterility, particularly when it came to people of color, women, and others whose uniqueness was rarely, if ever, accounted for within the confines of a particular theory or orientation. As a consequence, there was an intellectual explosion of sorts where psychologists and counselors of African, Asian, Native American/Indian, Latina/o, and other descents contributed scholarship that both critiqued traditional mainstream approaches, and also outlined their own cultural variations of how a particular theory should be manifest within the context of work with a particular demographic group. Additionally, and quite possibly more relevant to many communities of color, are the contributions of scholars who advocate for moving beyond simply modifying existing mainstream theories, but also creating new paradigms that draw upon indigenous healing practices. And yet, even with that progress and some very profound and meaningful contributions to theory, there was still a gap between those constructs and how a professional helper could apply those ideas in work with particular populations.

In celebrating this welcome addition to the profession, and inviting all of you to take a serious look at the content within, we also owe a special thanks to the editors and their team of collaborators. This volume of multi-perspective case studies invites the reader to be a consummate risk taker. In this regard, these chapters invite you to be a mental risk taker, daring to stretch your thinking in ways that expose greater possibilities. The chapters invite verbal risks, where each of you will be challenged to break the silence of your own personal silos and discuss these case studies with colleagues and co-workers. These narratives invite you to take behavioral risks, if you dare to step outside of your personal comfort zones to try a different intervention you learned about through reading this volume.

We as professionals are committed to serving the students we teach, the clients we treat, and researching the questions that provide meaningful answers that inform our work. However, we also need the best tools and strategies that assist us in becoming more competent and proficient in our approaches. This volume on *Case Studies in Multicultural Counseling and Therapy* is a tremendous asset to your repertoire, and I for one would strongly encourage you take full advantage of all of this rich content and information.

Thomas A. Parham, Ph.D
University of California Irvine
Distinguished Psychologist
Association of Black Psychologists.

---

* NOTE: Scenarios help frame issues and provide context that allow for the application of theory in addressing a particular situation and circumstance.

Introduction: Moving From Theory to Practice in Multicultural Counseling

Case Studies in Multicultural Counseling and Therapy presents descriptions of real-life clinical cases encountered by practicing experts in the field of multicultural psychology. The casebook illustrates general principles, practices, and issues related to multicultural counseling and therapy by providing numerous cases illustrating specific assessment, diagnostic, and treatment concerns associated with specific populations (e.g., women, specific ethnic or religious groups, etc.). In the work, we acknowledge the rich diversity within each population. The chapters in the collection explore the ways in which social identities intersect with one another to influence presenting concerns and the therapy process; for example, how race, gender, sexual identity, class, and immigration status may influence one's work within a specific ethnic group and social context. The casebook is written to specifically accompany the best-selling sixth edition of *Counseling the Culturally Diverse: Theory and Practice* (*CCD*; Sue & Sue, 2013), but it also may be used as a free-standing accompaniment to any course or workshop related to multicultural mental health practice. The impetus for the development of a multicultural clinical casebook came from two primary quarters.

First, the mental health professions have recognized the central importance of training clinicians to work with an increasingly diverse population. Nearly all of the helping professions representing psychologists, counselors, social workers, and psychiatric nurses have proposed standards of practice and codes of ethics to ensure culturally competent services to different sociodemographic groups. The importance and central role of culturally responsive care are reflected in the guidelines and practices produced by various professional organizations and accrediting bodies.

- In 2002, the American Psychological Association (APA) produced Guidelines on Multicultural Education, Training, Research, Practice, and Organizational Change for Psychologists (American Psychological Association, 2003).
- In 2003, the Association for Multicultural Counseling and Development published a stronger and updated version of its Multicultural Counseling Competencies (Roysircar, Arredondo, Fuertes, Ponterotto, Toporek, & Parham, 2003).
- In 2008, the Council on Social Work Education's Educational Policy Accreditation Standards (updated in 2012) fully endorsed the importance of cultural competency.
- In 2009, the Council for Accreditation of Counseling and Related Educational Programs (CACREP; being revised for 2016) included the centrality of "Social and Cultural Diversity" in curriculum standards for counseling specialties.

All these organizations share four common themes or goals in education, training and practice:

1. Clinicians need to develop cultural awareness, knowledge, and skills to work effectively with different groups.
2. Social justice and advocacy are central features of clinical practice.
3. Developing cultural competencies in the assessment, diagnosis, and treatment of disorders must be a top priority.
4. Ethical and legal decisions must be primary considerations when working with diverse populations.

In essence, a casebook approach bridges the gap between theory and practice.

A second impetus for the casebook came from numerous requests by faculty to supplement multicultural textbooks with practical clinical examples by which they could teach students to apply the theory, concepts, and research associated with culturally responsive care. Such requests came not only from teachers but from students and trainees desiring to advance their clinical skills in working with diverse populations in such fields as psychology, psychiatry, social work, and nursing. The use of these cases, however, assumes that trainees have been exposed to information related to the special populations covered in the text. Cases dealing with African Americans, people living in poverty, or immigrant populations, for example, are helpful only when trainees have been exposed to information about the specific client group under study. Thus, although each case comes with expert commentaries, none is sufficient for trainees to thoroughly master the concepts without additional resources provided through readings or by the expertise and guidance of faculty or other mental health professionals. The 17 core chapters in this book are organized around three categories; each chapter is focused on a specific population and provides background information about each case, a critical analysis of two case vignettes, reflections questions, and recommended resources. Thus, 34 real-life clinical case vignettes are presented.

Category I: Case Studies With U.S. Racial/Ethnic Minority Populations

- African Americans
- American Indians and Alaskan Natives
- Asian Americans
- Hispanic/Latino/a Americans
- Middle Eastern/North African and Arab Americans (MENA)
- Biracial and multiracial persons
- White therapists working with people of color

Category II: Case Studies Involving Special Circumstances With Ethnic Populations

- American Jews
- Immigrants
- Refugees

Category III: Case Studies With Other Multicultural Populations

- Women

- Men
- Transgender
- Lesbian, gay, and bisexual
- People in poverty
- Persons with disabilities
- Older adults

DEVELOPING REAL-LIFE DIVERSE CASES

We invited well-known mental health professionals who specialize in working with specific populations and who possess expertise in clinical practice to write chapters for each of the 17 diverse social identity groups. We asked contributors to produce two case studies to be used by trainees and mental health professionals in learning how to work with diverse populations. The cases they submitted are based on actual clients from current work or in the past, composites of clients from their caseload, and/or hypothetical creations based on their own experiences. In each case vignette, the authors and editors took care to remove identifying information and/or to change enough of the clinical information to ensure confidentiality and anonymity.

These 17 pairs of cases correspond to specific chapters of the newest edition of *CCD*; they highlight multicultural foundational clinical/counseling practices that provide readers with an overview of therapeutic/counseling considerations that address a range of diverse populations. Each contributor read the specific-population chapter from *CCD* carefully and was asked to consider the areas covered in the chapter when providing case vignettes for the casebook. This volume also includes chapters on working with men and transgendered populations and White therapists working with people of color. As we examined the comprehensiveness of the content of the casebook, we believed that the addition of these three chapters would enhance its overall utility, include critical areas of relevance, and advocate for the continued expansion of the intersection of social identity issues. We provided chapters from the *CCD* as a template for contributing authors to utilize, but the authors were authorized develop clinical vignettes they believed best represented the communities they were discussing. The contributors were encouraged to expand on the foundational considerations and provide an overview of specific cases reflecting these areas, but with a more detailed description of what real-world therapeutic encounters look like when working with culturally diverse individuals/families/communities.

EDUCATIONAL OBJECTIVES

The goals we hope to achieve in the casebook are to present therapeutic case vignettes as an educational tool to generate discussion among trainees and mental health professionals and to illustrate important principles of culturally responsive therapeutic practices. These cases can be used to help trainees and mental health professionals identify diversity issues in working clinically with a broad range of clients in terms of race, culture, ethnicity, nationality, gender, sexual orientation, ability/disability, class, and other important social identities. We fully understand that our lives are influenced by the intersection of multiple social identities. A Latino male client who is religious and in the process of coming out is an example of where ethnicity, religion/spirituality, gender, and sexual identity intersect. Intersectionality, as proposed by feminist and critical race theorists, was designed to encourage researchers and clinicians to consider the meanings and consequences of multiple social identities (Cole, 2009). Ultimately, when working within a therapeutic encounter, intersectionality situates the mental health professional to attend to the cultural and political histories of communities as well as how these social identities derive meaning from one another. Thus, we asked contributors to consider the ways in which social identities intersect to influence the presenting concerns, treatment plan, and, ultimately, therapeutic outcomes.

Additionally, we also wanted to help trainees and mental health professionals reflect on thematic issues that arise when working therapeutically with diverse clients. To this end, we asked contributors to reflect on the process of conducting culturally responsive therapy as they wrote the case vignettes. We encouraged them to think about questions such as: How do they address, therapeutically, the multiple ways in which people identify? Moreover, we encouraged them to reflect on their own social identities and how this may influence their work with clients. One of our educational goals in developing this casebook was to encourage trainees and mental health professionals to develop an enhanced awareness of who they are as cultural beings within the context of working therapeutically. While having behavioral skills certainly lessen the anxiety clinicians/counselors may experience when working with diverse communities they are not familiar with, behavioral skills may also provide a false sense of cultural responsiveness, without the necessary cultural mind-set and awareness needed as the precursor to successful therapeutic work with diverse communities.

Therefore, we urge faculty and workshop facilitators to encourage students and attendees to reflect on who they are in the context of providing services to diverse communities and how this meta-awareness (taking self-awareness itself as an object of attention) either enhances or potentially disrupts therapeutic work.

We are hopeful that the case vignettes capture and expand readers' understanding of significant sociocultural and political issues when they arise in counseling/therapy and the influence of these factors on clients' presenting concerns and in the development of treatment planning. Although the presenting problem of the client is important, we are interested in helping trainees and mental health professionals understand how ignoring or being unaware of the intersection of presenting problems with various social, cultural, and political issues could result in therapeutic impasses.

The contributors provide a critical assessment of each case by identifying and presenting a discussion of the therapeutic issues. In many respects, the points raised by the expert contributors provide tips, clues, or hints for trainees and mental health professionals to consider in their assessment and treatment plans. One of the main goals of the casebook is to have readers reflect on issues of relevance when attempting to situate problems within the therapeutic context. Our aim is to help trainees and mental health professionals better understand what clients bring to the therapeutic encounter and, most important, learn how to think critically about these issues as precursors to actual therapeutic encounters.

CHAPTER OUTLINE

To aid trainees and mental health professionals in learning about each specific population, we asked contributors not only to provide brief case descriptions but to supply focus questions, brief topical analyses of the case vignettes, and additional recommended resources. For the most part, each case vignette within each chapter is divided into four parts.

Part I: Case Description

Each case description has been purposely kept brief and succinct, but with enough descriptive information to capture the details of the client's presenting issues within sociocultural and sociopolitical frameworks. This was done for two primary reasons: First, we have found that the law of diminishing returns applies to longer cases and that too much information may confuse and/or restrict the ability of trainees and mental health professionals to freely speculate and consider alternative explanations. Thus, we specifically asked contributors to briefly identify several primary multicultural themes in the therapeutic encounter and to weave them throughout the case description. Although some authors did offer specific treatments and interventions for clients, we encouraged them to concentrate on providing clues by which trainees might incorporate the themes into their own treatment plans.

Second, the cases are meant to be interactive in classroom or workshop training in that they allow trainees and mental health professionals to freely discuss their analyses; to provide rationales for their assessment, diagnosis, and treatment of clients, families, and client systems; and to compare and contrast their approaches with each other. We are hopeful that such an approach enables trainees and mental health professionals to:

1. Become aware of their own biases and assumptions about human behavior.
2. Understand the cultural worldview of the client being discussed.
3. Develop culturally responsive intervention strategies.
4. Broaden their awareness of how systemic and contextual forces affect not only culturally diverse clients but the helping relationship as well.

Part II: Reflection and Discussion Questions

Besides the case vignettes, contributors provide a series of reflection and discussion questions for readers to contemplate and discuss. Focus questions for trainees and mental health professionals illustrate cultural, clinical, sociopolitical, ethical, or legal issues related to the cases. These questions have been found to be very educational in stimulating classroom or workshop discussions. They identify culture-bound, class-bound, and linguistic factors that may bias the assessment, diagnosis, and treatment of culturally diverse clients and highlight multicultural issues that must be considered in culturally responsive treatment. Instructors and trainees may desire to use these discussions in any number of ways: as free-standing questions to generate discussions, as guideposts that help in case analysis, or as essay exam questions to test how well trainees understand and have integrated the material.

Part III: Brief Analysis of the Case

All contributors have supplied a brief analysis of each case from a culturally responsive perspective. This brief analysis provides readers with clues regarding multicultural issues that may arise for that particular population. While some of the analyses reveal more detailed information, the challenge to trainees and mental health professionals is using this knowledge or insight and incorporating it into actual practice with clients. Many chapters provide tips and hints as to how a counselor/therapist would approach the therapeutic work with a client but leave the majority of the work for trainees and mental health professionals to integrate into a treatment plan.

The therapeutic questions and potential answers posed in each chapter are extremely enlightening and helpful in developing a treatment plan. Some additional key questions for trainees and mental health professionals to consider when conceptualizing culturally responsive care for diverse clients in the assessment, diagnosis, and formulation of treatment plans are given below:

- ◆ What does research tell us about working with diverse clients?
- ◆ Similarly, what if no or very little research exists regarding a particular community?
- ◆ Traditional research is often culture-bound and may prove culturally inappropriate in work with a different racial/ethnic minority and other special populations. How should clinicians use research or evidence-based practice in formulating treatment plans? (In this respect, it may be helpful to review Chapter 9, "Multicultural Evidence-Based Practice," from *CCD*.

    The APA Presidential Task Force on Evidence-Based Practice in Psychology (2006) defined evidence-based practice in psychology (EBPP) as "the integration of the best available research with clinical expertise in the context of patient characteristics, culture, and preferences" (p. 1). Ultimately, the contributors to this casebook provide a solid foundation by which readers can begin to conceptualize cases within a culturally responsive framework while utilizing research evidence, culture and context, and personal experiences in developing good evidence-based treatments. We hope that readers expand their perspectives of what accounts for legitimate "evidence" when responding to the needs of diverse communities. We advocate that readers consider EBPP from the perspective of not always privileging one component over another but implementing what is culturally congruent with the client/family while considering the historical context and political realities. In this regard, we also strongly urge readers to understand and implement culturally grounded and culture-specific approaches that are developed from a ground-up perspective and derived directly from the community as legitimate sources of evidence for use therapeutically.

• In what ways can your theoretical orientation facilitate or hinder culturally responsive care with your client? Almost all theories of counseling and therapy have something to offer in work with clients. However, it is important to remember that nearly all the traditional forms of counseling/therapy originated from Western/European civilizations and may prove culture-bound and culturally inappropriate in application to racial/ethnic minorities, for example. Culturally responsive approaches have long emphasized that attempting to fit clients into a rigid mold or framework may constitute cultural oppression rather than healing. Thus, techniques and strategies must be flexible and adapted to the life experiences and cultural values of clients. How might this latter point impact your work as a therapist?

• Where do the sociocultural and/or sociopolitical experiences of the client fit into your approach? For example, most people of color value a collectivistic identity rather than an individualistic one. Likewise, experiences of discrimination, prejudice, and stereotyping may affect both the identity and worldviews of culturally diverse clients. How do cultural values and experiences of oppression affect the therapeutic relationship between you and your client? We know, for example, that culture may influence the manifestation of symptom formation, how disorders are perceived, and what is considered appropriate treatment. Furthermore, experiences of oppression may result in cultural mistrust of the therapist and the therapeutic relationship and process. In light of these factors, how would you establish a respectful working relationship with clients who have been marginalized in society? What specifically would you do?

• Related to these questions, we can also ask more specifically in what ways should you take into consideration client systems (family, friends, religious institutions, schools, and other systemic entities) in your treatment of clients? Traditional clinical approaches often emphasized intrapsychic or person-centered change as most appropriate because the assumption is that problems reside within the person. Yet if we acknowledge that most socially devalued groups in our society have been victims of stereotyping, prejudice, discrimination, and oppression, is it possible that many of their concerns, or "problems," arise from the social system rather than within the client? If that is the case, where should therapeutic change be directed: at the individual level? At the systemic level? If the latter, what roles other than the therapist treating the client would you have to play? Would you feel comfortable or capable of playing such a role? How would you apply this approach to your culturally diverse clients? Is client self-disclosure always a precursor to therapeutic change?

◆ In culturally responsive therapy, the old adage "counselor know thyself" seems especially important in working with diverse clients who might not necessarily share the therapist's worldview, cultural assumptions, or values. How aware are you of your worldview, assumptions of human behavior, biases, values, and stereotypes? Worldviews determine how we perceive the world, our definitions of normality and abnormality, and how we define problems and solve them. Without this awareness, we may be guilty of cultural oppression or imposing our standards on culturally diverse clients who do not share our worldview. Rather than free or liberate, we may constrict, diminish, pathologize, or even harm clients. What personal challenges are likely to arise when therapists work with clients who differ from you in race, culture, gender, age, or sexual orientation, to name a few? If you believe, for example, that sexual orientation is a "choice" or that being gay is "immoral" or a "sin," how will these perspectives impact the therapist's work with lesbian, gay, bisexual, and transgendered (LGBT) populations? How aware are mental health professionals of hot-button issues that may impede their work with culturally different clients? Additionally, are clinicians aware of how they might be perceived by others with regard to their race, ethnicity, gender, class, and so on? How might this perception impact what happens therapeutically? For example, if practitioners are working with clients from working class backgrounds, how might the practitioners' privileged status impact what their clients choose to disclose or withhold in therapy? We encourage readers to critically self-evaluate how they come across to others and how this potentially impacts relationships with them, in particular with clients.

- What are the potential ethical issues that may arise in working with diverse clients? Are there potential conflicts in the ethical guidelines and standards of practice advocated by the American Counseling Association, APA, National Association of Social Workers, and other professional associations that may hinder culturally responsive treatment with diverse clients? Remember that ethical guidelines and practices of professional associations have been developed within a Western/European framework and often reflect the values and assumptions of that culture. For example, in *CCD*, we identified five therapeutic taboos that may be derived from these guidelines:

1. A therapist does not give advice and suggestions.
2. A therapist does not engage in dual role relationships.
3. A therapist does not barter services.
4. A therapist does not accept gifts from clients.
5. A therapist does not self-disclose.

Although professional organizations have begun to acknowledge the culture-bound nature of these standards, they have still not adequately addressed how they may be adapted. Thus, we can ask these questions:

- How might these therapeutic taboos and others affect therapist ability to provide culturally relevant services?
- How would they overcome them?
- What would practitioners do when culturally responsive care clashes with "ethical" dictates?

How therapists answer these questions may determine the degree to which they are able to provide culturally responsive care for clients. Developing multicultural counseling competencies and providing culturally responsive care is a process in which trainees and mental health professionals critically examine their values and assumptions, the theoretical and empirical literature on specific populations, and the intersection of the two on their clinical work with clients.

Part IV: Recommended Resources

To provide trainees with additional information on the specific topic associated with a particular case, our contributors have created a list of recommended resources. These resources generally fall into four main categories, although some authors have chosen to adapt them when the classification seemed too limiting:

1. Books and/or articles
2. Films and DVDs
3. Fiction/nonfiction readings
4. Inventories/Assessments

These resources provide a range of valuable information about each diverse population through academic channels, media productions, activities that allow for self-exploration, and the experiential realities of the group. They can provide trainees and mental health professionals with cognitive and emotive understanding of the groups they hope to serve. We have found these resources to be valuable tools in helping trainees and mental health professionals to understand the worldviews of their diverse clients and for stimulating excellent classroom or workshop discussions.

INTEGRATING CULTURAL FORMULATION INTO ASSESSMENT AND TREATMENT PLANS

[1]Accurate assessment, diagnosis, and case conceptualization, key prerequisites to the provision of culturally responsive treatment, are dependent on the characteristics, values, and worldviews of both therapist and client (APA, 2006). A critical point in treatment is the ability to gather culturally congruent and contextually appropriate information that guides clinical decisions. This is most represented in intake interviews. Most intake forms generally include questions concerning client demographic information, the presenting problem, history of the problem, previous therapy, psychosocial history, educational and occupational experiences, family and social supports, medical and medication history, risk assessment,

---

1   This section has been adapted from *Counseling the Culturally Diverse: Theory and Practice* (pp. 345–361), by D. W. Sue and D. Sue, 2013, Hoboken, NJ: Wiley.

diagnosis, and goals for treatment. Fisher, Jome, and Atkinson (1998) reviewed the evidence supporting what they term universal healing conditions or common factors in a culturally specific context. These scholars concluded that there are four common factors across all therapeutic healing approaches:

1. It is now widely accepted across all therapeutic orientations or approaches to psychotherapy that the *therapeutic relationship* serves as a base for all therapeutic intervention across all cultures.
2. A *shared worldview* or conceptual schema or rationale for explaining symptoms provides the common framework by which both healer and client work together.
3. The *client's expectation* in the form of faith or hope, in the process of healing, exists across all cultures.
4. The *therapeutic ritual or intervention* takes place in the form of a procedure that requires the active participation of both client and therapist, and the procedure is believed by both to be the means of restoring the client's health.

In summary, it is critical for trainees to: (1) develop culturally respectful relationships with their clients; (2) find avenues to mutually understand the creation and maintenance of presenting concerns; (3) provide clients with a sense of hope; and (4) provide clients with a sense that the work trainee and client embark on together has the potential to create change, ultimately leading to the codevelopment of interventions that are culturally and contextually meaningful and feasible to achieve for clients. We believe it is the combination of these common factors that serve as a solid therapeutic template for trainees and mental health professionals. We are hopeful that readers utilize the EBPP and common factors frameworks to develop culturally responsive services for diverse communities.

Many of the intake questions are focused primarily on the individual with little consideration of situational, family, sociocultural, or environmental issues. Although it may be difficult to modify standard intake forms used by clinics and other mental health agencies, consideration should be given to these contextual factors when gathering data. In the next sections, we present common areas of inquiry found in standard diagnostic evaluations and the rationale for each (Rivas-Vazquez, Blais, Rey, & Rivas-Vazquez, 2001).

We also include suggestions for specific contextual queries that can be used to supplement the standard interview and/or treatment for ethnic minorities and other diverse populations.

Identifying Information

Asking about the reason for seeking counseling allows the therapist to gain an immediate sense of the client and reason for seeking therapy. Important information typically gathered includes age, gender, ethnicity, relationship status, and referral source. When gathering and establishing information, it is critical to take the time to build culturally respectful relationships. Therapists must recognize that, for many diverse populations, the personal relationship holds more importance than rushing quickly to gather "clinical information." Additionally, it is important to inquire about cultural or social identity groups to which a client feels connected. For ethnic minorities or immigrants, immigration history and the degree of acculturation or adherence to traditional values is important to determine. If relevant, ask about the primary language used in the home or the degree of language proficiency of the client or family members. Determine if an interpreter is needed. (It is important not to rely on family members to translate when assessing clinical matters and to use interpreters only when absolutely necessary.) For other social identities, such as religion, sexual orientation, age, gender, or disability, it is important to consider if and how these factors influence the client's lived experiences or any of the difficulties the client is facing.

Presenting Problem

In order to understand the source of distress in the client's own words, obtain his or her perception of the problem and assess the degree of insight the client has regarding the problem and its chronicity. Some questions to consider as you explore a client's culturally embedded explanatory model include these: What is the client's explanation for his or her disorder? Does it involve somatic, spiritual, or culture-specific causes? Among all groups potentially affected by disadvantage, prejudice, or oppression: Does the client's own explanation involve internal causes (e.g., internalized heterosexism among gay males or lesbians or self-blame in a victim of a sexual assault) rather than external, social, or cultural explanations? What does the client perceive are possible solutions to the problem?

History of the Presenting Problem

To assist with diagnostic formulation, it is helpful to have a chronological account of the perceived reasons for the problem. It is also important to determine levels of functioning prior to the problem and since it developed and to explore social and environmental influences. When did the present problem first occur, and what was going on when this happened? Has the client had similar problems before? How was the client functioning before the problem occurred? What changes have happened since the advent of the problem? When was the last time the problem did not exist? What was different about that particular time? Note that problems can occur in multiple spheres, including interpersonal, intimate relationships, family, work, and school. Are there any family issues, value conflicts, or societal issues involving factors such as gender, ability, class, ethnicity, or sexual orientation that may be related to the problem?

Psychosocial History

Clinicians can benefit from understanding the client's perceptions of past and current functioning in different areas of living. Also important are early socialization and life experiences, including expectations, values, and beliefs from the family that may play a role in the presenting problem. How does the client describe his or her level of social, academic, or family functioning during childhood and adolescence? Were there any traumas during this period? Were there any past experiences or problems in socialization with the family or community that may be related to the current problem? McAuliffe and Ericksen (1999) describe some questions that can be used, when appropriate, to assess social background, values and beliefs:

> "How has your gender role or social class influenced your expectations and life plans?" "Do religious or spiritual beliefs play a role in your life?" "How would you describe your ethnic heritage; how has it affected your life?" "What was considered to be appropriate behavior in childhood, adolescence and as an adult?" "How does your family respond to differences in beliefs about gender, acculturation, and other diversity issues?" "What changes would you make in the way your family functions?" (p. 271).

These questions can be adapted, depending on the social identity and presenting concern(s) being addressed therapeutically.

Trauma History

Despite the potential importance of determining if the client is facing any harmful or dangerous situations, many trainees and mental health professionals do not routinely inquire about trauma and abuse histories, even with populations known to be at increased risk. In one study, even when the intake form included a section on abuse, fewer than one-third of those conducting intake interviews inquired about this topic (Young, Read, Barker-Collo, & Harrison, 2001). We encourage mental health professionals to attend to a range of abuse, including the types covered in most training programs, such as sexual, physical, and emotional abuse and neglect of children and adults. Additionally, it is critical to address any social and cultural issues and their contributions to histories of trauma in conjunction with background information, such as a history of sexual or physical abuse, as the culmination of these historical experiences can have important implications for diagnosis, treatment, and safety planning. As an example, these questions involve domestic violence for women (Stevens, 2003, p. 6), but can and should be expanded for use with other groups, including men and older adults:

- Have you ever been touched in a way that made you feel uncomfortable?
- Have you ever been forced or pressured to have sex?
- Do you feel you have control over your social and sexual relationships?
- Have you been ever been threatened by a (caretaker, relative, or partner)?
- Have you ever been hit, punched, or beaten by a (caretaker, relative, or partner)?
- Do you feel safe where you live?
- Have you ever been scared to go home? Are you scared now?

If a client discloses a history of trauma during the intake process and there are no current safety issues, the therapist can briefly and empathetically respond to the disclosure and return to the issue at a later time in the conceptualization or therapy process. Of course, developing a safety plan and obtaining social and law enforcement support may be necessary when a client discloses current abuse issues.

We also urge readers to pay attention to areas of abuse that are often overlooked in our training programs but are of critical importance for diverse and underrepresented communities. In particular, mental health professionals should explore trauma experiences or the emotional reactions to abuse and/or terrible events related to clients' social identities. Historical trauma and trauma associated with racism or immigration, to name a few, are directly connected to the cases illustrated throughout this casebook. These questions could be included in any intake protocol:

- Have you ever been discriminated against? If so, what events stand out to you the most?
- Do you think about this (these) experience(s)?
- Have one or both of your parent(s) experienced a significant form of discrimination? If so, describe the experience(s).
- If you have children, has one or more of your children experienced a significant form of discrimination? If so, describe the experience(s).

Strengths

It is important to identify culturally relevant strengths, such as pride in one's identity or culture, religious or spiritual beliefs, cultural knowledge and living skills (e.g., hunting, fishing, folk medicine), family and community supports, and resiliency in dealing with discrimination and prejudice (Hays, 2009). The focus on strengths often helps put a problem in context and defines support systems or positive individual or cultural characteristics that can be activated in the treatment process. This is especially important for ethnic group members and individuals of diverse populations subjected to negative stereotypes.

- What are some attributes that they are proud of?
- How have they successfully handled problems in the past?
- What are some strengths of the client's family or community?
- What are sources of pride such as school or work performance, parenting, or connection with the community?
- How can these strengths be used as part of the treatment plan?

Medical History

It is important to determine if a client has medical or physical conditions or limitations that may be related to the psychological problem and important to consider when planning treatment.

- Is the client currently taking any medications, using herbal substances, or using any form of folk medicine?
- Has the client had any major illnesses or physical problems that might have affected their psychological state?
- How does the client perceive these conditions?
- Is the client engaging in appropriate self-care?
- If there is some type of physical limitation or disability, how has this influenced daily living?
- How have family members, friends, or society responded to this condition?

These questions are especially important and relevant with older adults or elderly clients as aging comes with frequent major health risks and conditions.

Substance Abuse History

Although substance use can affect diagnosis and treatment, this potential concern is often underemphasized in clinical assessment. Because substance use issues are common, it is important to ask about drug and alcohol use.

- What is the client's current and past use of alcohol, prescription medications, and illegal substances including age of use, duration, and intensity?
- If the client drinks alcohol, how much is consumed?
- Does the client (or family members) have concerns about the client's substance use?
- Has drinking or other substance use ever affected the social or occupational functioning of the client?
- What are the alcohol and substance use patterns of family members and close friends?

Risk of Harm to Self or Others

Even if clients do not share information about suicidal or violent thoughts, it is important to consider the potential for self-harm or harm to others. What is the client's current emotional state? Are there strong feelings of anger, hopelessness, or depression? Is the client expressing intent to harm him- or herself? Does there appear to be the potential to harm others? Have there been previous situations involving dangerous thoughts or behaviors?

* * *

Diversity considerations can easily be infused into the intake process. Such questions can help the therapist understand the client's perspective on various issues. Questions that might provide a more comprehensive account of the client's perspective are listed next (Dowdy, 2000).

- *"How can I help you?"* This question addresses the reason for the visit and client expectations regarding therapy. Clients can have different ideas of what they want to achieve. Unclear or divergent expectations between client and therapist can hamper therapy.
- *"What do you think is causing your problem?"* The answer to this question helps the therapist to understand the client's perception of the factors involved. In some cases, the client will not have an answer or may present an explanation that may not be plausible. The therapist's task is to help the client examine different areas that might relate to the problem, including interpersonal, social, and cultural influences. However, the therapist must be careful not to impose an explanation on the client.
- *"Why is this happening to you?"* This question taps into the issue of causality and possible spiritual or cultural explanations for the problem. Some clients may believe the problem is due to fate or a punishment for "bad behavior". If this question does not elicit a direct answer or to obtain a broader perspective, the therapist can ask, "What does your mother (husband, family members, or friends) believe is happening to you?"
- *"What have you done to treat this condition?"* *"Where else have you sought treatment?"* These questions can lead to a discussion of previous interventions, the possible use of home remedies, and the client's evaluation of the usefulness of these treatments. Responses can also provide information regarding previous providers of treatment and client perceptions of prior treatment.

- *"How has this condition affected your life?"* Answers to this question help identify individual, interpersonal, health, and social issues related to the concern. Again, if the response is limited, the clinician can inquire about the impact on each of these specific areas.

Finally, we would like to refer readers to the changes being implemented in the fifth edition of the *Diagnostic and Statistical Manual of Mental Disorders* (American Psychiatric Association, 2011) that include not only a Cultural Case Formulation section but also a Cultural Formulation Interview that identifies major areas of psychological assessment and evaluation that we incorporate throughout this casebook. We believe that, although it is not mandated for use, the Cultural Formulation Interview serves as a useful tool for implementation therapeutically. Some of the areas include:

- *Cultural identity of the individual* (e.g., the individual's cultural reference groups, specifically relating to race, ethnicity, religion, social class and gender identity)
- *Cultural explanation of the individual's illness* (e.g., the meaning and perceived severity of the individual's symptoms in relation to norms of the cultural reference group)
- *Cultural factors related to psychosocial environment and levels of functioning* (e.g., environmental sources of stress)
- *Cultural elements of the relationship between the individual and the clinician* (e.g., What has it been like to describe and explain your problems and your situation to me?)
- *Overall cultural assessment for diagnosis and care* (e.g., discussion of how cultural factors affect diagnosis and determine treatment plan)

As trainees and clinicians begin the exploration of these multicultural cases, we hope that they will use a cultural formulation in the assessment, diagnosis, and treatment of clients. Culturally responsive assessment should be conducted in a manner that considers the unique background, values, and beliefs of each client. We hope that as mental health proviers proceed though these cases and read the chapters in *Counseling the Culturally Diverse* describing general characteristics and special challenges faced by various oppressed populations, they will remember that we are providing this information so they will have some knowledge of specific research or sociopolitical and cultural factors that *might* be pertinent to a client or family from this population. However, when counseling diverse clientele, it is critical to actively work to avoid succumbing to stereotypes (i.e., basing opinions of the client on limited information or prior assumptions). Instead, the task is to develop an in-depth understanding of each individual client, taking into consideration that individual's unique personal background and worldview. By doing this, therapists will be in a position to develop an individually tailored treatment plan that effectively addresses presenting problems in a culturally responsive manner.

REFERENCES

American Psychiatric Association. (2011). *DSM-5: The future of psychiatric diagnosis.* Retrieved from http://www.dsm5.org/pages/default.aspx

American Psychological Association. (2006). Guidelines on multicultural education, training, research, practice, and organizational change for psychologists. *American Psychologist, 58,* 377–402.

American Psychological Association Presidential Task Force on Evidence-Based Practice. (2006). Evidence-based practice in psychology. *American Psychologist, 61,* 271–285.

CACREP. (2009). *Council for Accreditation of Counseling and Related Educational Programs 2009 Standards.* Alexandria, VA: Author.

Cole, E. R. (2009). Intersectionality and research in psychology. *American Psychologist, 64*(3), 170–180.

Council on Social Work Education. (2008, updated 2012). *Educational Policy and Accreditation Standards.* Alexandria, VA: Author.

Dowdy, K. G. (2000). The culturally sensitive medical interview. *Journal of the American Academy of Physicians Assistants, 13,* 91–104.

Fischer, A. R., Jome, L. M., & Atkinson, D. R. (1998). Reconceptualizing multicultural counseling: Universal healing conditions in a culturally specific context. *The Counseling Psychologist, 26,* 525–588.

Hays, P. A. (2009). Integrating evidence-based practice, cognitive-behavior therapy change, and multicultural therapy. 10 steps for culturally competent practice. *Professional Psychology: Research and Practice, 40,* 354–360.

McAuliffe, G. J., & Eriksen, K. P. (1999). Toward a constructivist and developmental identity for the counseling profession: The context-phase-stage style model. *Journal of Counseling and Development*, *77*, 267–280. doi: 10.1002/j.1556–6676.1999.tb02450.x

Rivas-Vazquez, R. A., Blais, M. A., Rey, G. J., & Rivas-Vazquez, A. A. (2001). A brief reminder about documenting the psychological consultation. *Professional Psychology: Research and Practice, 32*, 194–199.

Roysircar, G., Arredondo, P., Fuertes, J. N., Ponterotto, J. G., Toporek, R. L., & Parham, T. A. (2003). *Multicultural Counseling Competencies*. Alexandria, VA: American Counseling Association.

Stevens, L. (2003, November 20). Improving screening of women for violence: Basic guidelines for physicians. *Medscape*.

Sue, D. W., & Sue, D. (2012). *Counseling the culturally diverse: Theory and practice*. Hoboken, NJ: Wiley.

Young, M., Read, J., Barker-Collo, S., & Harrison, R. (2001). Evaluating and overcoming barriers to taking abuse histories. *Professional Psychology: Research and Practice, 32*, 407–414.

About the Editors

Derald Wing Sue is Professor of Psychology and Education at Teachers College, Columbia University. He received his PhD from the University of Oregon and has served as a training faculty member with the Columbia University Executive Training Programs. He was co-Founder and first President of the Asian American Psychological Association, and past President of the Society for the Psychological Study of Ethnic Minority Issues and the Society of Counseling Psychology. Dr. Sue has served as Editor of the *Personnel and Guidance Journal* and Associate Editor of the *American Psychologist* and serves on the Council of Elders for *Cultural Diversity and Ethnic Minority Psychology*. Dr. Sue can truly be described as a pioneer in the field of multicultural psychology, multicultural education, multicultural counseling and therapy, and the psychology of racism/antiracism. His current research explores the manifestation, dynamics, and impact of racial, gender, and sexual orientation microaggressions. He currently applies this research to strategies for facilitating difficult dialogs on race in the classroom and public forums. He is author of more than 150 publications, including 16 books and numerous media productions. In recognition of his outstanding contributions, Dr. Sue has been the recipient of numerous awards from professional organizations, educational institutions, and community groups.

Miguel E. Gallardo is an Associate Professor of Psychology and Director of Aliento, The Center for Latina/o Communities at Pepperdine University, and a licensed psychologist. He received his PsyD from the California School of Professional Psychology, Los Angeles. He teaches courses on multicultural and social justice, intimate partner violence, and professional practice issues. Dr. Gallardo's areas of scholarship and research interests include understanding the psychotherapy process when working with ethnocultural communities, particularly the Latina/o community, and understanding the processes by which individuals develop cultural awareness and responsiveness. Dr. Gallardo is currently Director of Research and Evaluation for the Multiethnic Collaborative of Community Agencies (MECCA), a nonprofit organization dedicated to serving monolingual Arab-, Farsi-, Korean-, Vietnamese-, and Spanish-speaking communities. Dr. Gallardo has published refereed journal articles and book chapters in the areas of multicultural psychology, Latina/o psychology, and ethics and evidence-based practices. He coedited the book *Intersections of Multiple Identities: A Casebook of Evidence-Based Practices with Diverse Populations* and is coauthor of the book *Culturally Adaptive Counseling Skills: Demonstrations of Evidence-Based Practices*. Dr. Gallardo is a Fellow in the American Psychological Association.

Helen A. Neville is a Professor of Educational Psychology and African American Studies at the University of Illinois at Urbana-Champaign. She currently chairs the counseling psychology program and in the past was a Provost Fellow at the same institution. She received her PhD from the University of California at Santa Barbara in counseling psychology. Prior to coming to Illinois, she was on the faculty in Psychology, Educational and Counseling Psychology, and Black Studies at the University of Missouri-Columbia, where she cofounded and codirected the Center for Multicultural Research, Training, and Consultation. She is the lead Editor of the *Handbook of African American Psychology* and is a past Associate Editor of the *Counseling Psychologist* and the *Journal of Black Psychology*. Dr. Neville has been recognized for her research, teaching, and mentoring efforts including receiving the American Psychological Association Graduate Students Kenneth and Mamie Clark Award for Outstanding Contribution to the Professional Development of Ethnic Minority Graduate Students and the Charles and Shirley Thomas Award for mentoring and contributions to African American students and community. She is a Fellow in the American Psychological Association and recently received the Association of Black Psychologists' Distinguished Psychologist of the Year award.

About the Contributors

Julie R. Ancis, PhD, is an American Psychological Association (APA) Fellow and Associate Vice President for Institute Diversity at the Georgia Institute of Technology. She previously served as Professor of Counseling Psychology at Georgia State University. Dr. Ancis received the 2012 Woman of the Year Award from the Society of Counseling Psychology (Division 17) Section for the Advancement of Women and chairs the section. She has published and presented extensively in the area of multicultural competence, race and gender, university climate, women's legal experiences, and *DSM-5* proposals. She is the author of several books, including *The Complete Women's Psychotherapy Treatment Planner* (Wiley) and *Culturally Responsive Interventions: Innovative Approaches to Working With Diverse Populations* (Taylor and Francis). Dr. Ancis's professional activities include serving as Legal and Legislative Representative of the Georgia Psychological Association's Council on the Psychology of Women and Girls as a member of the committee for the development of the APA Guidelines for Psychological Practice with Girls and Women, and editorial board of the *Journal of Counseling and Development.*

Lucinda Bratini, PhD, is a psychologist, professor, and community organizer who received her degree in Counseling Psychology at Teachers College, Columbia University, from which she graduated with distinction after defending her dissertation titled: *"It Depends on Where You Go!" The Transnational Racial Consciousness of Dominican Immigrants.* She specializes in working with diverse individuals, groups, and families as well as youth living in poverty. She completed her EdM in Psychological Counseling at Teachers College and her Bachelor of Science in Human Development at Binghamton University, State University of New York. Currently she holds a position as both professor and clinician in the Department of Counseling at John Jay College of Criminal Justice, City University of New York. She is one of the faculty founders and leaders of the Participatory Action Research Collective at John Jay College, a research team comprised of students, professors, and mental health staff working on projects that seek to understand and address the impact of poverty and marginality on the first-generation student experience. Her interests focus on institutionalized and internalized oppression, intersectionality, Afro-Latina/o issues, and socially just mental health practice. A New Yorker of Dominican origin, Dr. Bratini is also an aspiring fiction writer

Christina M. Capodilupo, EdM, PhD, is Adjunct Professor at Teachers College, Columbia University. She was formerly Assistant Professor of Psychology in the Graduate Institute of Professional Psychology at the University of Hartford in Connecticut. While at Hartford, she was awarded the Faculty Excellence Award for teaching in the doctoral program. She has taught graduate and undergraduate courses that focus on multicultural psychology, gender issues, theories of counseling, and clinical practice. Dr. Capodilupo's areas of interest include the etiology of eating disorders and body image issues for women of color, intersections of racism and sexism with body image and eating habits, everyday experiences of oppression and their impact on mental health, and contemporary psychoanalytic theories. Her current research explores the role of everyday racism in Black women's appearance satisfaction, eating habits, and weight status. She and a colleague (Dr. Gina Torino) are in the process of developing a scale that measures gender microaggressions (i.e., everyday experiences of sexism). Dr. Capodilupo has served as a Clinical Supervisor and Psychotherapist at the Karen Horney Clinic in New York City. She engaged in a psychodynamic practice that focused on the role of sociocultural forces in the development of symptoms.

Kelly O'Shea Carney, PhD, CMC, is the Executive Director for the Phoebe Center for Excellence in Dementia Care, a Phoebe Ministries service located in northeastern Pennsylvania. She is a Licensed Psychologist and a Certified Geriatric Care Manager with over 25 years of experience in geropsychology. Dr. Carney's extensive clinical experience centers on providing behavioral health consultation and training to direct caregivers within long-term care settings. She has particular expertise in dementia care and currently provides leadership for the development and implementation of an array of community- and facility-based dementia services. Dr. Carney is a frequently invited speaker on a variety of eldercare topics, addressing professional groups including the American Psychological Association, the National Association of Professional Geriatric Care Managers, the Pennsylvania Bar Institute, the Pennsylvania Community Providers Association, and the Pennsylvania Long Term Living Training Institute. In addition to her clinical duties, Dr. Carney is actively engaged in varied efforts to promote and address the behavioral health needs of older adults. She served as the President of the Pennsylvania Behavioral and Health and Aging Coalition and is currently co-Chair of the APA Committee on Aging.

Debbie-Ann Chambers, PhD, is a counseling psychologist working in the areas of community mental health and development in inner-city Kingston, Jamaica. She facilitates individual and group counseling, community meetings, youth participatory action research, and after-school programming at the St. Anne's Roman Catholic Church, a Jesuit parish in Kingston. Dr. Chambers completed her doctoral degree at Teachers College, Columbia University, where she studied counseling trainees' perceptions of persons in poverty, participatory action research as a therapeutic intervention in marginalized communities, and the experiences of coping with unemployed poverty. She completed her American Psychological Association–approved clinical internship at Jacobi Medical Center, then worked in community mental health for one year before returning to Jamaica. In addition to being a counseling psychologist, Dr. Chambers is also a entering candidate of the Sisters of Mercy, Jamaica, and is involved in social justice initiatives on the island.

Cynthia de las Fuentes, PhD, is a Psychologist in independent practice in Austin, Texas. Dr. de las Fuentes earned a predoctoral Congressional Fellowship with the Women's Research and Education Institute and a Public Interest Directorate Fellowship with the American Psychological Association (APA) before graduating from the University of Texas at Austin. Among various roles within the APA, she chaired the Committee on Women in Psychology and is a former President of the Society of Psychology of Women. Currently Secretary on the Board of Trustees of the Texas Psychological Association, she is also a Professional Reviewer for the Ethics Committee of the Texas State Board of Examiners of Psychologists. Dr. de las Fuentes was tenured as an Associate Professor at Our Lady of the Lake University, where she taught in its APA-accredited doctoral program for 14 years, receiving numerous awards, including Texas Psychological Association's Outstanding Contributions to Education, the Society for the Psychological Study of Ethnic Minority Issues' Emerging Professional Award, the University of Utah's G. Jones and V. Jones Award, and the Kenneth and Mamie Clark Award for Mentorship from The American Psychological Association of Graduate Students. Dr. de las Fuentes's scholarship is in the areas of ethics and risk management and in multicultural, Latino, and feminist psychologies.

Michi Fu, PhD, is a Psychologist who is licensed to practice in the states of Hawaii and California. She specializes in conducting bicultural therapy with Taiwanese and other Asian populations. She teaches diversity courses and mentors students with regard to cross-cultural mental health issues at the California School of Professional Psychology of Alliant International University. She is also the Statewide Prevention Projects Director of Pacific Clinics, where her projects focus on reducing stigma and discrimination as well as mental health disparities among Asian Americans. She serves as a Primary Supervisor at an American Psychological Association–accredited internship. Her private practice is dedicated to those who need bilingual therapy in Taiwanese or Mandarin. Her particular areas of interest are trauma, sexual abuse, women's issues, relationship difficulties, mood disorders, and children's mental health. She enjoys utilizing nonverbal modes of treatment, such as play therapy, sand tray therapy, use of music or movement, and art therapy. She publishes in the areas of cross-cultural mental health, Asian American psychology, and women's issues.

Julie Hakim-Larson, PhD, received her doctoral degree in Life-Span Developmental Psychology from Wayne State University in 1984 and obtained postdoctoral training in the field of Clinical Child Psychology. She has been on the faculty of the University of Windsor in Windsor, Ontario, Canada since 1991, where she is a Professor of Clinical Psychology. Her publications and research interests include culture and emotional development within a global perspective, emotion in families, Arab ethnic identity in North America, and the promotion of mental health in Arab immigrants and refugees. She has collaborated on projects that have resulted in peer-reviewed articles, book chapters, a training video, and conference presentations involving her work with individuals of Arab ethnicity. She is currently working on several books and organizing an international study group on Arab youth identity issues funded by the Society for Research in Child Development and the Social Sciences and Humanities Research Council of Canada.

Douglas C. Haldeman, PhD, has been a Counseling Psychologist in independent practice in Seattle for 30 years. He serves as a Clinical Professor in the Psychology Department at the University of Washington and an evaluator for the Federal Aviation Administration. His long publication record includes issues of ethics; family systems; practice guidelines for marginalized groups; and competent treatment of lesbian, gay, and bisexual individuals and families. This scholarship has won him a number of awards, including a Presidential Citation from the American Psychological Association (2005), the John D. Black Award from the Society of Counseling Psychology (2007), and the Outstanding Achievement Award from APA's Committee on Lesbian, Gay, Bisexual and Transgender Concerns (2002). Dr. Haldeman has held a number of positions in American Psychological Association (APA) Governance, including a term on the Board of Directors (2006–2008), on the Board for the Advancement of Psychology in the Public Interest, and on numerous committees and task forces. He represents the Division of Independent Practice on APA's Council of Representatives and is a Trustee of the American Psychological Association Insurance Trust. Dr. Haldeman is an avid long-distance runner, competing in several marathons each year.

Shelly P. Harrell, PhD, is a Licensed Clinical Psychologist and Full Professor of Psychology at Pepperdine University's Graduate School of Education and Psychology, where she serves as Research Director for the Doctoral Program in Clinical Psychology program. She is active in chairing dissertations, clinical supervision, and teaching psychotherapy conceptualization and skills. After receiving her undergraduate degree from Harvard University in Psychology and Social Relations, she completed her doctoral degree in Clinical Psychology at the University of California–Los Angeles. Her primary areas of scholarship include multicultural and community psychology, the psychology of African Americans, culture and well-being, racism and mental health, and the development of culturally syntonic interventions with diverse populations. Dr. Harrell has published on topics such as racism-related stress, diversity principles, sociopolitical development, race and clinical supervision, and therapeutic empowerment journaling. As a Psychotherapist and Consultant, she also maintains a private practice where she works with individuals, couples, groups, and organizations from an integrative multicultural-humanistic perspective.

Anita R. Hund, PhD, is a Clinical Assistant Professor for the Division of Counseling Psychology in the Department of Educational Psychology at the University of Illinois, Urbana–Champaign, and a Licensed Clinical Psychologist with a private practice. She has presented nationally and regionally and published in peer-reviewed journals on topics of sexual orientation, gender identity, White individuals' responses to racism, eating disorders, and childhood trauma. She previously worked at the University of Illinois Counseling Center, where she was the specialist in clinical work and outreach programming with lesbian, gay, bisexual, and transgender students. In this role, she served as co-Chair of the university's Ally Network and as Chair of the LGBT Resource Center Advisory Board. Through her private practice, she has worked with a number of clients around issues of gender identity and sexual orientation. She also has experience with the treatment of eating disorders and trauma-related concerns.

Connie Hunt, PhD, is a Puyallup tribal member and was trained at the University of Vermont. She has served Native communities throughout her professional career as a Psychologist. She is a Consultant through Kinuk Sisakta Consultation, Training, and Research Group. Dr. Hunt specializes in Pediatric Psychology and Substance Abuse and is licensed in the state of Oregon. She has won awards for the management of deployed public health service employees to a suicide cluster, developments in health care, and contributions to public health. Dr. Hunt is active in Division 18 of the American Psychological Association (APA). She manages a listserv for this group of professionals committed to mental health care of American Indians/Alaska Natives. Dr. Hunt is a former APA Minority Fellowship Program recipient. She also is an APA HOPE Trainer and continues to be committed to the well-being and care of patients with HIV disease.

Diya Kallivayalil, PhD, is a Staff Psychologist at the Cambridge Health Alliance and an Instructor in Psychology in the Department of Psychiatry at Harvard Medical School. She received her doctorate at the University of Illinois at Urbana–Champaign in the Clinical/Community Psychology division. She completed a two-year fellowship at the Victims of Violence Program, Cambridge Health Alliance/Harvard Medical School, specializing in the assessment and treatment of psychological trauma. In addition to her clinical practice, her research is broadly concerned with psychological trauma. She has published in the areas of domestic violence, trauma recovery, feminist therapy, the impact of trauma and migration on mental health in minority and immigrant communities, narrative methods, political trauma, and homicide bereavement. She is the coauthor of the *Trauma Recovery Group* (2011) published by Guilford Press.

Nicholas Ladany, PhD, is Dean of the School of Education and Counseling Psychology at Santa Clara University in Santa Clara, California. He previously served as Director of the Counseling Program at Loyola Marymount University in Los Angeles, California, and Program Coordinator and Director of Doctoral Training of the Counseling Psychology Program and Chair of the Department of Education and Human Services at Lehigh University in Bethlehem, Pennsylvania. He received his PhD at the University at Albany, State University of New York, in 1992. He has published numerous articles and presented nationally and internationally in the area of counseling and psychotherapy supervision and training. His primary research interests include the interrelationships between supervision process and outcome and counseling and psychotherapy process and outcome, including such issues as the working alliance, self-disclosures and nondisclosures, multicultural training, ethics, and social justice. He has served as an Associate Editor of *Psychotherapy: Theory, Research, Practice, and Training* and has served on the Editorial Boards of the *Journal of Counseling Psychology*, *The Counseling Psychologist*, and *Counselor Education and Supervision*. He has published five books, including: *Practicing Counseling and Psychotherapy: Insights From Trainees, Clients, and Supervisors*; *Critical Events in Psychotherapy Supervision: An Interpersonal Approach*; and *Counselor Supervision* (4th ed.).

Peggy Loo, MA, is a doctoral student in the Counseling Psychology program at Teachers College, Columbia University. She received a Master of Arts degree in Clinical Psychology from Wheaton College in 2009 and practiced for three years as a Licensed Professional Counselor in the state of Illinois prior to her return to graduate studies. Her past clinical experiences include providing individual and group therapies in both community mental health settings and group private practice. She also received training in multisystemic therapy, an evidence-based treatment for high-risk youth and their caregivers. She currently works with Dr. Marie Miville of Teachers College, Columbia University, on multicultural gender roles, and is also cultivating further interest in participatory action research and interracial relationships.

Marie L. Miville, PhD, is an Associate Professor of Psychology and Education and Chair of the Department of Counseling and Clinical Psychology, Teachers College, Columbia University. Dr. Miville is the author of over 50 publications dealing with multicultural issues in counseling and psychology. She is the Editor of the Around the Winter Roundtable Forum in *The Counseling Psychologist* and is currently serving or has served on several editorial boards, including *Journal of Counseling Psychology*, *Journal of Latina/o Psychology*, *Cultural Diversity and Ethnic Minority Psychology*, and *Training and Education in Professional Psychology*. Dr. Miville is a past Chair of the Council of Counseling Psychology Training Programs (CCPTP) and was co-Chair of the joint Division 17/CCPTP Special Task Group that developed the Integrative Training Model, a competency-based model integrating multiple aspects of diversity. Dr. Miville also helped to develop the Counseling Psychology Model Training Values Statement Addressing Diversity (http://www.ccptp.org/trainingdirectorpage6.html) and was among a group of authors who won the 2009 Major Contribution Award for a series of articles about the statement published in *The Counseling Psychologist*. Dr. Miville is Historian of the National Latina/o Psychology Association and a Fellow of the American Psychological Association (Division 17 and 45).

José Montes, PhD, is a graduate of the California School of Professional Psychology, Los Angeles. Currently he is a Staff Psychologist at California State University Northridge (CSUN). He completed an American Psychological Association internship at the University of California–Irvine and a postdoctoral fellowship at the University of California–San Diego. Dr. Montes came from Mexico at the age of 15 and has made Southern California his home ever since. Before embarking on formal education, he worked as a farm laborer in Bakersfield, California. He graduated from community college, and the California State system (Cal State–Los Angeles). Dr. Montes considers himself a Chicano psychologist who is influenced by his lifelong activism in social rights, equality, and fairness. His clinical sub-emphasis focuses on community psychology. In this regard, he has worked with community members bridging the gap of traditional mental health services within disfranchised communities. He also teaches a course at CSUN aimed at empowering students to reach their true academic potential.

Ora Nakash, PhD, is an Assistant Professor at the School of Psychology at the Interdisciplinary Center in Herzeliya, Israel. She earned her doctorate in Clinical Psychology at Boston University and completed postdoctoral training at the Cambridge Health Alliance/Harvard Medical School and at the Stone Center/Jean Baker Miller Training Institute. Following her training, she served as a Research Associate at the Center for Multicultural

Mental Health Research/Harvard Medical School and as a Staff Psychologist at the Program for Psychotherapy at the Cambridge Health Alliance/Harvard Medical School. Since her return to Israel, she served on the faculty of the School of Psychology at the Interdisciplinary Center, Herzliya, and as Director of the Center for Cross Cultural Clinical Research. Her research focuses on the study of the effects of social and cultural factors on mental health with specific interest in mental health disparities with the goal of improving the access, equity, and quality of these services for disadvantaged and minority populations. She has a private practice in Modiin, Israel.

Sylvia C. Nassar-McMillan, **PhD,** is Professor and Program Coordinator of Counselor Education at North Carolina State University. Her professional background spans multicultural, gender, and career development issues, with a special focus on Arab Americans. She has published over 65 books, refereed articles, and other instructional materials. Dr. Nassar-McMillan currently serves on the CACREP Standards Revision Committee and has served as Board Member for the Census Information Center advisory board to the Arab American Institute, National Board for Certified Counselors, and North Carolina Board of Licensed Professional Counselors. She is past Associate Editor for Multicultural Issues for the *Journal of Counseling & Development*, for which she currently serves as Senior Associate Editor. Her recent National Science Foundation– and NASA-funded projects have examined career stereotyping and evaluated curriculum tools. Dr. Nassar-McMillan is currently co-Editor for the upcoming book *Biopsychosocial Perspectives on Arab Americans: Culture, Development, and Health* (Springer).

Rhoda Olkin, **PhD,** is a Distinguished Professor at the California School of Professional Psychology at Alliant International University, where she has been teaching clinical skills, diagnosis, case formulation, and family therapy and working with clients with disabilities for over 20 years. She is the Founder and Executive Director of the Institute on Disability & Health Psychology, which conducts research, training, and consultation, and is currently partnering with the Northern California MS Society to evaluate outcomes of a phone and Internet stress and pain reduction intervention. She is the author of the book *What Psychotherapists Should Know About Disability* and the training film *Disability-Affirmative Therapy: A Beginner's Guide.* She developed disability-affirmative therapy as a method to help therapists conceptualize clients with disabilities. Dr. Olkin has presented and published extensively on the intersection of disability and psychology. She has a private practice in the San Francisco East Bay and does expert witness work related to disability, such as wrongful termination or discrimination. She is completing a book of short stories, *Blue Zone*, which contains multiple stories with characters with disabilities.

Gregory J. Payton, PhD, is a Lecturer in the Department of Counseling and Clinical Psychology of Teachers College, Columbia University. Dr. Payton's clinical, teaching, and research interests include identity development, risk, and resiliency within LGBTQ populations; HIV/AIDS stigma and access to care; health disparities among marginalized populations; multicultural competency; and evidence-based practice. Additionally, Dr. Payton has written on issues of substance abuse, harm reduction, and gay/lesbian parenting. Dr. Payton is also a Licensed Psychologist in private practice.

Indhushree Rajan, MA, is an American-born South Indian woman who grew up in Southern California. Indhushree has a Master's in Postcolonial and Postmodern Literature and Critical Theory from California State University, Fullerton, and is currently finishing her doctoral degree in Clinical Psychology at Pacifica Graduate Institute in Carpinteria, California. She has done therapeutic work with physically and sexually abused children and adolescents, adult victims of rape and domestic violence, and at-risk youth and families with criminal, psychiatric, and substance abuse histories for the past 16 years. More recently, Ms. Rajan has been doing research and therapy work with sex trafficking survivors in Kolkata, India, and Los Angeles, California. Her passion for working with these girls and young women compelled her to create Project Satori, a nonprofit organization committed to providing mental health and trauma care for sex trafficking survivors, both domestically and in developing countries.

Martha Ramos Duffer, PsyD, is a Licensed Psychologist with a doctorate in Clinical Psychology from Baylor University. She serves as a motivational health and wellness speaker, trainer, and consultant based in Austin, Texas. She is the owner and Founder of Quantum Possibilities, which provides a broad array of consulting, training, coaching, and therapeutic services focused on personal and spiritual growth for individuals, healing and joyful relationships for couples, and peak performance and healthy systems for organizations. She has taught undergraduate and graduate psychology courses at several universities in Texas and served as the Executive Director of a nonprofit organization focused on social and economic justice. She has provided psychological services through various agencies, hospitals, and her own private practice and has spoken widely nationally and regionally. She has also worked with various organizations, developing programs and providing training to their boards of directors and staff, helping them gain the skills and create the systems necessary to sustain a healthy workforce and to increase effectiveness. A frequent guest on Univision's *Despierta Austin,* Dr. Ramos Duffer has become a sought-after speaker and trainer in the areas of motivation, empowerment, growth, communication, multicultural competence, health, and wellness.

Jane E. Reid, PhD, MSW, is a Licensed Clinical Social Worker in independent practice. She is trained both as a philosopher (PhD, University of North Carolina at Chapel Hill), with a specialization in ethics, and as a clinician (MSW, Smith College School for Social Work). She has presented locally and nationally on a range of issues salient to clinicians, particularly in the areas of ethics and clinical practice and in psychoanalytic theory and practice. Recent presentations include a paper exploring the clinical implications of therapist pregnancy, arguing for a more flexible understanding of this phenomenon than those represented in the historical psychoanalytic literature; a paper analyzing therapist sexual orientation, how clients construct meaning and use therapist sexual orientation in the service of the clinical work, again arguing for a more idiosyncratic understanding, depending on the particular dyad of therapist and client, than the extant literature allows; and a presentation on the implications of technology, particularly social media, for clinical practice. Her previous position was at the University of Illinois student Counseling Center, where she was the Specialist in Clinical Work and Programming for lesbian, gay, bisexual, and transgender students.

Daniel C. Rosen, PhD, is an Assistant Professor at Bastyr University (Kenmore, WA) in the Department of Counseling and Health Psychology. He earned a PhD in Counseling Psychology from Arizona State University after completing his predoctoral internship at the Center for Multicultural Training in Psychology at Boston Medical Center/Boston University School of Medicine. He completed his postdoctoral clinical fellowship at Cambridge Health Alliance/Harvard Medical School in the Behavioral Medicine Program. Dr. Rosen's scholarship is focused in the area of multicultural psychology and has explored issues of American Jewish identity, social justice in mental health, addressing disparities in access to and quality of mental health services, interpersonal complementarity, and the experiences of persons' with disabilities. He is the Founder of the nonprofit organization

AWARE, whose mission focuses on enhancing the effectiveness of health care practitioners by providing opportunities for cross-cultural learning and exchange. Dr. Rosen has a private practice in Seattle, Washington.

Daryl M. Rowe, PhD, is a Licensed Psychologist and Full Professor of Psychology, teaching in both the doctoral and master's programs in Clinical Psychology, at the Graduate School of Education and Psychology of Pepperdine University. He teaches courses on sociocultural influences and theories and strategies of clinical intervention; provides clinical supervision; and chairs and serves on dissertation committees. He received his undergraduate degree in Psychology from Hampton Institute and completed his master's and doctoral degrees in Counseling Psychology from the Ohio State University. His term as President of the Association of Black Psychologists begins in July 2013, and he is the former Chair of the African Psychology Institute, where he helped develop a comprehensive curriculum for African psychology. His primary areas of scholarship include African-centered psychology; and theory, practice, prevention, and treatment that aid the functioning of persons of African ancestry. Dr. Rowe has published on topics such as African-centered theory, treatment and training, marital relations, cultural competence, and religious leadership and diversity. He has presented at professional organizations, nationally and internationally. As a Psychotherapist and Consultant, Dr. Rowe maintains a private practice emphasizing the psychological needs of African Americans, focusing on marital and family relationships.

Laura Smith, PhD, received her doctoral degree in Counseling Psychology from Virginia Commonwealth University. Now an associate professor in the Department of Counseling and Clinical Psychology at Teachers College, Columbia University, Dr. Smith previously worked in a variety of applied settings in New York City. She was formerly the Director of Training of the American Psychological Association–accredited predoctoral internship program at Pace University, the founding Director of the Rosemary Furman Counseling Center at Barnard College, and the Director of Psychological Services at the West Farms Center, where she provided services, training, and programming within a multifaceted community-based organization in the Bronx. Dr. Smith's research interests include social class and poverty, the influence of classism on psychological theory and practice, the development of socially just practice models for psychologists at the community level, and participatory action research in schools and communities.

Mark Stevens, PhD, is Director of the University Counseling Services at California State University Northridge (CSUN). Prior to his position at CSUN, he was the Coordinator of Internship Training and Assistant Director at the University of Southern California (USC) Student Counseling Services for 19 years. Dr. Stevens has written and presented extensively in two clinical areas: (1) counseling and psychotherapy with men and (2) rape prevention and education workshops for college students. He was the co-Editor of the first *Handbook on Counseling and Psychotherapy with Men* (Sage, 1987). His most recent book (co-edited with Dr. Matt Englar-Carlson) is titled *In the Room With Men: A Casebook of Therapeutic Change*, was published by the American Psychological Association in 2006. Dr. Stevens is also the featured therapist in an APA-produced video (2003) on counseling and psychotherapy with men. For the past six years he and Dr. Englar-Carlson have been facilitating retreats for men at Esalen Institute in Big Sur, California. Dr. Stevens is a Fellow of the American Psychological Association and past President of APA Division 51, the Society for the Psychological Study of Men and Masculinity. In 2007, Dr. Stevens coordinated the first National Psychotherapy With Men Conference at CSUN.

Joseph B. Stone, PhD, *Okie* is our traditional Blackfeet (Aamskapipi-kuni) greeting, and I am Joseph B. Stone, PhD, SAC III, ICADC, CADC III, Director: Kinuk Sisakta Consultation, Training, and Research Services. Dr. Stone is an enrolled member of the Blackfeet and a descendant of the Sioux (Lakota), with Turtle Mountain Chippewa lineage. He was trained by the American Indian Support Project at Utah State University in the Professional-Scientific Psychology program and holds multiple certifications in addictions counseling. Among the Blackfeet, Dr. Stone is known as *Omahkapi'si Iniskim*, or Wolf Buffalo Stone. Dr. Stone is an expeditionary veteran of the U.S. Navy and currently lives in Gallup, New Mexico.

Pratyusha Tummala-Narra, PhD, is Assistant Professor in the Department of Counseling, Developmental and Educational Psychology at Boston College. She is a Teaching Associate at the Cambridge Health Alliance/Harvard Medical School and has a clinical practice. Dr. Tummala-Narra received her doctoral degree from Michigan State University and completed her postdoctoral training in the Victims of Violence Program at the Cambridge Hospital in Cambridge, Massachusetts. She is the recipient of the Scholars in Medicine Fellowship from the Harvard Medical School. She has presented nationally and published peer-reviewed journal articles and book chapters on the topics of immigration, ethnic minority issues, trauma, and psychodynamic psychotherapy. Her research concerns the areas of racial and ethnic discrimination and mental health issues among ethnic minority communities. Dr. Tummala-Narra has served as the Chair of the Multicultural Concerns Committee and Member-at-Large for Division 39 (Psychoanalysis), as a member of the Committee on Ethnic Minority Affairs (CEMA) in the American Psychological Association, and as a member of the American Psychological Association's Presidential Task Force on Immigration.

Melba Vasquez, PhD, ABPP, is in Independent Practice in Austin, Texas. She is a former President of the American Psychological Association (APA, 2011), and is the first Latina and woman of color to serve in that role. Dr. Vasquez has served in other leadership roles, including a term on the APA Board of Directors, as President of the Texas Psychological Association, and of APA Divisions 35 (Society of Psychology of Women) and 17 (Society of Counseling Psychology). She is a co-Founder of APA Division 45, Society for the Psychological Study of Ethnic Minority Issues, and of the National Multicultural Conference and Summit. She has published over 70 books, book chapters, and journal articles in the areas of ethics, ethnic minority psychology, psychology of women, counseling and psychotherapy, and supervision and training. She is a Fellow of 10 divisions of the APA, holds the Diplomate of the American Board of Professional Psychology, and has received numerous awards for distinguished professional contributions, career service, leadership, advocacy, and mentorship.

Oksana Yakushko, PhD, received her doctoral degree in Counseling Psychology and a graduate minor in Women and Gender Studies from the University of Missouri–Columbia. Her scholarly interest is focused on immigration, including xenophobia, gendered adaptation, irregular migration (human trafficking), social class issues, and career development in the lives of recent immigrants and refugees. She has been a part of an international collaboration to create a psychometrically valid and cross-culturally meaningful scale that assesses xenophobia toward refugees and immigrants in countries such as Norway, the Netherlands, South Africa, and the United States. In addition, she has been a part of community collaborative qualitative research partnerships that seek to understand adjustment concerns of recent immigrants and refugees. She has written on mental health and treatment of recent immigrants and refugees who have limited English proficiency and has been involved in training interpreters. She works as a Core Faculty and a Research Coordinator at Pacifica Graduate Institute.

PART I
Case Studies With U.S. Racial/Ethnic Minority Populations

1

Clinical Applications
With African Americans

Shelly P. Harrell and Daryl M. Rowe

AND STILL I RISE: THE STORY OF NIA

Case Description

Nia, a 16-year-old African American girl self-referred for therapy, was accompanied to the first session by her mother, Joyce, a 52-year-old woman who worked as a professor of nursing at the local state university. Nia was nearing the end of her sophomore year at a public high school in a large urban city. Nia described bad grades, outbursts of crying and anger, problems with peers at her school, and conflict with her father, Eric, as her reasons for wanting to come to therapy. Nia had tried speaking with a counselor at her school but told her mother that "the lady talked to me like I was stupid." Joyce disclosed in the first session that Nia had said in one of her tantrums that she wanted to kill herself but that she did not believe Nia really meant it.

Nia lived alone with her mother. Her parents had never married, and she was 2 years old when they split up. She had a 23-year-old half-brother (father's son) who was married and living in another state. They had begun to form a relationship as she got older, and she spoke with him regularly. Their father was currently married to another woman, and Nia had two younger half-sisters, ages 5 and 8. Nia's relationship with her father was characterized by starts and stops, hopes and disappointments. She described her father as always "depressed and complaining" and that he had lots of health problems. She shared that her father blamed her for the problems in their relationship, telling her that she should call and check on his well-being more often. She was very distraught regarding her father's inability to tolerate hearing about her concerns and his inappropriate disclosure to her that he wanted to kill himself. Joyce was a quiet woman who was very thoughtful in her speech. She took great care in providing a strong extended family kinship network for Nia that included numerous uncles, aunts, and cousins not related by blood. She engaged intentionally in racial socialization by exposing Nia to books and events related to African and African American history as well as cultural organizations. Joyce practiced Buddhism but shared multiple religious traditions with Nia, including African American Christianity and Black Liberation theology, traditional African religious beliefs, and contemporary metaphysical spirituality. Nia liked all of them and felt like she should not have to choose one. Nia's father was very critical of Joyce's spirituality and commitment to African cultural and racial socialization. He stated, "That's why Nia is all messed up . . . all that African crap you constantly shove down her throat."

Nia reported feeling isolated at school. She was very critical of the Black girls, stating that they were superficial and that she "hates them." She felt that teachers at school saw her as intimidating and stereotyped her as probably being in a gang based on her large stature, clothing choices, and "dark" complexion. She talked about the "light girls with good hair or weaves" who just wanted to talk about fashion, shoes, sex, and how they were going to get a man with "long bank" and have his baby. She tried befriending the "smart, good girls" but shared that they all seemed to be really religious and told her she was going to hell when she disclosed that she liked to do Buddhist chants with her mother. One day she said, "I'm not anybody's homegirl, I'm not a gold digger, I have no plans to have babies and be on welfare, and I'm not trying to be a holier-than-thou church lady, so where do I fit in?" She perceived that the Black boys were attracted to the "gold diggers." She had a couple of good friends but felt that "the religious thing" was a barrier. Nia had played competitive soccer where she was top scorer, and although she made the varsity team at school, she reported being marginalized and treated more harshly than her mostly Latina teammates. She loved to read and tried to participate in class discussions but reported that teachers completely ignored her when she raised her hand, responded to her questions as if she were challenging them, or shot down her ideas completely. She described a paper she wrote for a history class and being upset about her "liberal" White male teacher's comment that slavery and racism had destroyed culture for Black people and that there was no such thing as positive African American culture. This teacher also frequently made reference to his African American wife. Nia was focused on attending a historically Black college and university school with her dream college being one of the most highly competitive. She expressed significant fear and worry that her grades were going to ruin her dream and disclosed that she became particularly anxious when preparing for and taking a test. In addition, Nia reported that it was really hard to study, that she would get distracted by thoughts about her father and things that had happened at school during the day, and that she replayed past negative events in her mind repeatedly.

Nia shared that she did not want to burden her mother with her problems because she knew how hard her mother worked and how much she was trying to be a good mom. She experienced significant guilt that she was causing her mother stress. However, Nia also reported that she felt her mother did not really understand how much pain she was in and would just tell her that she was "beautiful." Nia felt that she should be able to handle her life better like her mother, whom she perceived as "above my petty concerns." She also felt she would be disappointing her mother if she didn't have high self-esteem and conduct herself with dignity and pride as a woman of African descent.

Reflection and Discussion Questions

1. What internal and external strengths can you identify for Nia?
2. Do you think that therapy with Nia should include attention to racism and social justice themes? Why or why not?
3. What ways do the various stereotypes about African American girls and women potentially play a role in this case (consider Nia, Joyce, teachers and coaches, peers)?

4. What role might Nia's parents' experiences and cultural identity play in their expectations of and responses to Nia's distress?

5. How might the concepts of internalized racism, colorism, racial identity, racial socialization, and stereotype threat be helpful in conceptualizing this case? For understanding Nia? For understanding Nia's peers and family members?

6. How are issues of intersectionality and negotiation of multiple (and sometimes conflicting) dimensions of diversity relevant in this case?

7. In what ways were cultural considerations integrated into treatment strategies used with Nia?

8. What treatment and conceptual ideas may have been dominant if culture were not considered? How might a therapist have conceptualized and worked with Nia if culture were not a central consideration? What would be the risks of a non–culture-centered approach in working with Nia? With Joyce?

Brief Analysis of the Case

♦ Diagnostically, Nia fit criteria for generalized anxiety disorder accompanied by sadness, loneliness, and difficulty with emotion regulation. Primary themes of treatment included identity, racism, and relationships (family, peers, interracial). Nia requested that she be seen individually, and I honored this despite cultural "cookbook" recommendations that one should always see African Americans as a family. I saw Joyce separately approximately once every three weeks with sessions focused on parenting and how she could support Nia. Toward the end of treatment I saw them together for a few sessions.

♦ I worked with Nia from an integrated multicultural-humanistic orientation with a postmodern sensibility that values transparency, collaboration, technical flexibility, self-determination, and experiential awareness, and supports therapist self-disclosure where clinically indicated. I am a 50-plus-year-old, married African American woman with two adolescent sons. Over the course of therapy with Nia, I made these disclosures, as well as others related to my religious/spiritual journey and experiences coping with racism. We read Maya Angelou's poetry and autobiographies, sharing a particular love for the poem "Still I Rise." Nia was already familiar with meditation and chanting. We identified the phrase "I rise" as her personal mantra and integrated it into breathing, meditation, visualization, and chanting processes to address her excessive worry and rumination. Her name, which means "purpose" in Swahili, served as an organizing frame for working on issues related to identity and achievement of her goals.

• Nia's case raises many multicultural considerations that are important when working with African American clients:

   ♦ In addition to differential diagnostic procedures, early assessment should be culture and context centered. The genesis and maintenance of symptom expression can be understood, in part, as a function of the cultural and racial dynamics of the contexts of daily life. For example, assessing the racial-ethnic composition of Nia's environments (e.g., neighborhood, school, etc.) and the cultural norms and behaviors of the contexts within which she functioned (e.g., "soccer" culture) were very important to getting a comprehensive understanding of this client.

   ♦ Specific treatment strategies should be a culturally syntonic fit with the client's sociocultural experience, identities, and sensibilities. Treatment should be informed by examining how the intersections of person, culture, and context, and the congruence (or incongruence) between them, contribute to the African American client's internally experienced and externally expressed distress. Central to case conceptualization and treatment planning with Nia was constantly keeping in mind the interrelationships between her multiple cultural identities, her personal and psychological characteristics, and relevant contextual considerations. The use of bibliotherapy focusing on Maya Angelou's work was an example of selecting and implementing an intervention strategy that was a cultural fit for Nia.

   ♦ Conceptually, psychotherapeutic work with African American clients should be understood as treating the whole person-culture-context transaction, as a person cannot be understood or understand themselves outside of the relationships and contexts that make up their entire field of experiences. In an African-centered context, it is limiting to restrict oneself to a therapy that artificially separates the interconnected person-culture-context experience into segmented "types" of therapy. Even in meeting primarily with Nia in one-on-one sessions I conceptualized my client not as Nia the individual but rather as "Nia in context," which included Joyce, her father, Eric (whom I never met), her brother in another state, other friends and family members, her school, as well as the African American community as a whole.

- It is important to identify not only a client's individual strengths but also strengths of African culture and the African American community and how these are manifested in the client's life. Therapeutic practice with African American clients benefits from infusing a strengths-centered perspective into the work. Nurturing confidence, self-efficacy, and empowerment are important treatment goals to consider. Joyce's parenting practices had integrated and capitalized on many cultural strengths, and it was important to highlight and affirm these strengths regularly with both Nia and Joyce.

- Identifying and challenging internalized racism is critical in work with African American clients. The insidious and pervasive presence of racism and anti-Black sentiments results in inevitable exposure to negative images, dominant narratives, and socialization messages that pathologize and devalue people of African descent. Historical hostility and internalized racism were conceptualized within a larger understanding of Nia's developing identity and relationships with her parents, teachers, coaches, and peers. With Nia, this issue was approached using an acceptance-based orientation. Interventions were designed to help Nia move from "fusing" with her negative thoughts as reflecting a reality about herself or others to experiencing her thoughts and feelings as completely understandable, given her familial and sociopolitical contexts. We worked with self-compassion as a path to freeing herself from the emotional hold of her negative self-judgments that kept her paralyzed with overwhelming emotions and prevented her from making choices and changes.

- Incorporating attention to a client's multiple and intersecting dimensions of diversity that can contribute to the development of a healthy identity characterized by a sense of wholeness and pride is important. With Nia, it was critical to implement exposure to socialization messages and experiences that took into account issues of intersectionality, multiple identity dimensions, and ecological niche. Generating opportunities for Nia to feel a sense of belonging, of being accepted, required creative and collaborative brainstorming. After assessment, a particular race-gender-religion ecological niche was identified as a potential microcommunity of belonging and acceptance for Nia. We researched opportunities where she might interact with other African American adolescent girls who were spiritually centered but did not hold a fundamentalist Christian belief system.

- Assessing racial socialization and increasing positive socialization opportunities is often very helpful in work with African American clients. Racial socialization includes not only the increasing familiarity with and affirming culture but also preparation for dealing with racism (Hughes et al., 2006). Joyce's racial socialization efforts were both a significant strength and a source of grounding for Nia. They also provided content for intrapersonal, familial, and peer conflict. While Joyce had engaged in proactive racial socialization efforts with Nia that had contributed to Nia developing a strong and positive core racial identity, it appeared that she had unintentionally but simultaneously communicated to Nia that it was unacceptable to feel negatively toward other African Americans or have negative thoughts about herself. The manner in which Nia's racial socialization occurred was related to Joyce's personal coping style of keeping "negativity and negative energy out of her space." This understanding of Joyce's coping points to the importance of working with racial socialization as more than simply a present or absent parenting activity. The context within which socialization messages are delivered and received is critical to explore. In addition, Nia had a limited repertoire of racism-related coping methods and needed to build these up in order to manage the manifestations of racism that she experienced with both staff and students at her school. Therefore, treatment included identifying, applying, and debriefing diverse strategies for coping with the racism-related stress that she experienced (Harrell, 2000).

- Suicide is an understudied phenomenon among African Americans and should be understood in both its active and passive dimensions.

Processing Nia's suicidal ideation revealed that her underlying need was to get her mother to take the severity of her distress more seriously. She assured me repeatedly throughout treatment that she had no intention of harming herself. She disclosed that she often hesitated to share her thoughts and feelings with her mother. She felt that Joyce minimized her problems and did not seem to understand how distressed she really was. Nia experienced significant guilt, feeling that she was letting Joyce down by having negative self-esteem and conflicts with her African American peers at school. While I continued to check in with Nia regarding suicidal ideation and intent throughout treatment, our discussions pointed to the importance of increasing Joyce's awareness of these dynamics and a need for conjoint sessions with Joyce and Nia at an appropriate point in therapy.

- Therapeutic work with African Americans may benefit from incorporating some attention to the development of critical consciousness. This work involves processing the client's own race-related life experiences and observations, relating them to the sociohistorical and sociopolitical dynamics of racism, and exploring the implications of these understandings for one's choices and actions. Roderick Watts's theory, intervention program, and research on sociopolitical development emerge from liberation psychology and are very helpful in learning how to utilize critical consciousness interventions (Watts, Williams, & Jagers, 2003). With Nia, we drew on her increasing consciousness of the dynamics of race and culture to manage her feelings of "hate" toward her African American peers at school. Nia's negative judgments of and emotional reactivity to her peers decreased as she developed alternative ways to understand their behavior in sociopolitical and historical contexts.

- Authenticity, transparency, and an emphasis on expression of experiential processes can be effective in work with African American clients. This approach is consistent with the common African American sensibility of "keeping it real." The two-faced nature of racism (e.g., smiling to our faces and calling us "nigger" behind our backs) has contributed to an African American ethos that places high value on knowing where someone is coming from. In addition, the attention to the experiential is also quite consistent with African cultural sensibilities around expressiveness and the African American music-based experience of "soul" (i.e., being deeply moved). The importance of needing to get a "feel" for a person and needing to be "felt" are critical aspects in the development of interpersonal relationships in an African American context. A contemporary question in conversations between African American youth is "You feel me?" This has a meaning similar to "Do you understand me?" but places more emphasis on relational interconnectedness and affective attunement. These cultural understandings provided support for a relatively high level of transparency and disclosure regarding the person of the therapist and the therapeutic process in working with Nia and Joyce. Selective disclosure was an intentional decision in order to promote trust, model self-acceptance, and normalize the experience of race-related stress. Therapist disclosure may facilitate trust and credibility in the therapeutic relationship with African American clients as well as provide affirmation of the client's racial and cultural experiences.

Recommended Resources

Books and/or Articles

Belgrave, F. Z., Cherry, V. R., Butler, D. S., & Townsend, T. G. (2008). *Sisters of Nia: A cultural enrichment program to empower African American girls.* Champaign, IL: Research Press.

Boyd-Franklin, N. (2006). *Black families in therapy: Understanding the African American experience* (2nd ed.). New York, NY: Guilford Press.

Bridges, F. W. (2001). *Resurrection song: African American spirituality.* Maryknoll, NY: Orbis.

Jones, C., & Shorter-Gooden, K. (2003). *Shifting: The double lives of Black women in America (based on the African American Women's Voices project).* New York, NY: Harper.

Nasir, N. S. (2012). *Racialized identities: Race and achievement among African American youth.* Stanford, CA: Stanford University Press.

Poussaint, A., & Anderson, A. (2001). *Lay my burden down: Suicide and the mental health crisis among African-Americans.* Boston, MA: Beacon Press.

Vanzant, I. (1999). *Don't give it away! A workbook of self-awareness and self-affirmations for young women.* New York, NY: Fireside Press.

Williams, A. K. (2001). *Being Black: Zen and the art of living with fearlessness and grace.* New York, NY: Penguin Books.

Videos

Chapman, V. & McKay, E. (Producers/Directors). *For our daughters: A film for Black girls . . . and those who care about them.* [Motion picture]. (2012). United States: Draxum Media Group. Available at http://www.4ourdaughters.com

Fiction and Biography

Angelou, M. (1994). *The complete collected poems of Maya Angelou.* New York, NY: Random House.

Angelou, M. (2004). *The collected autobiographies of Maya Angelou.* New York, NY: Random House/Modern Library.

Willis, J. (2001). *Dreaming me: Black, Baptist, and Buddhist: One woman's spiritual journey.* Somerville, MA: Wisdom Press.

Websites/Blogs

www.afrobella.com
Afrobella celebrates women all shades and textures of beautiful.
www.positivepropoganda.com
This site inspires, educates, and empowers Black women and girls to create healthy perceptions of self while campaigning for global perception change.

REFERENCES

Harrell, S. P. (2000). A multidimensional conceptualization of racism-related stress: Implications for the well-being of people of color. *American Journal of Orthopsychiatry, 70,* 42–57.

Hughes, D., Rodriguez, J., Smith, E. P., Johnson, D. J., Stevenson, H. C., & Spicer, P. (2006). Parents' ethnic-racial socialization practices: A review of research and directions for future study. *Developmental Psychology, 42*(5), 747–770.

Watts, R. J., Williams, N. C., & Jagers, R. (2003). Sociopolitical development. *American Journal of Community Psychology, 31,* 185–194.

REDEFINED: THE STORY OF ANDRE

Redefined: The Story of Andre discusses psychotherapy with an African American man, grappling with multidimensional identities, using an African-centered modality.

Case Description

When Andre first came to therapy, he was 22 years old, single, and described himself as a third-generation, African American Pentecostal minister. At intake, he lived with his mother and did not disclose his sexual orientation. Both his father and grandfather were preachers, as were two of his uncles. Andre arrived with his hair in braids—he shared that he was "starting to loc"— wearing jeans and an oversize T-shirt and jewelry. His left earlobe was pierced; he had rings and bracelets on both hands and a huge silver necklace around his neck.

Andre presented to therapy upon referral from his uncle, the senior pastor at his church, who was concerned that Andre was suffering from "delayed grief." Andre was very skeptical of therapy, feeling that if God abandoned him, how could anyone else help him? He reluctantly agreed to therapy because his uncle told him that he would keep him on the church payroll only if he sought help. The church was paying for treatment and wanted monthly updates that Andre was coming to therapy—they did not require updates on therapy content or progress.

Andre grew up in the Pentecostal church. His activities were strictly monitored, and he had very restricted habits. As a child he went to religious school and spent most of his "free" time singing in church, practicing his music, and in Bible study and prayer groups. Andre is very bright, articulate, and a passionate public speaker; he was being groomed to become senior pastor at his grandfather's church. His peers led similar lives. Currently he is on leave from the church, where he served as the minister of music and led several youth groups. Both his father and grandfather were deceased; however, both had been very active in advocating civil and human rights for African Americans. Thus Andre had been reared with a very strong racial-ethnic identity and envisions himself as an activist minister. Andre's father's died when he was 15 from a long-term illness.

Andre was born a twin; his sister, Andrea, died mysteriously approximately two years ago. She was found in an empty storehouse at the bottom of some stairs, with massive head trauma. She was pronounced dead upon arrival to the hospital. Although the circumstances of her death remain cloudy, the police ruled the death accidental. Andre was devastated and began to question his commitment to the church and God. He reported that "God abandoned him" and he was unwilling to continue his involvement in the church.

After about 12 sessions, discussing the story of his sister's death and his conviction that it was "not an accident," he began to address his "real problem." Andre reported that he is "same-gender loving,"[1] that he has had several same-sex experiences, and that he thinks he is "in love" with another man. He expressed some confusion about how to integrate his sexual identity with his strong ethnic identity and deeply held religious faith.

Upon the suggestion of the therapist, Andre had begun working at a community agency doing outreach with HIV-positive African American men. He reported that this work gave him a chance to engage in important social activism work while getting to experiment with his same-sex identity. Although he reported that he was comfortable with his sexual identity, he experienced conflict between his identity and the strong conviction that he had been "called" to the ministry and wanted to remain a minister at his church. He reported that he had conversations with both his uncle and mother about his sexual identity, although neither of them "took me seriously." He is balancing moving in with his "lover" versus staying with his mother, who continues to grieve about the loss of his sister.

Andre presented as a strong, African-centered social activist, steeped in a deeply held Pentecostal faith tradition, emerging ownership of his SGL sexuality, devoted son and surviving twin, bright, educated, middle-class, African American male.

Reflection and Discussion Questions

1. What role do you think Andre's religious heritage and affinity has on his identity?

---

[1]   Same-gender loving (SGL), a term coined for use by activist Cleo Manago, is a description for same-sex oriented men and women, particularly in the African American community. It emerged in the early 1990s as a culturally affirming same-sex identity. SGL is an alternative to Eurocentric same-sex identities—gay and lesbian—that do not culturally affirm or engage the history and cultures of people of African descent.

2. What do you know about the social values of the Pentecostal denomination?
3. What is the significance of Andre defining himself as a same-gender-loving man?
4. How does this definition conform with or differ from being an African American gay man?
5. What primary diagnostic impressions are best to consider for Andre? At intake? After 12 sessions?
6. Given Andre's skepticism about the value of counseling and psychotherapy, what role, if any, might therapist self-disclosure have on establishing a strong therapeutic alliance with him?
7. What are the primary dimensions of Andre's identity, and how might a culturally competent therapist begin to prioritize targets of treatment with Andre?
8. How difficult might it be to address each of the major dimensions of Andre's identity? What role, if any, do the therapist's multidimensional identities play in Andre's treatment planning?

Brief Analysis of the Case

◆ The critical challenge with this client was to develop a perspective for therapy that could privilege his multiple, varied contextual identities, each of which had strong meaning and definition for Andre. Although there might be a variety of ways of conceptualizing therapy with Andre, given his status across multiple dimensions of his identity, it was important to approach work with him from a nontraditional conceptual framework. Current traditional models of mental health practice may not be particularly helpful with any of his primary identities, let alone with all of them combined.

◆ An African-centered approach to treatment allowed Andre to find himself in a culturally affirming fashion that focused on his strengths, interdependence, and spirituality. Key points in the analysis of this case are presented within an African-centered conceptual framework that articulates and centers "five healing aims" for the treatment of African-descended clients. African proverbs were incorporated throughout sessions to help Andre situate his challenges within an African worldview and served as a catalyst for him to envision a better tomorrow (Rowe & Rowe, 2009).

First Healing Aim: Remembering or Re-Memorying

- Healing involves the process of "re-memorying"—reconstructing our stories (spirits, bodies, families, and psyches) from fragments of memory, gossip, and news. Memory and storytelling are reconnective processes that can help us live more harmoniously with our self, family, community, and the past (Akinyela, 2005).

  Andre entered therapy with the second author, a middle-age African American male, and established rapport through initial emphasis on shared strong ethnic identification and social activism. This provided an opportunity to focus on grief issues in a more culturally syntonic fashion.

  Andre explored the loss of his sister, his twinship, and the resulting emptiness by examining the role of twins and loss in traditional African spirituality (Ephirim-Donkor, 1997) and comparisons to his Pentecostal faith. This exploration enhanced therapist credibility, since it supported Andre's ethnic identity, supported the deep loss he was experiencing, and created a sense that therapy would be nontraditional, thus challenging and expanding his perspective about its perceived helpfulness. Andre settled on an understanding that his sister would always live within him, and he could maintain his regular communing with her during his daily prayer time.

Second Healing Aim: Realignment

- Reconnecting a sense of personhood—spiritual, communal, cultural (physical/environmental), and personal potentials (Grills & Rowe, 1998) is a second healing aim of treatment with clients of African descent.

  It was during those discussions that Andre reported that the loss of his twin and sense of abandonment by God had given him permission to explore his sexual identity, which he had suppressed for most of his life. His same-sex orientation had been a secret he and his sister shared; her loss propelled him to act on it.

  A referral was made for Andre to volunteer within a culturally specific HIV service agency to give him a chance to try on aspects of his sexual identity without having to become public, thereby letting him challenge some of his negative stereotypes about nonheterosexuals (Herek & Garnets, 2007). Through his volunteer experiences, he found a number of African American men who had crafted a different perspective regarding their same sexual orientations: same-gender-loving. He was also surprised to find a number of these men who retained their deeply held religious beliefs.

Third Healing Aim: Rebuilding

- "Rebuilding" refers to developing sociocommunal systems that replicate and reflect African notions of human beingness, features of human functioning and optimal human development. Rebuilding fractured spirits requires collective, communal, and cultural practices; one cannot address symptoms of disorder by imposing or reinforcing isolation to reinstitute order within the person.

  Rebuilding was the most important aspect of Andre's work; the aim was to give him an opportunity to experiment with the fullness of his emerging identity. Andre began to explore the role of his Pentecostal faith, its impact on his current functioning, and the possibility of merging his faith tradition with his social activism and sexual identity. He began to study the history of the Pentecostal movement and discovered that African Americans were integrally involved in its formation and development at a time when integrated church services did not exist in the United States.

Fourth Healing Aim: Revitalization

- Grounded in the importance of spiritual experience for mental health, the healing aim of revitalization focuses on helping persons see themselves as spirit manifest. Ongoing healing becomes the process and state of guiding and/or developing the person's ability to experience the extraordinary, special, and divine spirit within (Nobles, King, & James, 1995).

  This aspect of treatment resonated strongly with Andre, as it fit with his faith traditions and inspired him to consider a future that merged his multidimensional contextual identities: He began to claim the possibility of being a sociocultural activist and same-sex-oriented minister for underserved men of African ancestry.

Fifth Healing Aim: Restoration

- Restoration—the fifth healing aim—promotes renewal through strengthening interdependence; fostering a sense that life unfolds in intimate reciprocity; and regaining the capacity to experience life with a fullness of being.

As therapy progressed, Andre reported sleeping well, regaining the 20 pounds he had lost following his sister's death, having an increase in energy and concentration, and recognizing his integrated goals and aims: "I know who I am and what I'm supposed to do," he stated.

• The emphasis and continuity across the healing aims on *"re"* processing is intentional. A central component of an African-centered approach is orienting to psychotherapy as a healing and revealing process. Therapists are grounded in the understanding that our primary task is to help clients reconnect with their core spiritual identity and culturally experienced humanity that already exist within them and link them across time and place to ancestors, family, and all persons. This cultural grounding helps to minimize the overpathologizing of symptom expression and contributes to a therapeutic process that is ultimately liberating, affirming, and empowering.

Recommended Resources

Books and/or Articles

Harawa, N. T., Williams, J. K., Ramamurthi, H. C., Manago, C., Avina, S., & Jones, M. (2008). Sexual behavior, sexual identity, and substance abuse among low-income bisexual and non-gay-identifying African-American men who have sex with men. *Archives of Sexual Behavior, 37*, 748–762.

Jones, R. (2004). *Black psychology* (4th ed.). Hampton, VA: Cobb & Henry.

Knight-Lapinski, M., Braz, M. E., & Maloney, E. K. (2010). The down low, social stigma, and risky sexual behaviors: Insights from African-American men who have sex with other men. *Journal of Homosexuality, 57*, 610–633.

Nobles, W. W. (1998). To be African or not to be: The question of identity or authenticity—some preliminary thoughts. In R. L. Jones (Ed.), *African American identity development* (pp. 183–206). Hampton, VA: Cobb & Henry.

Parks, C. W. (2001). African-American same-gender-loving youths and families in urban schools. *Journal of Gay & Lesbian Social Services, 13*(3), 41–56.

Pendeno, F. J., Antoni, M. H., Schneiderman, N., Ironson, G. H., Malow, R. M., Cruess, S., & LaPerriere, A. (2001). Dysfunctional attitudes, coping, and depression among HIV-seropositive men who have sex with men. *Cognitive Therapy and Research*, *25*(5), 591–606.

Piper-Mandy, E., & Rowe, T. D. (2010). Educating African-centered psychologists: Towards a comprehensive paradigm. *Journal of Pan-African Studies*, *3*(8), 5–23. Available from http://www.jpanafrican.com/docs/vol3no8/3.8EducatingAfrican.pdf

Wester, S., Vogel, D. L., Wei, M., & McLain, R. (2006). African American men, gender role conflict, and psychological distress: The role of racial identity. *Journal of Counseling and Development*, *84*(4), 419–429.

Popular Books

Marcell, D. (2011). *Saved, sanctified, and same-gender loving*. Corona, CA: Trinity Learning Community.

A proclamation of reclamation for all African American SGL men who have lived conflicted lives, tormented by indoctrinated fears of eternal damnation, terrified of being rejected by God and family. In this book, Marcell presents personal stories that illustrate his struggle to reconcile his spiritual and sexual identities; he also challenges other African American SGL men (whether openly gay, closeted, down-low, or transgendered) to confront their own identity.

Stewart, J. (1997). *African proverbs and wisdom: A collection for every day of the year, from more than forty African nations*. Secaucus, NJ: Carol Publishing Group.

A poignant compendium of wise sayings, proverbs, legends, riddles, and tales, this work can serve as an adjunct to therapy to provide clients with reflective space to contemplate how their particular challenges fit within an African-centered worldview.

Videos

Evans, R. (Producer & Director). (2004). *Brother to brother* [Motion picture]. United States: Wolfe Releasing.

Opposites attract when an elderly homeless man named Richard, once a literary legend of the Harlem Renaissance of the 1920s, befriends gay art student Perry in this sensitive, introspective drama.

Fairchild, H. H. (2012). *Joseph White, father of Black psychology: An interview* [Motion picture]. Available from http://www.youtube.com/watch?v=2bm6ek6swGg

An interview with Dr. Joe White, founder of the Association of Black Psychologists and retired professor at the University of California, Irvine. Dr. White is at the 40th Annual Convention of the Association of Black Psychologists in Oakland, August 2008. Copyright by the Association of Black Psychologists.

Johnson, H. (Director). (2009). *Black faith* [Motion picture]. United States: Music Video Distributors.

In this fascinating documentary, director Howard Johnson delves into the storied history of the Black church and examines the ways the diverse religious institution has influenced the lives of African Americans throughout time.

Websites/Blogs

Christian meta-groups: Pentecostal group of denominations: http://www.religioustolerance.org/chr_pent.htm

REFERENCES

Akinyela, M. M. (2005). Testimony of hope: African-centered praxis for therapeutic ends. *Journal of Systemic Therapies, 24*(1), 5–18.

Ephirim-Donkor, A. (1997). *African spirituality: On becoming ancestors.* Trenton, NJ: Africa World Press, Inc.

Grills, C., & Rowe, D. (1998). African traditional medicine: Implications for African-centered approaches to healing. In R. L. Jones (Ed.), *African American mental health: Theory, research and intervention* (pp. 71–100). Hampton, VA: Cobb & Henry.

Herek, G. M., & Garnets, L. D. (2007). Sexual orientation and mental health. *Annual Review of Clinical Psychology, 3*(3), 353–375.

Nobles, W. W., King, L., & James, C. B. (1995). *Health promotion and disease prevention: Strategies in the African American community.* African American professionals health promotion and disease prevention focus group report submitted to the Congress of National Black Churches, Washington, DC: The Association of Black Psychologists.

Rowe, D. M., & Rowe, S. L. (2009). Conversations in Marriage™: An African-centered marital intervention. In M. E. Gallardo & B. McNeill (Eds.), *Intersections of multiple identities: A casebook of evidence-based practices with diverse populations* (pp. 59–84). New York, NY: Routledge.

2

Clinical Applications With American Indians and Alaska Natives

Joseph B. Stone and Connie Hunt

TREATING "DEPRESSION" IN A DYING
NATIVE RELATIVE: THE STORY OF WILL

Case Description

I (Joseph Stone) am an enrolled Blackfeet tribal member and a practicing clinical psychologist with an exclusively Native caseload for the past 17 years. Some years ago, I was working at a tribal clinic in a western location. A physician appeared at the door and said, "This man is depressed because he is dying and I have work to do. Would you handle this?" Away he went.

"Will" (for confidentiality purposes) came in and sat down. We looked at each other quietly, as is often the case when tribal men first meet. Will said, "You look Native." I replied, "Joe, Blackfeet from Montana." He named his tribe. Then he said, "What's wrong with that guy?" We laughed—much was not stated between us, but clear mutual understanding of "that guy" and the meaning he brought to our universe was apparent. It required no dialogue.

Will said, "I don't think I am depressed, but I am dying, and soon. It is a natural thing. How do your Blackfeet handle it?" I talked about our practices around the transition of the spirit from this existence into the next. "It is a natural thing." He nodded. I nodded. That was the extent of our dialogue around "depression," or dying. But Will stayed with me for 36 sessions after this initial one. He stayed until his spirit made the transition to the other world (in other words, he died).

Will simply started telling me his story that day, and he returned weekly to tell his story. This story was of life, his life, and it was a good one: He spoke of being raised in a tribe in a western state. Of the rituals and ceremonies and culture and language and traditional practices he learned as a boy. He spoke of his family and respected tribal members. Not only did he speak, but Will often asked me about my tribe, my ceremonies, my rituals, my elders, our ways. In many respects, our life stories were the same.

Will spoke of his losses and those of his people—loss of land, culture, traditions, and, ultimately, their very identity. The U.S. federal government had engaged this small western tribe in the policy of termination, a process by which the government provided a cash payout to each tribal member, nationalized all tribal holdings, and declared the tribal members to no longer be Indians/First Nations. Will said, "I asked myself continually, who am I, after that occurred. I spent the money on alcohol to drown the pain of not knowing. The money went quickly. After, I worked, as did everyone else, in the logging industry and I became a blacksmith—a good one."

"Of course, we were always treated badly and we stayed to ourselves, unless we were drinking. There were many deaths—they say from disease, but I know better; it was sadness and loss. But we did hold on to our ceremonies and practices in secret. Do you know anything of your ways, young man?"

Will was my elder and, within our First Nations, he had the right to confront me about traditional and spiritual matters and, further, to instruct me in areas where I might be deficient.

Will spoke about the practices, beliefs, values, and ceremonies of his people and asked me to describe the Blackfeet culture and spirituality. He encouraged me to continue to participate and to enhance and increase my participation in traditional spirituality. "A man must know these things." I shared openly with him and I solicited his advice on spiritual practices—that was culturally appropriate for a younger man, therapist or not.

Will talked about the "restoration" day when his tribe was recognized again as a tribe by the federal government. "That was a great day," he said, "a great day. Now we have regained our dignity. We are no longer White men, we are Indian. I didn't like being a White man." He laughed. Will spoke about the advances and strides his tribe had made in business and health care and education, and he was proud. I was too.

Will described his immediate family. His wife was deceased and his adult children were successful and out on their own. "They did good. My wife was a good woman, good to me and to them, and I was fortunate to have her. I can't wait to see her again, and soon enough, I will." He smiled. "I have missed her." Then he talked about the disease, it was rare, one in a million, unusual and invariably fatal. "It takes me home to her," he said, and smiled again.

One day, Will came in and said, "I have always loved the game of horseshoes and so I have sold everything, my house, my car, all my stuff, and I have taken the money and hired a band and I am getting a caterer and setting up some horseshoe pits and we are going to have a tribal horseshoe tournament in honor of"—he winked—"me. Will you come to it? There will be prizes," he asked. I did attend and I played, badly, but I had fun. I won a cash prize, as did all the attendees, and I had a good meal and I laughed with Will that afternoon. I never saw him alive again. He passed two days later to the spirit world.

We told stories about Will at his wake and we laughed: We laughed about Will, we laughed at Will, we laughed at ourselves, and, I think, Will laughed with us. After the internment, I returned to the grave site, I had a final task, a ceremony Will had described to me. He had said, "A man must know these things." So, I learned and I practiced it that day to help ease my older brother, my relative on his journey to the spirit world. I imagined his wife had greeted him in the spirit world warmly with food, drink, and love—that is our way.

Will died well, and for us, in the First Nations, that is important. It was his final spiritual gift to a younger man—he showed me how to die well, and when that time comes for me, I will know how that is done and I will die well. Then I'll laugh with Will again. Perhaps he will tell me stories and teach more—that's okay. This is what we believe.

Reflection and Discussion Questions

1. What model of therapy did the therapist use here? Is it a common model? Is it taught in graduate schools? How could it have been improved?

2. How might a therapist who was not of Native heritage or who was not familiar with Native peoples have worked best with Will?
3. Was Will in "denial" of depressed mood? Should Will's lack of acceptance of "depression" as a diagnosis have been confronted more aggressively? Would antidepressant medication have benefited Will?
4. Would classic cognitive, psychodynamic, or behavioral therapies have improved this therapy? Why or why not?
5. Did the counselor err in his open disclosures and dialogue with Will? If so, how could that have been improved? Is it ethical to accept spiritual instruction from a client?
6. Was the counselor's decision to spend time with Will outside of therapy a problem? Was it culturally responsive? Was it unethical?
7. Is the therapist's use of and adherence to the constructs and language of traditional Native practices appropriate? If not, what would a viable alternative be? Has the therapist overly identified with Will and lost objectivity? Is objectivity desired when a First Nations therapist meets with a First Nations relative for counseling?

Brief Analysis of the Case

Native or First Nations relatives (I do not like the terms *client* or *clients*) are often impacted by a sequence of the effects of colonization and historical trauma with ongoing intergenerational developmental, social, economic, and cultural loss and disruption. These themes are the backdrop of any therapy for a First Nations relative on any topic, and they emerge in most therapeutic interactions. Many times, a First Nations relative will move from the presenting problem to a discussion of these dynamics: colonization and recovery from colonization in therapy.

♦ When working with First Nations relatives, it is important for therapists to consider colonization, culture, spirituality, political, economic, racial, class, and social issues. Tribal communities are impacted by a historical trend of violence, trauma, genocide, and postcolonial stress perpetrated by the clash of cultures between Native cultures and tribes and the dominant or affluent Euro-American culture and colonists to America. This clash of cultures has incorporated numerous systemic influences on tribal persons and communities across history, including but not limited to these:

- Dispossession of lands and property
- Biological warfare through introduction of foreign diseases in blankets and other gifts
- Disruption of language and culture
- Indian wars and massacres
- The federal and religious boarding schools (disruption of family and language, which is the carrier of culture)
- Federal polices of governmental termination of tribal and Native status
- Federal relocation programs of Natives to cities
- Modern sociological influences on urban and rural tribal people and communities including, but not limited to, gangs and drugs (in particular, methamphetamine)

• Each of these systemic influences on Native people and communities has underlain chronic stress within specific generations, in turn, predisposing less-than-adequate parenting practices within specific generations in the tribal communities and negatively impacting the neurodevelopment of Native youth. In addition, negative influences of trauma on neurodevelopment led to unregulated arousal, decreased resilience, and increased risk (compromised behavioral immunity). Understanding this systemic intergenerational process of historical trauma and postcolonial stress affecting tribal communities and individuals gives the professional behavioral health worker insight into the depth and breadth of the underlying dynamic that often manifests itself in the form of psychiatric disorders and addictive behaviors, which are natural consequences of intergenerational trauma, postcolonial stress, and genocide across time. Reclaiming tribal identity and spirituality are of great importance, therefore. Some methods for doing so are described and recommended.

• Colonization and historical trauma are critical shaping mechanisms in most, if not all, experiences of First Nations relatives. But of greater importance are the ways within which First Nations individuals, communities, and tribes are ameliorating the effects of colonization by restoring traditional beliefs and practices, building viable economic bases, developing pride and dignity about heritage and beliefs, and increasing use of ceremony and ritual.

• There are a growing number of tribal professionals trained as psychologists, counselors, and other mental health workers. The training is most often in the classical Euro-American and Westernized methods. However, Native workers often bring in their own reservoirs of traditional and spiritual knowledge and a shared understanding of the unspoken issues with the relative (client) being treated, including a shared perspective on racialism, colonization, second-class citizenship, poverty, and the like.

• Other mental health workers from outside the First Nations culture must seek and develop a sense of cultural understanding through training and dialogue with both experts in cross-cultural counseling and from First Nations persons. It is critical that non-Native workers must forge relationships within the First Nations communities in order to best obtain the consultations necessary to serve First Nations relatives. There are many and sundry methods of working with a First Nations relative that bear no resemblance to those taught in Westernized graduate schools. These ways are often more effective in ameliorating the issues of the First Nations relatives than the standardized Western "best practices."

• In addition to the use of scientific literature and consultation with experts, either Native themselves or those familiar with Native issues, it serves non-Native workers well to form professional collegial relationships with local experts in tribal culture and spirituality. These relationships provide a resource to justify moving from the predominately non-Native methodologies, such as cognitive-behavioral or psychodynamic, into the realm of individualizing treatment based on integration of tribal/Native spiritual and cultural values, traditions, beliefs, and practices. The therapy described here relied highly on those perspectives, but just because I am Native does not imply that a well-trained non-Native worker could not learn and integrate a Native perspective into his or her preferred treatment model.

• Not only is it critical to develop a larger and more comprehensively trained group of Native professionals and to educate non-Native workers, but it is important to consider the entire paradigm of mental health for applicability to First Nations relatives, communities, and their issues. It is important to think through and address the effects of colonization and the methods to ameliorate those effects. Do the classical Westernized "best practices" of cognitive therapy and other Euro-American interventions work best, or must they be replaced? Based on this writer's clinical experience, it is clear that a new Native-based paradigm of mental health must replace that of the classic Western model.

Recommended Resources

Books and/or Articles

Bullchild, P. (1985). *The sun came down: The history of the world as my Blackfeet elders told it.* Lincoln, NE: University of Nebraska Press.

Deloria, V., Jr. (1995). *Red earth, white lies: Native Americans and the myth of scientific fact.* New York, NY: Scribner.

Lowe, J. (2002). Balance and harmony through connectedness: The intentionality of American Nurses. *Holistic Nursing Practice, 16*(4), 4–11.

Lowe, J. (2002). Cherokee self reliance. *Journal of Transcultural Nursing, 13*(4), 287–295.

Marks, P. M. (1998). *In a barren land: American Indian dispossession and survival.* New York, NY: Morrow.

Stone, J. B. (1998). *Traditional and contemporary Lakota death, dying, grief, and bereavement beliefs and practices: A qualitative study* (Unpublished dissertation). Utah State University Psychology Department, Logan, Utah.

Stone, J. B. (2012, Spring). First Nations historical trauma: A path analysis. Native American culture and the Western psyche: A bridge between. *Spring: A Journal of Archetype and Culture, 88.*

Struthers, R., and Lowe, J. (2003). Nursing in the Native American culture and historical trauma. *Issues in Mental Health Nursing, 24*(3), 257–272.

Training Lecture

Stone, J. B. (2010, September 17). *Depression: Causes and treatments—Native American behavioral health training.* Western New Mexico University, 2055 State Road 602, Gallup, NM.

Videos

Forsen, J. (Producer), & Stevenson, R. (Director). (2006). *Expiration date* [Motion picture]. United States: Roadkill Productions LLC.

Fiction Reading

Alexie, S. (1986). *Indian killer.* New York, NY: Warner Books.

Momaday, N. S. (1969). *The way to Rainy Mountain.* Albuquerque, NM: University of New Mexico Press.

Welch, J. (1979). *The death of Jim Loney.* New York, NY: Penguin Books.

Welch, J. (1986). *Fools crow.* New York, NY: Penguin Books.

TREATING "DEPRESSION" IN A DEEPLY BEREAVED AND TRAUMATIZED CLIENT: THE STORY OF MARY

Case Description

I (Connie Hunt) am an enrolled Puyallup tribal member and a practicing clinical psychologist with an exclusively Native caseload for the past 19 plus years. Some years ago, I was working at a Western model community mental health clinic in a rural, western location. A tribal woman from more than 250 miles away in a neighboring state made an intake appointment through the appointment management system. The woman came in deeply saddened and curled up in the chair and whispered, "I have lost my grandmother."

Let's call her "Mary" for confidentiality. Mary's eyes were turned down toward her knees as she sat with her knees tucked under her chin. A tear trickled down her cheek. We looked at each other. "I'm Connie," I told her softly. She glanced at me and replied, "I'm Mary, and I'm afraid I am losing my mind." After quietly reassuring her, I redirected her to an intake interview. She understood that it was part of the policy at the agency I worked for. She told me, "I have come a long way tonight to see you. I had heard there was a Native woman here. You are the only Native therapist in the entire region." There was a silence as we acknowledged the reality of the health care world interface with tribal communities and the deeply disparate way that tribal community members must seek care. It required no dialogue.

Mary said, "I think I'm depressed. I have waited for the pain to pass, but it hasn't. My grandmother raised me after I was removed from the home of my alcoholic mother and her husband who sexually abused me. The tribe picked me up and dropped me off with my grandmother. She adopted me. She took care of me, and no one ever hurt me again. She was my mother and my family. How do you make the pain go away? She was the only good thing in my life." Tears streamed down her face as she hugged her knees tighter to her chest. "She was always there." We spoke of grief and the passage to the other side. We talked about what her grandmother believed and what she believed. We spoke of giving grief time and honoring the old ways. A deep silence followed. "It is the way of things," she whispered.

After a long silence, Mary looked up at me and said, "She came to me, you know. . . . It's been a year since she passed. We did the traditional giveaway." A giveaway is a traditional giving of gifts that is a common practice across tribes after the death of a loved one. The length of time between death and the giveaway varies but often is about one year. The ritual acknowledges a time of closure surrounding grief, among other things. "I thought I was all right, but I hurt. I came home, and it was late. I'd gone to bed but woke up. I walked out into the living room and the moonlight was coming in the window. She was there, sitting in her rocking chair. She spoke and called me by my traditional name in our language. I remembered her speaking to me in the past in our language and how kind and strong she was." Tears continued. "Am I losing my mind?" Mary asked.

Mary was frightened and deeply bereaved. She was willing to make a long journey to make her way to the place where healing might begin. She knew the traditions of meeting and learning from those she was intended to meet with and learn from. She remembered the stories that her grandmother told her and knew of and practiced the ways and rituals of her people.

Mary struggled with tears and further asked what I thought. We spoke of beliefs and variations between and among tribes. She asked about my people and if we ever saw the dead. I shared our beliefs surrounding seeing others after their passing. She thought about my words and continued, "How can you tell whether someone has seen their grandmother or is simply seeing things?" Mary and I talked about cultural context. We talked about the words she heard her grandmother use. She told me she felt loved and cared for when her grandmother had come to her in the moonlight. I asked Mary, "Was it fitting for her to come with the moon?" Mary smiled a ghost of a smile, and we closed.

Of the rituals, ceremonies, culture, language, and traditional practices she had learned as a child, Mary was sure of herself. She continued to return for several months. Her grandmother never reappeared to her, but she acknowledged knowing that her grandmother was watching over her. Mary was confident enough to begin her own work on her personal history of abuse. She held her grandmother's strength in mind and in her heart.

Mary was much younger than I but was willing to sit in silence and ground herself in her own beliefs. She was mindful, did not drink, and felt torn apart from the person she most dearly loved and trusted. She was poor but had a job. She had the home her grandmother had left her. Before her last visit, she spoke of her hope and dream of love and family. She prayed that her history of abuse would never touch the dream of the future.

Mary was quiet and accepting. She learned with grace and worked to find balance within herself. She found the ability to honor the passing of her grandmother. Her parting words to me were "I was afraid to tell you that I had seen my grandmother. I was afraid you would just think I was crazy and lock me up, but you understood. I never really believed that you or anyone would. I didn't believe that you wouldn't judge me. . . . Thank you."

As quietly as she had arrived, she departed.

Reflection and Discussion Questions

1. Was it problematic for the therapist to frame the "seeing" of a deceased relative as anything other than visual and auditory hallucinations? Might a different therapeutic approach have worked with this client? What might it have been?

2. Should the therapist have advised a medication evaluation? Why or why not? What are the possible benefits or negative consequences from possibly supporting medication in a case like this? How would you have discussed this "seeing" if you had seen this client?

3. Do you understand the utilization and sharing of names among Native peoples? Supervisors and attending non-Natives often see informality with clients as being discourteous or promoting inappropriate boundaries. How do you interpret the use of first names between therapist and client?

4. The therapist saw Mary's symptoms as indications of a culturally valid experience. Western theory may consider her "seeing" or hallucinations as a form of a psychotic episode associated with major depression and/ or posttraumatic stress disorder. What do you think? What explanations are you willing to consider? In the end, does it make a difference?

5. Linguistically, the client and therapist were from different language groups with only English in common. Does this change therapy? If

this therapeutic session were carried out in the client's primary Native language, would this even have been considered therapy? Is there any meaning to the client's grandmother speaking in the primary language? How does that affect the interpretation of the client's perceptual experience?

6. What type of therapy would you recommend for Mary? Is there any room for consideration of a culturally relevant approach? Would you consider seeing a client like this who traveled a great distance to see you? What are the risk factors? Are these acceptable living and working conditions based on your frame of reference? How do you view health care disparities after considering these questions? Can you devise a specific step-by-step culturally appropriate treatment plan?

7. Are you familiar with any spiritual practices of Native peoples? Are you bound by the cultural conditioning of therapeutic practice, or is that in and of itself unprofessional or unethical? Do either of these queries have any bearing on this case?

8. Can the Western construct of the therapeutic session be considered a barrier to health care? Is the formal intake itself a barrier? Do the costs of nonparticipation in reimbursement, billing, and credentialing outweigh the needs of the client? How might we be able to find a middle ground and resolve competing requirements? How would this alleviate systemic inhibitors that may interfere with services for the client, and how might this reduce compassion fatigue for the provider?

9. Discuss whether telepsychology is a viable option. What aspect of mental health do providers lose if they never know where their clients live, how to sit with a client, or how to communicate with culturally appropriate phrases and intonations? What happens when we do not learn the finer arts of communication (verbal and nonverbal) necessary to practice therapeutic techniques? Can mental health professionals actually effectively advocate for the health care of their clients without any contact with the world of those clients?

Brief Analysis of the Case

This example illustrates the importance of the cultural experience and belief systems for Native peoples. It also focuses on perceptions, interpretation, judgment, and socioeconomic and geographic issues, and touches on linguistic and cultural differences even within the context of being Native. Historical context is also an abiding issue for Native peoples due to the knowledge and trauma that it has left behind.

• The forbidden or hidden qualities of Native cultural practices has led Native peoples to be viewed as individuals with spiritually magical properties. This creates a layer of complexity for the therapist or mental health professional. The therapist is left to learn about the client's culture. Further, the impact of history on the client is a critical aspect of treatment. The popular and politically correct method of working with the culturally different client is to develop culturally responsive methods; however, it is difficult to embrace something that may lie outside the parameters of conventional therapies. How to know that which is unknown is difficult but not impossible. Western training develops boundaries within the professional that makes it difficult to question the therapeutic approaches promoted by graduate school. Western modalities assume a power differential. Traditional Native methods largely promote a power parallel model.

• Mary's "hallucination" may have many causes. Even if mental health practitioners do not view themselves as embracing of various cultural phenomenological sets, therapists can "Fake it until they make it." Regardless of theoretical orientation, spiritual beliefs, or preference in practice, clinical clarifications are in order. If the client is not a danger to self or others, is not truly a candidate for in-client care, has no overt organic conditions, and has a solid understanding of his or her own beliefs, therapists can restructure their own beliefs to view such hallucinations as bereavement hallucinations or illusions. The client will go on with therapy and the therapist will be thanked in the end. A cognitively flexible therapist will adapt and seek to learn more, creating a new therapeutic repertoire. In fact, therapists from any theoretical orientation can learn to differentiate such disorders as *ghost sickness*, which is a culturally bound disorder. However, whether therapists embrace such diagnoses has to do with the therapists themselves and their workplace.

• Another consideration in the life of Mary may be her geographic isolation, lack of access to health care, and perceived lower socioeconomic status. Have Mary's life circumstances affected her clinical presentation? Even if they have, does it change the approach taken in quality health care or therapeutic practice? Could Mary's life circumstance simply be an artifact of the inability of an observer to accept that this is an external stimulus that is not well understood in the Western world? Therapeutic practice relies on the therapist to consider all possibilities, no matter how uncomfortable. Whether practitioners believe as clients do is immaterial to the practice of therapeutic techniques.

• Among Native peoples, all aspects of the therapeutic practice are considered an essential part of the concept of "healing." Clients who have the means to drive to an appointment are not considered impoverished within the community. Nonetheless, a drive from another state would indicate motivation on the part of the client. Even if the client's disadvantaged position from a Western perspective is considered, has this client changed prognostic indications by objective and quantifiable commitment? Is the trip a quantifiable and holistic part of the healing journey?

• Would we consider denying this client the best-fit therapeutic process to force the issue of evidence-based, Western practices?

• We know that boarding schools created a variation in marital patterns among Native groups. Native genetic pools were altered, and language changes were forced. Adaptive language changes were created by relationships between individuals from different linguistic groups as well as the dynamic shared languages their children spoke or creoles (languages used by in-groups) or pidgins (used to communicate with those outside of the group). Psycholinguistically, cognitive sets within linguistic groups would be dynamically altered to accommodate these language changes. These observations by linguists also give us a peek into the unique development of communication sets within Native communities and clues as to how subsequent generations remain affected by primary languages. These affects may linger for what is postulated to be several generations. Linguistic, cognitive, and emotional barriers may delay therapeutic goals as these are the major media in which therapeutic process is effective. Care and consideration are essential (see Arends, Muysken, & Norvul, 1995).

• While clients may utilize a version of standard English in the therapeutic interface, therapist likely will miss nuances or the importance of specific events from the clients' perspectives. Ultimately there would be a linguistic/cognitive/behavioral bias on the part of the therapist. It is not the client's responsibility to acquire greater skill; it is the therapeutic responsibility of the therapist. Contrary to the belief of most radical behaviorists or psychoanalysts, the therapeutic relationship requires that nurturing regardless of therapeutic modality and/or agreed-on treatment plan.

◆ Although the case example did not require it, near some reservations, the use of interpreters is essential. Their use, however, places serious limitations on therapeutic exchanges. There are numerous perceptual and conceptual variations in Native primary languages that have no adequate translations in standard English.

◆ Native peoples have a number of culturally and historically bound issues that they may not be able to adequately address if the therapeutic process becomes a parallel process. Although the individuals who created traumatic experiences within Native communities have long passed, Natives continue to have unresolved grief and trauma issues. Traumatic stress issues from the past affect current traumas, and therapists should be mindful that clients may have behaviorally compromised immunity. Caution with client well-being is always wise. Parallel processes may either exacerbate these issues or be used effectively to assist the client in the therapeutic relationship.

◆ Finally, Native peoples face numerous barriers in seeking health care. Engage in an exercise of the imagination. Use a computer and create the mental health care world of the Blackfeet Nation in Montana. (Remember, this nation is the southern branch of the Blackfeet peoples, a nation that reaches far north into Alberta. This area is also the traditional gene pool of these peoples.) Locate the primary health resource on the Blackfeet Reservation. Locate the nearest off-reservation clinics (remember that health care across the northern border into Canada is normally not approved by third-party insurance). See where the nearest outpatient psychiatrist is located. Find out what type of payment is accepted and what the wait time is. Figure out the drive and potential weather conditions during four different seasons of the year. Locate the nearest psychiatric hospital. Find out whether the State of Montana screens for alcohol and substance abuse as a prohibition to hospitalization if a client is a danger to self or others. Determine whether the Blackfeet population on the reservation is likely to have private third-party insurance by looking at the U.S. Census findings. Look at the Medicaid recipient distribution for the state. Use an Internet search to take a look at the suicide rates of Natives. Attempt to estimate the number of gatekeepers a Native client will have to get past to access care. Try to assess how likely it would be for a mental health provider to facilitate appropriate mental health care for a client from this reservation. Now consider how possible it is for an individual with approximately an eighth-grade education to accomplish this task.

Recommended Resources

Books and/or Articles

Clarke, J. (2009). *A gathering of wisdoms: Tribal mental health a cultural perspective.* LaConner, WA: Swinomish Indian Tribal Community.

Cox, G. R. (2010). *Death and the American Indian.* Omaha, NE: Grief Illustrated Press.

Danieli, Y. (1998). *International handbook of multigenerational legacies of trauma.* New York, NY: Plenum Press.

Duran, E. (2006). *Healing the soul wound: Counseling with American Indians and other native peoples.* New York, NY: Teachers College Press.

Duran, E., & Duran, B. (1995). *Native American postcolonial psychology.* Albany, NY: State University of New York Press.

Manson, S. (2000). Mental health services for American Indians and Alaska Natives: Need, use, and barriers to effective care. *Canadian Journal of Psychiatry, 45,* 617–626.

Mathieu, D. J. (2013). *Way of wakan: Reflections on Lakota spirituality and grief.* n.p.: Author.

O'Nell, T. (1998). *Disciplined hearts: History, identity, and depression in an American Indian community.* Berkeley, CA: University of California Press.

Stone, J. B. (1998). *Traditional and contemporary Lakota death, dying, grief, and bereavement beliefs and practices: A qualitative study* (Unpublished doctoral dissertation). Utah State University Department of Psychology, Logan, Utah.

Sue, D. W., & Sue, D. (2012). *Counseling the culturally diverse: Theory and practice* (6th ed.). Hoboken, NJ: Wiley.

Videos

Eyre, C. (Director). (1998). *Smokesignals* [Motion picture].United States: ShadowCatcher Entertainment in association with Sherman Alexie & Welb Film Pursuits, Ltd.

Jutra, C. (Director). (1976). *Dreamspeaker* [Television movie]. Canada: Canadian Broadcasting Corporation.

Duke, Daryl (Director). (1973). *I heard the owl call my name* [Television movie]. United States: Tomorrow Entertainment.

Fiction Reading

Craven, M. (1991). *I heard the owl call my name.* New York, NY: Fitzhenry & Whiteside. (Originally published 1973)

REFERENCE

Arends, J., Muysken, P., & Norvul, S. (1995). *Pidgins and Creoles: An introduction.* Amsterdam, The Netherlands: John Benjamins.

3

Clinical Applications With Asian Americans

Michi Fu

FIGHTING CHANCE: THE STORY OF DONNA

Case Description

Donna was a 17-year-old Cambodian American bi-curious female. She was referred for counseling with me at a local Asian Pacific Family Center for getting into fights at school. She was experiencing academic failure due to multiple suspensions for fighting with gang members. Her mother, who barely escaped from the Khmer Rouge, was receiving medication for her own depression and symptoms of posttraumatic stress disorder. Her younger brother was referred for mental health treatment for his acting-out behaviors (e.g., getting into fights, petty theft, academic failure). Donna claimed that her mother was "crazy"—oftentimes displaying extreme behaviors such as emotional smothering (not allowing client to have her own space at home and listening in on her telephone conversations) or abandonment (throwing Donna and her possessions out of the house when she misbehaved). She often fought with her mother and reported that her father, who remarried when Donna was 5 and had other children, has not been a big part of her life. She had difficulty accepting her mother's new identity as a lesbian (and her female partner) and secretly fantasized that her parents would someday reunite despite not being together for more than a decade.

Initial phases of treatment consisted of Donna boasting to this therapist of how many times she had been in fights with her classmates and the number of sexual escapades she had had with multiple partners. She also relayed that she was able to be financially independent by supporting herself as an import model (she received minimal compensation for modeling bikinis or appearing seminude in exotic automobile advertisements). She seemed amused when she fought with her mother and unaffected by her father's absence.

Although Donna was enthusiastic and willing to self-disclose, developing a genuine connection was initially a challenge due to her inability to recognize her contributions to the dynamics surrounding her. The focus of her treatment was delivered via individual therapy, especially since family therapy seemed to aggravate her acting-out behaviors. Donna also had difficulty seeing how her behaviors could be considered sexually risky. My own countertransference regarding her sexually risky behaviors prevented me from being completely present with her, leading me to openly question her self-destructive behaviors. Why would she allow her boyfriend to share her with his friends? Did she understand that not using contraceptives could lead to unintended pregnancy and other health risks? Challenging her with my own values and assumptions without fully comprehending the root of her sexual acting-out behaviors made her wonder whether I aligned more closely with her mother or her.

Eventually it became clear that building rapport would take more time than I initially thought since she was suspicious of other females. Her mother had failed at creating a trusting bond. Her mother's female partners prevented her from seeing Donna as a priority with her mother. I inadvertently became a maternal figure that could fail her as well.

Treatment slowly challenged her to consider the consequences of her own actions. This happened over time and by using nonverbal techniques. We discussed her disappointment in her father, anger toward her mother's inability to take care of Donna and her brother, and difficulties obtaining positive attention from her peers and romantic interests. We worked together for a year and a half, during which time Donna was better able to communicate with her mother without getting angry, reduced the number of fights she got into with gang members, found a stable romantic relationship, and began to work toward financial independence from her family of origin.

Reflection and Discussion Questions

1. If you were Donna's therapist, what are some assumptions you might make about her based on her demographics?

2. Both the client and this therapist are Asian American. What aspects of this case study highlight similarities and differences between the therapist and client? What aspects of this case address assumptions about two Asian Americans working together therapeutically?

3. Both the client and this therapist are females. What does this case study address about the client and therapist both being female?

4. What are some of the ways in which Donna departs from the model minority myth?

5. What types of countertransference might you have when working with someone similar to Donna?

6. What are ways of reducing the barriers to treatment for someone who is underage, living with a caregiver with a mental illness, and financially insecure?

7. What types of treatment techniques do you think should have been considered when working with someone like Donna?

8. The therapist in this case initially had stereotypes about the client's mother that were incongruent with her sexual orientation. What are some assumptions you may have when considering a first-generation female refugee from Cambodia?

9. What are some treatment techniques you could incorporate to help Donna feel safe and engage in self-exploration?

10. What are some theoretical orientations that may be appropriate for someone such as Donna, given her cultural background and presenting issues?

Brief Analysis of the Case

My work with Donna taught me lessons about working with Asian Americans who do not fit the model minority myth. As an educator, I have often decried the stereotype, yet as a clinician, my own biases led me to have expectations of my clients that may have inadvertently damaged our relationships. Here are a few parts of Donna's identity and struggles that I had to accept before I could be of true assistance to my client:

• Donna came from a broken home. The majority of Asian Americans I know of come from intact families, even if the marriage is loveless or intimate partner violence is a part of family life. I spent time helping Donna grieve the loss of her nuclear family and helped her envision the type of family life that she would want for herself someday. We explored the types of role models she had had while growing up and what she could do to ensure that she could help to break unhealthy cycles of being in a relationship.

• Her mother identified as a lesbian. To my knowledge, I have never met someone from an Asian American, first-generation refugee background who identified as a lesbian. Her mother was very matter-of-fact about her relationship with her partner, but it took me some effort to get over my own biases regarding what I believed her sexual orientation ought to be, given her generation level and age. I had to recondition myself to accept that Asian Americans who were born and raised in Asia could have fluid concepts of sexuality, even though the Asian part of my cultural identity had taught me that women of my mother's generation engaged in sexual activity only for the purposes of procreation. I also had to allow myself to see that Donna's mother chose safety in the arms of a woman, thus breaking my own misconceptions of what traditional relationships were supposed to look like for people who were born and raised in Asia.

• The client lived well below the federal poverty level. Donna believed that she needed to sell images of herself in order to obtain the things she wanted in life. She was not yet of legal age, and I had difficulty understanding how people could get away with taking compromising pictures of her. Because she was not actually nude, there were no child reporting laws I could invoke to protect her. Instead, I had to work on empowering her and offering her alternative resources. For example, case management focused on learning how to navigate the public transportation system and applying for other such benefits. Donna eventually learned that resources available to her meant that she did not need to earn money by selling compromising images of herself.

• Donna was experiencing academic failure. This may have caused her feelings of unease since she did not fit the model minority stereotype of excelling in academics. Not only did she not care about school; it seemed that her school did not care about her. I had difficulty accepting that school administrators could give up on her just because she got into fights with peers. She had been suspended multiple times, and I felt that part of my position was to advocate on her behalf with school personnel. I initiated and attended multiple individual education plan meetings. I ensured that there was adequate linguistic facilitation available for such purposes so that her mother could be involved with Donna's educational goals. I encouraged the school to consider modifying Donna's curriculum in a way that would make sense for her achievement level. She was able to resume her coursework due to the persistence of the treatment team advocating for her needs with the school. It is important to note that I played the role of cultural broker and moved away from being in the role of the "traditional" therapist. Much of the work involved helping to bridge the cultural gap between the school and the family.

• Donna engaged in extremely risky sexual behavior. She discussed being in relationships with males and females and boasted of having sex with multiple partners at the same time. I was worried about her physical health and potential consequences of such risky behaviors since she did not see the need to protect herself. I was constantly concerned that her partners were using her since she never demanded that they use protection. Much of our work was spent on psychosexual education regarding potential consequences of sexual behaviors.

• As mentioned earlier, nonverbal therapy techniques were key to having her express herself during treatment. Donna responded well to requests to draw how she wanted her family life to look. She was able to express herself through poetry about the anger she felt toward the insecure attachments she had with both of her parents. At one point, she began to understand how she gave her power away by not taking control of her sexual health. She developed a consciousness in regard to why her partners might feel free to sexually share her, and she developed an awareness of how to protect herself from being exploited in her sexual relationships, thus enabling her to be more selective in her choice of mates.

• Examination of the impact of her family of origin on her relationships was also part of the treatment. I utilized an objection relations approach, in which I helped her to believe that she was worthy of respectful relationship dynamics. She was able to engage in nonverbal therapies as a shortcut to expressing how she felt in relationships and about herself. For example, she created wire sculptures to share how angry her parents' divorce left her. She used sand tray therapy to reenact family dynamics. She also utilized talk therapy to examine her contributions, the role models she had while growing up, and societal factors in her romantic pursuits and exploitation. The power dynamics between herself and others were also at the heart of the latter stages of treatment.

All of the above considerations were difficult for me to conceive since my prior work with Asian Americans confirmed the model minority myth of high achievers, law abiding, respectful of authorities, comfortable socio-economic status, and the like. My client was able to demonstrate to me that Asian Americans are a bimodal population. Southeast Asians in particular tend to experience hardships that are not seen as often in those of East Asian background. For example, Southeast Asians are often refugees rather than immigrants. This usually means that there may have been little or no preparation for the migration process. Refugees may have needed to flee their countries of origin involuntarily in order to avoid persecution, war, or other adverse conditions. This could lead to high rates of posttraumatic stress disorder, among other serious mental illnesses. After a year and a half of working together, we were finally able to help her to engage in less risky behaviors, experience fewer family conflicts, and create a path toward independence for her. I am always grateful to clients such as Donna for being willing to openly share their lives with me.

Recommended Resources

Books and/or Articles

Becker, E. (1986). *When the war was over.* New York, NY: Simon & Schuster.

Chandler, D. P. (2007). *A history of Cambodia* (4th ed.). Boulder, CO: Westview Press.

Him, C. (2000). *When broken glass floats.* New York, NY: Norton.

Kamm, H. (1998). *Cambodia: Report from a stricken land.* New York, NY: Arcade.

Ratner, V. (2012). *In the shadow of the banyan.* New York, NY: Simon & Schuster.

Yathay, P., & Man, J. (1987). *Stay alive, my son.* New York, NY: Simon and Schuster.

Zhou, M., & Xiong, Y. S. (2005). The multifaceted American experiences of the children of Asian immigrants: Lessons for segmented assimilation. *Ethnic and Racial Studies: The Second Generation in Early Adulthood, 28*(6), 1119–1152.

Videos

Glatzer, J., & Courtney, C. (Producers), & Glatzer, J. (Director). (2003). The flute player [Documentary film]. United States: Over the Moon Productions.

Joffé, R. (Director), Puttnam, D., & Smith, I. (Producers). (1984). The killing fields [Motion picture]. United Kingdom: Warner Bros.

Lin, K. (Writer/Director). (2005). Perfection [Motion picture]. United States: IMDbPro.

Marcarelli, R. (Director). (2010). *Awakening Cambodia* [Motion picture]. United States: Vision Video.

Other Readings/Resources

BBC Cambodian History http://news.bbc.co.uk/2/hi/asia-pacific/133533.stm

Cambodia: Book Reviews and Recommended Reading: http://www .mekong.net/cambodia/reading.htm

Cambodia American Resource Agency: http://www.caraweb.org

Ung, L. (2000). *First they killed my father: A daughter of Cambodia remembers*. New York, NY: Harper Collins.

INTERGENERATIONAL EFFECTS OF WAR: THE STORY OF WADE

Case Description

Wade was a 32-year-old, fourth-generation Japanese American male who grew up in Hawaii. He lived with his mother, a second-generation Japanese American who lived through World War II, and was self-referred due to social anxiety. He longed for meaningful relationships with his peers, especially a romantic relationship, but struggled with severe anxiety whenever presented with an opportunity to speak with others outside of the classroom environment. In short, he had no friends and had never been involved with a significant other. The only person he spoke to on a regular basis was his mother. She raised him to pray over difficulties, not to discuss them openly with strangers. Therefore, he learned to pray to God whenever he was feeling nervous or lonely but did not actually have any successful interactions with people of his own age.

Over the course of treatment, it became clear that Wade was heavily impacted by his mother's own mental illness. As a result of her hoarding behaviors, she had accumulated many objects, which greatly limited his ability to live comfortably at home. Broken furniture shoved into the den rendered that room unusable. Heaps of toilet paper rolls on the sofa meant the living room area was not an inviting area to entertain or relax. Wade became aware that his home would never be a safe place to entertain his peers and grew to be somewhat hopeless regarding his situation.

At one point, I asked him what would happen if he were to "assist" his mother by helping her to remove some of the stacks of newspaper that were infested by silverfish or to slowly throw away some of the rows of decomposing plastic bags so as to create safe passageways to move freely from one room of the house to another. Around this point in treatment, Wade took an unannounced break from therapy. After three attempts to coax him back to therapy, he eventually responded by returning a few weeks later.

From then on, we utilized nonverbal therapy techniques to augment his treatment since speaking about his living conditions, abysmal social life, and relationship with his mother were often so difficult that at times he would appear somewhat catatonic. Over time, Wade joined a civic club on campus and practiced daily the relaxation techniques that he had acquired through therapy. He was able to identify two friends by the time our two-year treatment terminated. He considered one of the biggest successes to be convincing his mother to clear a path from the living spaces in the house to his room. Upon graduation from therapy, he reflected feeling more hopeful that he could recognize when his anxiety was provoked and how to engage in exercises to better manage his feelings.

Reflection and Discussion Questions

1. What about this client's family history warrants more exploration?
2. Would there be any type of countertransference to consider when working with this client?
3. What steps would you need to take to prepare yourself to work with someone like Wade if you were assigned as his therapist?
4. Would you have felt comfortable offering a home visit? Family therapy?
5. What are some assumptions you may have as a therapist when working with someone from this geographic region, generation level, and so on?
6. What are the cultural factors that influence the presenting issues?

7. How would you address Wade's reliance on prayer to address his life challenges? Is this a strength? A potential challenge? Both?
8. What learning opportunities might there be regarding how to work successfully with someone from this historical/cultural background based on the vignette provided?
9. What diagnostic issues, if any, are culturally responsive and culturally congruent with this case example?

Brief Analysis of the Case

When I initially began working with Wade, I did not realize that my own biases may have prevented me from fully appreciating his history. Here are some of the issues that I needed to realize before we could make progress:

♦ I had very little understanding of the Japanese American experiences of intergenerational traumatization due to World War II and Pearl Harbor. My supervisor at the time educated me regarding the type of discrimination Japanese Americans faced during the war. For example, internment camps and other such government restrictions were examples of institutionalized racism. It is clear that Wade's mother was influenced by growing up during such an era. The within-group differences between Asian Americans were highlighted by the interaction between myself (a second-generation Taiwanese American) and himself (third generation Japanese American). My first-generation Taiwanese American upbringing did little to prepare me to work with a postwar, traumatized family of Japanese descent.

♦ It did not dawn on me until later that Asian Americans who grew up in Hawaii had very different concepts of racial and ethnic identity from Asian Americans who grew up on the "mainland." Being born and raised on the mainland meant that my own identity development was contextualized. I made an assumption that we had similar processes. I later learned that those from the Hawaiian Islands tend to identify primarily as "local" versus "nonlocal" more so than actual ethnic background.

♦ It was difficult for me to understand how my client seemed so debilitated by his mother's hoarding behaviors when he appeared somewhat intelligent. I admittedly had countertransference toward his tolerance to live in such conditions. How could they have let their possessions control their lives? Why couldn't he help her to clean up? There was a part of me that did not want to believe someone's parent needed their own help. His mother was fortunate to have such a compassionate son. I became frustrated by his hopelessness and seeming inability to stand up to his mother's living conditions, thus not fully appreciating the precarious balance they achieved after his father passed. In order to help him to let go, we had to engage in grief and loss work. This meant that I needed to spend time allowing him to talk about how the dynamics of his family changed when his father passed and his mother elevated him to the status of partner and friend rather than maintaining his position in the family as a son. In the Asian family structure, this may not be uncommon, but his Americanized upbringing did not prepare him to take on such a role. Eventually, we were able to process the loss of his childhood, male role model, and mother as an effective caregiver. Such work revealed an underlying anger that he learned to mask through depression.

• Wade's mother was a religious woman who encouraged him to use religion as a coping strategy. Depending on the specific ethnic background and acculturation level, some Asian Americans are more likely to be Buddhists than Christians. Therefore, it may be beneficial to inquire about religious/spiritual beliefs upon the intake process. Although Wade was unsure of the efficacy of prayer, he utilized this "coping" mechanism often in lieu of other social supports. He once asked if I would be comfortable praying with him. We did not engage in a discussion of whether my own spiritual beliefs were aligned with his. Instead, it seemed more important for him to demonstrate how he lifts himself out of his depression. Therefore, I allowed him to pray in my presence and encouraged him to do whatever it took to make him feel more connected. This was one of his existing coping mechanisms we examined closely while helping to equip him with more. For example, we used role-plays to practice interactions he could have with peers to foster social supports. This resulted in him joining a service organization and developing relationships with a couple of club participants.

• Since Wade initially had reservations about divulging his reasons for seeking treatment, we needed to engage him with more creative techniques. Nonverbal therapy was utilized since Asian Americans are often taught that "dirty laundry" needs to stay within the home and that sharing such shameful family secrets can be a source of "loss of face."

Techniques used included sand tray therapy, which Wade initially was reluctant to use since it was so foreign to him. Over time, he would request sand tray therapy and divulge important bits of information regarding how he saw the world socially (e.g., one person sitting outside a circle and not knowing how to engage with others). We also used drawings for him to convey how he felt about his mother's hoarding behaviors (angry and hopeless).

♦ There were times when I wondered if being an Asian American female therapist might have helped or hindered the therapy process. On one hand, Wade may have felt a sense of familiarity with me based on phenotype. On the other hand, there could have been a heightened sense of awareness that family secrets were not to be shared with outsiders. I was able to assess his acculturation level by asking him a series of questions, and we ascertained that it would be appropriate for him to be seen by me as opposed to a "haole" (White person). It may be helpful to assess the acculturation level of one's client to determine optimal therapist match.

It was not until I recognized some of my countertransference and blind spots could I begin to gain my client's trust. Fortunately, he was very patient with me and willing to explore some of the painfully shameful patterns that had been developed. Eventually he was able to set some boundaries with his mother and establish relationships with a couple of peers before we terminated therapy. I am grateful to Wade for his willingness to stick with me despite my initial misassumptions, which could have led to more distance in the therapeutic relationship.

Recommended Resources

Books and/or Articles

Inouye, D. K. (1967). *Journey to Washington*. Englewood Cliffs, NJ: Prentice-Hall.

Okada, J. (1976). *No-no boy*. Seattle, WA: University of Washington Press.

Sakauye, E. E. (2000). *Heart mountain: A photo essay, reflection on the Heart Mountain relocation center*. n.p.: Author.

Ty, E., & Goellnicht, D. C. (2004). *Asian North American identities: Beyond the hyphen*. Bloomington, IN: Indiana University Press.

Videos

Bass, P., et al. (Producers), & Hicks, S. (Director). (1999). *Snow falling on cedars* [Motion picture]. United States: Universal.

Colesberry, R. F., & Nugiel, N. (Producers), & Parker, A. (Director). (1990). *Come see the paradise* [Motion picture]. United States: 20th Century Fox.

Korty, J. [Director]. (1976). *Farewell to Manzanar* [Television drama]. United States: NBC.

Other Readings/Resources

Going for broke Japanese American veterans honored http://abcnews .go.com/blogs/politics/2011/11/going-for-broke-japanese-american-veterans-honored-with-congressional-gold-medal/

Heart Mountain Interpretative Center: http://heartmountain.org/ EDUCATION.html

History Channel, Japanese-American relocation: http://www.history.com/ topics/japanese-american-relocation

Japanese American Legacy Project, Denshō website: http://www.densho .org/

Japanese American National Museum: http://www.janm.org

Popular Japanese American books: http://www.goodreads.com/shelf/show/ japanese-american

National Education Center website: http://www.goforbroke.org

Smithsonian Education, Letters from the Japanese Internment: http://www .smithsonianeducation.org/educators/lesson_plans/japanese_internment/ lesson1_main.html

4

Clinical Applications
With Latina/o Americans

Melba Vasquez, Martha Ramos Duffer, and Cynthia de las Fuentes

---

MARGARET CAN'T DO IT ALL (BY HERSELF) ANYMORE

Case Description

Margaret is a 38-year-old Mexican American mother of an 8-year-old son and married to a Latino who was her high school sweetheart. They grew up in central Texas, their families were from the working class, and their parents encouraged and promoted education. Both she and her spouse were first-generation college graduates and had good jobs. Margaret was working on a graduate degree when she initiated therapy. Margaret's advisor referred her to work with one of the authors specifically because she had also been a first-generation college student and is a Mexican American from central Texas. The advisor had heard the author speak at a meeting and thought that she would be a good fit for Margaret.

Margaret's presenting concerns included anxiety and stress in her graduate program, which she had undertaken while maintaining a full-time job. Margaret described other stressors, including feeling burdened by having too much to do and the fact that her husband, although generally supportive, did not do enough, in her view, to "pull his weight." She also felt that one of her professors was judgmental of her tardiness to an early-morning seminar and feared another professor was less than understanding when she had to leave a seminar twice because of her son's illness.

The precipitating event that led Margaret to enter psychotherapy, however, occurred upon the death and funeral of a paternal uncle ("Sam") who had sexually abused her when she was a young girl. When she was a teenager, she told her mother about the abuse in order to explain why she did not want to be around her uncle. Her mother, while upset for her and supportive, counseled her to not share the information with her father, as the mother indicated he would be devastated. Margaret agreed and never shared the information with anyone; however, she was angry and bitter that the uncle "got away" with it, believing he never had to experience consequences for his abusive behavior. As the oldest in her family, Margaret had taken it upon herself to make certain that none of her siblings was alone with her uncle, and generally tried not to think of the abuse. She acknowledged that her mother also seemed to ensure that the children not be left alone with the uncle; however, he was occasionally inappropriately invasive at family gatherings.

When her cousin, with whom she had been close during childhood, asked her to provide a eulogy at Sam's funeral, Margaret's rage resurfaced. The cousin explained that she asked Margaret because she was a good writer and orator and was very good at conveying respect for elders. Margaret "broke down" and told her cousin why she could not do so. Her cousin, shocked and devastated, understandably did not press her further. When Margaret asked her if Sam had also abused her, her cousin responded that her father had not and conveyed deep sorrow that he had done so to her. Unfortunately, two weeks following the funeral, her cousin miscarried a pregnancy. Margaret felt responsible for the additional stress she had placed on her cousin during an already difficult time and was angry that she felt guilty for something that the uncle had perpetrated.

Margaret so desperately wanted to "get past" this additional burden because it was interfering with her capacity to function effectively at home, work, and school. She had sleep disturbance and trouble concentrating, was highly irritable, and was feeling a lot of pressure to perform well at work and school. She felt that her current state was leading her to "take out" her frustrations on her spouse and son.

Reflection and Discussion Questions

1. What gender and cultural issues are present in the tension between Margaret and her spouse?
2. What gender and cultural issues may be present in Margaret's family responsibilities that may affect her timeliness and attendance in the academic setting?
3. What complex factors contribute to Margaret's feelings of burden of being a survivor of sexual abuse? In what ways does her value and prioritization of family help and/or detract from healing from the abuse? Similarly, in what ways did her mother's expression of *familismo* help and/or detract from Margaret's healing?
4. What assumptions do you make (and need to confirm or disconfirm) about Margaret's needs? What implications does this have for the direction in psychotherapy?
5. What traditional diagnoses (*DSM/ICD*) might you consider? Are there alternative nosologies, or clinical conceptualizations, that incorporate a better understanding of the gender and cultural dynamics in this case?

Brief Analysis of the Case

Possible considerations in providing culturally responsive services for Margaret are discussed next:

• Margaret's psychotherapist provided support in general and specifically for the trauma around the sexual abuse that had resurfaced as a result of the perpetrator's death. Therapists working with trauma survivors must take into account the complexity of an individual's multilayered identities. Multicultural therapists, as a result, typically draw on multiple strategies for treating clients with these presenting concerns. For example, a gender and culturally aware psychotherapist is sensitive to issues of privilege and its intersection with her or his own identities and cultures. In this case, client and therapist came from similar cultural (Mexican American) and economic (working-class) backgrounds; the therapist was also a first-generation college student and a firstborn child in a large family. Although these congruencies can be facilitative, caution should be taken because the privilege of holding a doctorate and serving in the psychotherapist's role constitutes an important power differential.

• Clinicians should be mindful that applying culturally appropriate understandings and interventions should not also inadvertently re-create the felt empathic failures by the client's mother (e.g., who did not confront the uncle or hold him accountable by outing him to her husband or extended family) or support a patriarchal norm that values men over girls. In this case, Margaret was raised in a traditional Mexican American family where elders and men in general were to be respected and protected, and a priority was the family remaining intact. As a result, Margaret's father's emotions were protected and prioritized over her own, her abuser continued to enjoy the privilege of being part of the family, and her trauma was hidden and silenced. Thus, the positive Mexican value of *familismo* had elements that interfered with a more ideal reaction/response from Margaret's mother. Helping Margaret come to terms with the complexity of her family's values and how her mother acted within that milieu has to be explored as part of the impact of the trauma on her.

• As an adult and mother however, Margaret did "out" her uncle—after his death, and to her beloved cousin, his daughter. She felt tremendously guilty that her cousin miscarried soon thereafter and feared that the stress of the knowledge could have triggered that devastating loss. Exploration of her intent, her refusal to collude with the protection of an abusive man, and her need to empower herself by no longer holding a toxic secret would be helpful to her. Teaching her self-compassion can enable her to accept that her disclosure was not intended to harm her cousin or her pregnancy but to relieve herself from the crushing pressure to sacrifice herself yet again for her abuser.

• Margaret's irritability, difficulty sleeping, poor concentration, and mediocre functioning were likely symptoms of chronic posttraumatic stress. She needed to feel safe and to understand the full impact of the trauma, which included anger at authority figures, including her professors, her spouse, and others who either did not treat her fairly and/or whom she *perceived* did not treat her fairly. Learning how to validate her anger and to transfer that angry energy into healthy action on her own behalf could be helpful goals in reducing her symptoms and empowering her.

• Margaret may have also been experiencing micro-aggressions in the form of subtle racism and sexism on the part of her professors whom she experienced as being judgmental of her difficulties in participating as the "perfect" student on those occasions when she needed to prioritize her son and family. Margaret sensed her professors' disapproval for her tardiness and skipping classes because of her family responsibilities. Some racism and sexism is so subtle that it is hard for the victim to state confidently that an experience was one of bias yet it is important for the therapist to explore the possibility to (a) raise awareness, (b) avoid silently colluding with the bias, and (c) explore, affirm, and support our clients' experiences and decision making.

◆ Women who strive for excellence in their work and school have cited the importance of family support in reaching their goals. Latinas, in particular, who are married and have families frequently wish to embrace both their family and their work/study roles. The opportunity for psychotherapy to play a positive role in facilitating this goal might involve the exploration and development of strategies that redefine roles and norms. For example, Margaret does not have to do it all herself. Some combination of engaging a supportive spouse, extended family, and hired help may be important. Encouraging Margaret to choose courses at times that reduce the likelihood of tardiness, which may appear to faculty as lacking in commitment, would further empower her to see the ways she can structure her environment to mitigate her stress.

◆ Mentoring is one of the key factors in success, especially for women and racial/ethnic minorities. People who have been negatively stereotyped in particular require positive, optimistic mentor–student relationships. Therefore, suggesting that Margaret seek out either formal or informal mentoring in her graduate program may be an additional supportive strategy for her as she learns to structure more support for herself in her program and family life.

Recommended Resources

Books and/or Articles

Bernal, G., & Domenech Rodriguez, M. M. (Eds.). *Cultural adaptations: Tools for evidence-based practice with diverse populations.* Washington, DC: American Psychological Association.

Brown, L. S. (2008). *Cultural competence in trauma therapy: Beyond the flashback.* Washington, DC: American Psychological Association.

Catalyst. (2005). *Women "take care," men "take charge": Stereotyping of U.S. business leaders exposed.* Retrieved from http://www.catalyst.org/publication/94/

women-take-care-men-take-charge–stereotyping-of-us-business-leaders-exposed.pdf. Catalyst Publication Code D62; ISBN#0-89584-252-1.

Cheung, F. M., & Halpern, D. F. (2010). Women at the top: Powerful leaders define success as work + family in a culture of gender. *American Psychologist, 65*, 182–193. doi:10.1037/a0017309

Comas-Diaz, L. (2012). *Multicultural care: A clinician's guide to cultural competence.* Washington, DC: American Psychological Association.

Sue, D. W., & Sue, D. (2012). *Counseling the culturally diverse: Theory and practice* (6th ed.). Hoboken, NJ: Wiley.

Vasquez, M. J. T., & Daniel, J. H. (2010). Women of color as mentors. In C. A. Rayburn, F. L. Denmark, M. E. Reuder, & A. M. Austria (Eds.), *A handbook for women mentors: Transcending barriers of stereotype, race and ethnicity* (pp. 173–188). New York, NY: Praeger.

Videos

Arau, A. (Producer & director). (1992). *Like water for chocolate* [Motion picture]. Mexico: Arau Films International.

Arredondo, P. (2005, March). *Counseling Latina/Latino clients* [Videotape]. Multicultural Counseling Video Series. Washington, DC: American Psychological Association. Videotape Series V. Item no. 4310617.

Cervantes, J. M. [Host]. (2009, October). *Counseling Latina/Latino clients using a family systems perspective* [DVD]. Multicultural Counseling Video Series. Washington, DC: American Psychological Association.

Hays, P. A. (2012, May). *Culturally responsive cognitive-behavioral therapy in practice* [DVD]. Multicultural Counseling Video Series. Washington, DC: American Psychological Association.

Vasquez, M. J. T (2010, January). *Multicultural therapy over time* [DVD]. Multicultural Counseling Video Series. Washington, DC: American Psychological Association.

Other Readings/Resources

Anzaldua, G. (1987). *Borderlands la frontera: The new mestiza.* San Francisco, CA: Aunt Lute Books.

Cisneros, S. (1991). *Woman Hollering Creek and other stories.* New York, NY: Random House.

Cisneros, S. (2002). *Caramelo.* New York, NY: Random House.

MULTIPLE ROLES, MULTIPLE IDENTITIES:
THE STORY OF ELISANDRO

Case Description

Elisandro was a 30-year-old Afro-Latino male whose family emigrated from the Dominican Republic when he was an infant. Elisandro grew up in the greater Houston area and was the second youngest child in a family of five siblings. He had two older brothers and an older and a younger sister. He was employed as a legal assistant and lived with his male life partner of 10 years and their 7-year-old son when he reluctantly came to therapy seeking help with symptoms of anxiety and depression that had been increasing during the last two months due to family tensions and difficult decisions regarding his parents' care and support. He explained that no one in his family had ever gone to therapy, and he was raised to believe that only people who were severely mentally ill had to go to therapy. He admitted to having obsessed about whom he was going to hire for a therapist, interviewed friends, did online research, and met with two other psychologists who were not quite right before finding a good fit with a single-mother queer Latina of mixed heritage with an islander background.

Elisandro described multiple challenges growing up, including his youngest sister's drug use and what he perceived as his mother's refusal to see what was occurring. He reported that his father was an alcoholic who had had multiple affairs. Despite the family being very poor, his mother made valiant, stoic daily efforts to secure education for her children and propel the family forward, despite her own illiteracy and frequent conflict in her marriage. One of the many traumatic events Elisandro shared was of the time one of his sisters came home in the middle of the night after being stabbed and how she bled all over the living room. Due to the significant life stressors his family faced, Elisandro received the message early on that there was no time or attention left over for his feelings in the family; therefore, feelings were an annoyance and could be seen only as a source of weakness. As a young child he vowed to himself that he would simply no longer feel. A primary goal he identified in therapy was to access and integrate his emotions in order to live more authentically.

The precipitating incident that brought Elisandro to therapy was his mother's sudden decline in health that led to his decision to have her come stay with him in his home. Elisandro's youngest sister was still addicted to drugs and lived in their mother's home "rent free" in exchange for the family's expectation that she was to help their mother manage her medications and ensure a proper diet. After a few trial months, it became evident that his sister was unable to hold up her end of this arrangement due to her drug addiction. Medication errors and poor eating habits were identified as the culprits in their mother's decline in health. Fortunately, after staying with Elisandro for a couple of months and eating the appropriate foods and taking her medication regularly, his mother's health stabilized.

During the course of therapy, Elisandro expressed significant distress over the differing expectations his family had about his role in the care of his parents compared to the expectations of his straight brothers and even of his sisters (one was married and the other was a drug addict). He felt that due to their marital status, sexual orientation, and gender, his siblings were often excused from full participation in the difficult decisions that had to be made in the care of their parents and in the division of labor in executing these decisions. Elisandro was led to feel that if he did not step up and play a primary role, the care his parents needed would not be provided. Rather than provide support, his siblings reported problems of their own, which led Elisandro's mother to worry about them and plead with Elisandro to help them. Although one sister was more involved in his parents' care than the brothers, the familial expectation that her primary responsibility was to her husband shielded her somewhat from the full impact of the responsibilities Elisandro felt compelled to take on. Elisandro felt that because his relationship was with a man and they had a son together, it was taken less seriously and given less accommodation by the family, despite their best efforts to be accepting of the relationship.

Elisandro also felt tension in his own relationship with his partner, a White man, who struggled to understand why Elisandro found it necessary to sustain such a high level of involvement in the care of his parents at the expense of his own peace of mind and time for their family and his career. As we explored Elisandro's feelings about his partner's concerns, we found that his partner was to some degree mirroring Elisandro's own internal conflict regarding the role he wanted to play in his parents' care. Elisandro felt the acculturative stress generated by his Latino cultural expectations of caring for aging parents juxtaposed with his adopted cultural expectations of focusing on his created family and career and was stressed by the pressures on either side.

As treatment progressed, Elisandro reported experiencing an increased ability to focus and make decisions, improved memory, increased access to his emotions, and greater experienced authenticity. He became better able to balance seemingly conflicting values in order to exercise clarity as he made the difficult choices of what he was and was not willing to do for his family members. One day as he began his therapy session, he said, "I don't understand how all of this works, but it's like I am finally able to quiet the noise around me and just get to be me."

Reflection and Discussion Questions

1. What cultural differences may be implicated in the tension in Elisandro's relationship with his partner as he negotiates his parents' care and his relationships with his siblings?

2. If you were his therapist, what assumptions about what Elisandro should do in this situation might have come up for you that you need to explore? How might these (in)validate and (de)value Elisandro's cultural perspectives and values? His sexual orientation identity?

3. What sociocultural forces are impinging on Elisandro as he attempts to navigate the already difficult developmental task of making decisions regarding the finances and health care of aging parents?

4. How are Elisandro's multiple identities both an asset and a challenge?

5. What assumptions do you make as you consider the situations and choices of Elisandro's family members?

6. How can a queer affirmative multicultural approach to counseling help you understand Elisandro's frustration at his family's choices?

7. Considering contributions from relational cultural theory, what factors may have contributed to Elisandro's reports of improved memory, focus, energy, and decision making?

Brief Analysis of the Case

Multiple sociocultural forces must be considered in providing culturally responsive therapy in this case. For example:

  • Elisandro embodied multiple socioculturally dictated identities as a gay Latino father in a long-term relationship who grew up poor and is now middle class. The intersectionalities of ethnicity, gender, class, and sexual orientation collided in his world, leading to significant challenges in his development of his sense of self and understanding of himself in relation to others. Each of these identities carried with it assumptions and expectations about access to voice and space.

• In order to enter into a therapeutic working alliance with Elisandro, the therapist must be knowledgeable about the challenges and lived realities of each of his identities while exploring their salience in different situations and in his different relationships. For example, his identity as a son may be less salient when he is engaged in his role as a father with his own son, but both of these and the additional one of being a partner may come up and confound him in discussions with his partner.

• Like many Latinos, Elisandro grew up thinking that therapy was not a resource and would be indicative of weakness and severe mental illness. He previously believed that coming to therapy would reflect his own failure as a man and as a father, son, and partner. It is important for the therapist to sit with this conflict and understand how foreign therapy is as a source of support to many individuals while affirming its value as an avenue toward health and remaining patient as the client explores whether, and if so how, therapy can be useful.

• It would be easy to assume that the task was for Elisandro to "assimilate" into one culture or another without recognizing the immense value he can provide by contributing his unique perspective to both. This process is vital to his own developing sense of integrated identity and self-esteem, as he understands the validity and value of his own lived experiences. It also reflects an often-misunderstood aspect of diversity. The value of diversity is not found in different people being allowed "in" and having access to become like the others who are already there but rather in people with different backgrounds and experiences contributing from their own lenses in order to enrich and expand communities beyond what they could have ever been without the integration of multiple ways of being and knowing.

• Making choices about an aging parent's care is a challenging developmental life task for many adults. In this case, several sociocultural considerations added complexity to the challenge. Elisandro grew up learning not only that the family was the utmost priority in every decision but that, by definition, family members took care of each other, no matter what. As a gay man, Elisandro was committed to questioning gender and sexual orientation narratives and assumptions regarding his role as a man in both of his families. As a loving son, he was committed to doing all he could to minimize his parents' struggle and suffering, but as a partner and father, he has had to learn to do the same for his husband and son. It is critical to support Elisandro in understanding what is being asked of him, how it feels, and what feels right. Doing this requires making sense of how multiple dominant narratives are written and upheld in his family as well as in society in general, without critiquing or judging his family values and choices.

Recommended Resources

Books and/or Articles

Cortez, J. (1999). *Virgins, guerrillas & locas: Gay Latinos writing on love.* San Francisco, CA: Cleis Press.

de las Fuentes, C. (2012). Working with men in the minority: Multiple identities, multiple selves. In H. Sweet (Ed.), *Gender in the therapy hour: Voices of female clinicians working with men* (pp. 149–170). New York, NY: Routledge/Taylor & Francis Group.

Glave, T. (2008). *Our Caribbean: A gathering of lesbian and gay writing from the Antilles.* Durham, NC: Duke University Press.

Ibañez, G. E., Van Oss Marin, B., Flores, S. A., Millett, G., & Diaz, R. M. (2012). General and gay-related racism experienced by Latino gay men. *Journal of Latina/o Psychology, 1*(S), 66–77. doi:10.1037/2168-1678.1.S.66

Ocampo, A. (2012). Making masculinity: Negotiations of gender presentation among Latino gay men. *Latino Studies, 10*(4), 448–472. doi:10.1057/lst.2012.37

Quiroga, J. (2000). *Tropics of desire: Interventions from queer Latino America.* New York, NY: New York University Press.

Ramirez-Valles, J. (2007). "I don't fit anywhere": How race and sexuality shape Latino gay and bisexual men's health. In I. H. Meyer & M. E. Northridge (Eds.), *The health of sexual minorities: Public health perspectives on lesbian, gay, bisexual, and transgender populations* (pp. 301–319). New York, NY: Springer Science +Business Media.

Rodriguez, R. A. (1996). Clinical issues in identity development in gay Latino men. In C. J. Alexander (Ed.), *Gay and lesbian mental health: A sourcebook for practitioners* (pp. 127–157). New York, NY: Haworth Press.

Ruiz, E. (2005). Hispanic culture and relational cultural theory. *Journal of Creativity in Mental Health*, *1*(1), 33–55. doi:10.1300/J456v01n1_05

Videos

Kilik, J. (Producer), & Schnabel, J. (Director). (1993). *Before night falls*. United States: El Mar Pictures and Grandview Pictures.

5

Clinical Applications With Individuals of Middle Eastern and Northern African Descent

Sylvia C. Nassar-McMillan and Julie Hakim-Larson

HARNESSING FEARS DURING A MEDICAL EMERGENCY: THE STORY OF JACOB M.

Case Description

Jacob M. was admitted into the emergency room of a community hospital in Florida after passing out in a grocery store. He underwent blood tests and other medical procedures that indicated he is diabetic. Apparently, his regular physician had provided this diagnosis previously, along with a recommendation for specialized medical treatment, but Jacob had failed to follow up on those recommendations for the past two years. This was his first experience with passing out, and he was scared. He was referred to a health clinician for consultation before being released from the hospital and is open about his feelings for the first time. The clinician provided information to Jacob about his condition, along with prescriptions for short-term treatment and referrals to a specialist in the community for a more regular, longer-term treatment plan, plus a series of hospital-based educational sessions and a support group for newly diagnosed patients with diabetes. The clinician suggested that ongoing treatment would be most effective if he would come back for follow-up individual appointments to work on learning biobehavioral techniques that, once learned, can be self-administered. With some basic biopsychosocial questions about Jacob's medical and mental health history and adaptive life conditions, the clinician could easily discern that Jacob's life has some significant stressors in it that may be contributing to his condition. Among these are poor nutrition and other unhealthy lifestyle habits. Thus, the clinician then also referred Jacob to a therapist affiliated with the hospital to help with that aspect of treatment.

Jacob decided to follow up with a specialist to get immediate medical attention for what he gradually accepted as his health condition. Rather than attending the educational and support group sessions, he opted to schedule an appointment with the therapist, viewing this as being both more direct and focused as well as more confidential. The therapist, Dr. Smith, did not move immediately into discussing the medical diagnosis and corresponding biobehavioral treatment plan with Jacob. Rather, he told Jacob that his professional procedure in opening a case includes conducting a thorough biopsychosocial assessment because he views patients' conditions from a holistic perspective, wherein many factors may contribute to the manifestation of their actual presenting medical condition. He explained that this process may take their entire session that day and will require, at minimum, a few additional sessions for them to discuss any diagnoses or treatment plans.

Through Dr. Smith's biopsychosocial assessment, the following information about Jacob was revealed:

+ Jacob was in his mid-50s.
+ Jacob immigrated to the United States as an adolescent in the late 1960s with his parents, due to sociopolitical tensions in the region.
+ His family settled in Florida, where they all still live, near an Egyptian community that is active but not particularly densely populated with other Egyptian Americans.
+ Jacob's father regularly sent money back to Egypt to help support his own and his wife's families of origin, and Jacob has continued that tradition.

- In addition, since Jacob's small business has expanded, he has donated money to charitable organizations in Egypt and in the surrounding region.
- Jacob married in his early 40s to an Egyptian woman, Najwa, who immigrated at the time of their marriage.
- Both Jacob and Najwa come from Coptic Orthodox (i.e., Christian) faiths.
- Their marriage was not an arranged one per se but was facilitated by the family and community of origin, with full approval of Jacob and Najwa.
- Najwa supports the continuance of the Arab cultural traditions (e.g., Arabic cooking and meals) from Jacob's childhood and early adulthood, particularly given her recent immigration, more than the types of meals he ate in his earlier years.
- Jacob and Najwa have five children, ranging from 4 to 15 years of age: Jamil, 15; Tarek, 14; Gabriella, 13; Rosina, 11; and David, 4.
- So far, Jacob and Najwa have held traditional Arab cultural roles in their child rearing: Jacob has provided the primary income and Najwa has been a homemaker. Jacob has been a supportive spouse and parent but has had a relatively low involvement in parenting.
- Recently, tensions have arisen as Jacob and Najwa's two daughters have reached adolescence. They have made increasing requests for interactions with other girls, particularly those outside the Egyptian community.
- Najwa has been exploring the possibility of sending their children, particularly the girls, back to Egypt during the summers so that they can practice their Arabic language skills and learn some of the more traditional ways.
- This dialogue has caused considerable tension in the household, and Jacob has felt "caught in the middle."
- Approximately five years ago, Jacob's business was under investigation for charitable contributions to a nonprofit organization based in Egypt; Jacob and his key financial and other staff members were questioned and his financial records were subpoenaed.
- As a result, he was arrested and put on trial. He hired an attorney specializing in immigration law and was acquitted of all charges.
- Since that time he has had trouble sleeping and has had recurrent nightmares.

- Jacob was diagnosed with diabetes approximately two years ago by his primary physician, but the myths and misconceptions he believes about diabetes, along with shame and self-perceived weakness, have prevented him from seeking help or even sharing his diagnosis with his wife.
- Jacob is a longtime smoker.

At the conclusion of the biopsychosocial assessment process, Dr. Smith commented on the nature and severity of some of the stressors currently in Joseph's life and, in particular, validated the impact of the traumatic experiences that Jacob has suffered with the legal system. He explained that, at their next session, he would like Jacob to fill out some questionnaires that would help to clarify some additional potential diagnoses. He also mentioned to Joseph that he is aware of a diabetes education program and support group at the other local hospital, which is located within a part of the community with a substantial Arab American population. However, Jacob indicated that he has been aware of those services in the past few years but has been unwilling to go there. Although he is somewhat connected with that community, he was opposed to attending either an educational or a support group because, as he stated, "Everyone would have to know about my personal business." Jacob did, however, agree to continue with an additional appointment with Dr. Smith.

Reflection and Discussion Questions

1. How do you think the legal case might have affected Jacob's emotional functioning?
2. What modalities and approaches do you think might be helpful in working with Jacob?
3. To what extent, if any, do you believe that other family members should be involved in Jacob's therapeutic treatment? Which family members? Which treatments?
4. What sources of social support are present in the immediate environment for Jacob? Are there other potential sources of tangible or emotional support from others that could be tapped with the help of his doctors or therapist?

5. How comfortable does Jacob seem to feel about seeking medical help? Psychological help? What factors are playing a role in his differential views on help-seeking?

6. Aside from administering the assessment tools, would it be helpful for Dr. Smith to seek additional information from the Arab American community in terms of medical treatment? Psychological treatment? Legal services?

7. How might a psychologist go about collaborating with other professionals to provide the best care for Jacob? Within the current hospital system? With a different hospital system? With another therapist?

8. In what ways could legal or legislative information be helpful, and how might a psychologist gain this additional knowledge?

Brief Analysis of the Case

• *Therapist credibility and preference issues.* Dr. Smith began the session by establishing positive rapport with Jacob. He explained how the process would work, which is important for any patient or client but particularly one potentially coming from a culture of origin in which help-seeking behaviors might be limited to a religious cleric (such as a priest or minister for Christians or an imam for Muslims) or some other authority figure within the community. Dr. Smith did well to ask Jacob if he would have a preference for working within the Arab American community, as many individuals might feel more secure with a therapist from within their own culture. However, Jacob clearly stated his preference for keeping his affairs outside the community. This preference is particularly relevant given the nature of his presenting concern—the diabetic symptoms and diagnosis, with their corresponding potential need for education and psychosocial support groups in the future.

• *Effective treatment approaches.* Jacob responded positively to Dr. Smith's explanation of the biopsychosocial assessment plan and process as well as his stated need for further assessment of trauma, depression, and anxiety symptoms to reach a more conclusive diagnosis and treatment plan. Within traditional Arab and Muslim American culture, credentials such as those held by medical and other clinical professionals are valued highly, and those holding them are often revered. Moreover, although Jacob reported resistance to accepting his diagnosed medical condition and corresponding need for medical help, he, like other individuals in general from Arab and Muslim cultures, is more likely to seek medical than mental health treatment (the latter being highly stigmatized). In this case, Jacob's reluctance to accept his medical diagnosis seems to have been more related to the misconceptions and myths he had about the condition itself. For example, he had associated diabetes with stress and felt ashamed that he could "not handle" his stressors, such as the legal incident and the emergent parenting challenges. Moreover, he feared that once he began using insulin, he would always be dependent on it. However, once he conceded to seek medical treatment as a result of the hospitalization and the reality of his health risks, it became easier for him to seek therapy as an "adjunct" to the medical treatment. Dr. Smith's approach in supporting that view helped to assure Jacob that the primary issue was indeed medical versus psychological and that, in fact, even the psychological components could be concrete, measurable, and treatable. Developing rapport and a working alliance with clients who have participated in the creation of a treatment plan is critical to providing effective treatment to Arab and Muslim American clients.

A helpful treatment approach for therapy with Jacob would be a cognitive-behavioral approach, because of its relatively concrete nature and thus the measurability of hopefully positive results. This approach can be applied to address issues of trauma, depression, and anxiety as well as the lifestyle changes Jacob needs. In later stages of therapy, it might be appropriate to bring Najwa in for marital sessions, with the same or another therapist. Family interventions, if handled sensitively in light of culturally appropriate roles for both Jacob and Najwa, could serve to enhance the couple's communication and reduce marital discord.

• *Holistic, cultural, and collaborative considerations.* Continued collaboration within the health care system will be critical in supporting Jacob's educational process. He will need to be educated about the risk factors that nutrition, exercise (or lack thereof), and smoking play in contributing to diabetes. Moreover, he will need education about the medical treatment options and the prognoses with each. Although Dr. Smith may not himself provide this information, he will need to be kept abreast of the information that is provided as well as the corresponding homework assignments to facilitate healthy lifestyle changes. Through the use of strategies such as biofeedback sessions, breathwork, and other mindfulness techniques, Jacob's adjunct therapy can help him more effectively navigate these changes.

From a cultural perspective, it is also important to recognize that the health benefits of the Arab diet have declined within both Arab and Arab American communities as people adopt a relatively more unhealthy American diet. When a healthy lifestyle in one culture and geographic region is transplanted to another, ultimately it will change. For example, after Jacob's parents moved to the United States, his mother no longer had access to the same ingredients. Furthermore, by the time Najwa immigrated, Egypt had undergone rapid urbanization characteristic of economically wealthy developing countries, causing the diet even in the home country to have become unhealthy. Exercise was not an inherent part of the native lifestyle, and thus Jacob never developed healthy exercise habits. Finally, while his father was a social smoker in Egypt and in the United States, Jacob has been a heavy smoker for most of his life. He needs to learn about the effect of smoking on diabetes. Jacob will need support in learning smoking cessation strategies or at minimum be encouraged within the adjunct therapy sessions. Some helpful resources are the Centers for Disease Control and Prevention (http://www.cdc.gov/tobacco/campaign/tips/) and the National Tobacco Cessation Collaborative (http://www.tobacco-cessation.org/resources/programs.html).

SILENCED: THE STORIES OF DALIA AND NABILA

Case Description

Mrs. Lovett, a school psychologist in a large urban school system in California, responded to a referral from a school principal to work with a teen in one of the system's high schools based on a suicide threat made by the student. She noted that 15-year-old Dalia is a minor. Because Dalia's parents are divorced, she contacts the custodial parent, Dalia's mother, Nabila, to inform her about the potential suicide risk and to obtain informed consent for providing counseling services to the girl. Although Nabila was resistant and insisted that Dalia's claim could not have been a sincere threat, Mrs. Lovett explained the seriousness of such a threat from a psychological perspective as well as the school's legal obligation to investigate it. After obtaining reluctant approval from Nabila, Mrs. Lovett then scheduled an appointment with Dalia and a separate follow-up one with Nabila.

During the session with Dalia, Mrs. Lovett first conducted a suicide risk assessment, followed by a full biopsychosocial assessment through direct questions and behavioral observations. She noted that Dalia appears to be embarrassed by her suicide threat yet does display some low-level risks, such as having thought about the means (i.e., overdosing on her mother's medication) and timing of a suicide plan. Dalia reported that there are certain circumstances under which she finds herself more desperate and hopeless than others. These include being around both parents during heated arguments. Family conflicts include her father's unwillingness to support a college education for Dalia (while planning to support her younger brother's) and, relatedly, Dalia's knowledge of her mother's inability to pay for college. When she hears her father make derogatory comments toward her mother, Dalia becomes upset and defensive. As a solution to this issue, Dalia has heard her parents talk about the possibility of sending her to stay with extended family members in Egypt or Sweden, where an arranged marriage could be planned. Mrs. Lovett's goal in conducting the broader assessment interview was to determine possible ways to defuse or otherwise minimize some of the precipitating stressors.

Mrs. Lovett observed that Dalia does exhibit depressed affect; her appearance was clean but disheveled and not very stylish. She wore a hijab, or traditional Muslim head covering, which in Dalia's case was a plain scarf that did not coordinate with her outfit very well. Within the somewhat affluent school system, this mode of dress would easily cause her to stand out. Dalia did, in fact, talk about feeling isolated at school and not having many friends. One issue that her parents did agree on is that she should not closely associate with her peers, whether they are Iraqi or not. They have warned her to share limited information about her background. In terms of family history, her family was caught up in the insurgency resulting from the U.S. invasion of Iraq in 2003. In 2007, they escaped Iraq, seeking temporary asylum in a refugee camp in Syria while waiting for entry into the United States. Separated from extended family members who ultimately were granted permanent resettlement status in Egypt and Sweden, Dalia and her brother and their parents lived in the refugee camp in Syria for three years prior to being granted permanent resettlement status by the United States. Dalia reported that her parents have been divorced for almost one year. She also reported tension between herself and her younger brother. Dalia was guarded in sharing information with Mrs. Lovett, who made a note to attempt to gather more information about the family history from Nabila. Despite these challenges, Dalia's grades have been in the above-average range, suggesting normal to high-level intelligence and resilient academic skills.

Mrs. Lovett closed the session by making a behavioral contract with Dalia, getting her to agree that she would contact the psychologist's office immediately if she began to feel suicidal. She could not, however, get her to agree that she would call 911 after school hours. Mrs. Lovett told Dalia that in order to remain enrolled in school, she would need to consent to continue receiving counseling services. Mrs. Lovett also told Dalia that she would recommend that the upcoming work with her would be geared toward creating a network of friends and exploring options for seeking financial aid for a college education. She explained that the sessions might touch on Dalia's religion and how it could become a source of support for her as she reached out to a broader social circle.

In Mrs. Lovett's subsequent interview with Nabila, her intent was to advocate for Dalia's pursuit of a college education, help her to expand her social network and personal autonomy, and glean any supplementary information that could help her develop the best treatment plan for Dalia. When Nabila arrived, Mrs. Lovett noted that she appeared to be quite tense. Mrs. Lovett noted Nabila's obesity and heavy breathing from the walk up the several flights of stairs to her office.

After Mrs. Lovett reiterated the reason for the session, she asked Nabila to help fill in some of the pieces that Dalia had not been willing or able to answer. She could tell that Nabila, too, seemed quite reluctant to share information. Mrs. Lovett was able to use some of the general knowledge she had gained to frame the interview with Nabila, such as asking about her divorce and the impact on Dalia and the overall family unit. Nabila shared that while divorce is not taboo within the Iraqi culture per se, it is viewed more conservatively within the Muslim community, even here in their urban California residence. She also shared the difficulty in being isolated from her siblings who had been relocated to other countries. Although she did not share much about the family's guardedness, she did mention the risks involved in their immigration process, including those within their resettlement communities. This included fear of retribution and retaliation toward themselves or family members still residing in Iraq by individuals who may have been in opposing factions. With regard to questions about family members' health status, it became apparent that Nabila was embarrassed about her obvious obesity.

She also expressed frustration about her inability to work, due to her Iraq-based education and career credentials as a nurse not being transferable to the United States. Although she was unwilling to disclose much about her husband, it was apparent that the dynamics of that relationship were a major source of stress and depression for Nabila. Nabila also reported that, although her former husband, Samir, had been an attorney in Iraq and also unable to recover his career credentials in the United States, he had acquired some financial assets in this country despite his emergent gambling addiction. Mrs. Lovett discussed with Nabila her recommendation that she support Dalia's growing need for independence by helping her daughter to develop a peer support group. Additional recommendations made for Nabila were that she meet with a college-preparatory financial aid official in the school system to learn more about how to get help for her daughter and that she work on her self-esteem by attending a self-esteem group at the local women's resource center. Mrs. Lovett also reiterated the requirement that Dalia be reevaluated at several subsequent points during the academic year as a stipulation for her continued enrollment in the public school system. She also strongly recommended that Dalia seek, with Nabila's blessing, support from one of the school counselors at her school.

Nabila refused to comply with the recommendations offered and did not seek services from the women's resource center or elsewhere. She forbade Dalia from seeking out the school counselor. While she felt sorry for what she now understands to be Dalia's pain, she was more worried about their safety and the safety of their other loved ones. Thus, she threatened Dalia, saying that if she ever speaks of suicide again, she will tell her father about the situation, thus diminishing further any level of potential or future support for her college education.

Reflection and Discussion Questions

1. What stereotypes about Arabs and Muslims seem supported or challenged in this case study?
2. What personal reactions did you have while reading the case study?
3. Which aspects of the school psychologist's interview strategies seemed effective? Ineffective? Explain/discuss.
4. What are some other approaches or strategies that could have been employed in the case example? Are there additional ones that could have been avoided? Which strategies could foster resilience?

5. How do you think Nabila and Dalia might feel about counseling?
6. What ethical issues are raised in this case study?
7. If Dalia were to seek out counseling either at the school or at a community mental health agency, what issues would need to be addressed, and why?

Brief Analysis of the Case

• *Therapist credibility.* Although Mrs. Lovett began the sessions by explaining the school system's protocols relative to suicide intervention, she did not employ specific measures to establish positive rapport with either Dalia or her mother, Nabila. Perhaps she viewed her role as merely to provide immediate or crisis-based intervention, yet based on her offer of follow-up sessions, it can be inferred that her intent was to see the client unit again. She did not appear to check with her clients on their respective understandings or views of the issues. Moreover, she did not appear to have a working understanding of Arab or Muslim cultural values generally or those specific to recent Iraqi immigrant refugees. She did not offer or intend to consult with professional colleagues in the local community who might have a better understanding or knowledge base about such issues. Finally, her diagnoses and treatment planning were based on mainstream therapeutic principles, with little or no sensitivity to cross-cultural issues. Had Mrs. Lovett been somewhat more attuned to the culturally based protection of privacy and confidentiality, particularly for clients speaking to an "outsider" to their ethnic community and particularly in the case of recently traumatized refugees who have legitimate reason to link secrecy with security, both Dalia and Nabila might have been more trusting and willing to engage in the counseling process.

• *Effective treatment approaches.* Dalia's family has undergone serious premigration traumas in the past two decades, due to the Gulf War, the U.S. invasion of Iraq, and the subsequent insurrections. Among their immigration traumas were the refugee experience, especially spending three years in a transitional refugee camp while awaiting asylum in yet a third country. Currently, they were experiencing the postmigration traumas of a disintegrated family system and memories of the horrific traumas undergone by families surviving a dictatorship and its subsequent demise. In a mainstream scenario of a family in the aftermath of trauma, therapy for the family unit as well as some of its individual members might be prescribed. In the case of Dalia's family, it is unlikely that the father, with his own disease of addiction in full swing, would be open to therapy or even recognize any of the dysfunctions in the unit. Rather, the dysfunctions themselves are self-perpetuating in his life. Thus, the most "systemic" treatment one could hope for is to explore issues in the context of the various traumas as well as the familial context, recognizing the absence of various key players in the overall family constellation. For example, Dalia might benefit from understanding more about the behavior of each of her parents in the context of their collective trauma, such as her father's need for control and dominance (vis-à-vis his active addiction dynamics) over her mother and even herself. She needs to understand that it is likely that her parents will be reluctant to complete any financial aid or other government paperwork.

Nabila does need to work on self-esteem issues. However, it will be critical for her to recognize and acknowledge the various reasons for her low self-esteem as well its strong correlation with her (justifiable) depression. As well, the abuse (emotional if not physical) from her husband concomitantly contributes to her depression and low self-esteem. It will be important for her to work with a therapist who is either familiar with her cultural background or open to learning from Nabila. The importance of the immigration trauma, which also includes her inability to transfer her professional credentials and, therefore, her professional identity, need to be addressed, not to mention her economic stability and corresponding dependence on an abusive relationship.

Career development from an action-oriented stance could be among the treatment goals, so that Nabila can become more self-sufficient and less dependent on her former husband. The role and importance of Nabila's religion and faith need to be explored as well, including the role of fate in her worldview. Perhaps most important for Nabila are to identify and engage any possible support networks. Within the local networks, it is already clear that Nabila has some issues to reconcile, such as her status as a divorced woman. Developing these networks will also help her to support Dalia's development as she ages and will help mediate any separation anxiety the two will suffer as a result of their migration trauma.

• *Holistic, cultural, and collaborative considerations.* From a biopsychosocial perspective, Nabila and Dalia both would benefit from psychological testing to measure their posttraumatic stress and related symptoms (depression and anxiety, among others). Both also need a thorough physical exam if they have not had one recently. Although they might have had exams upon entry into the United States, now that they are more settled it would be important to identify any physical or medical manifestations that might be associated with longer-term or lingering impacts of immigration. Nabila's obesity needs to be addressed from these contexts as well. Joining a medically supervised weight management support group might be an important first step for Nabila to improve her overall health and begin the process of improving her self-esteem. Wherever therapy might originate (such as in the school system as described in the case description), it ought to include consultation with professionals within the Arab American community's health (and mental health) care systems. If there is a self-esteem group offered there, it will be more likely to incorporate culturally appropriate perspectives and interventions, particularly for refugee women, many of whom may be experiencing similar dynamics and issues as are present in this family. Alanon and other 12-step intervention programs might be available and would be more culturally appropriate as well, as Dalia and Nabila both need support in dealing daily with a person in active addiction.

Recommended Resources

Books and/or Articles

Hakim-Larson, J., Kamoo, R., Nassar-McMillan, S. C., & Porcerelli, J. H. (2007). Counseling Arab and Chaldean American families. *Journal of Mental Health Counseling, 29,* 301–321.

Hakim-Larson, J., & Nassar-McMillan, S. C. (2013). Counseling Middle Eastern Americans. In G. McAuliffe (Ed.), *Culturally alert counseling: A comprehensive introduction* (2nd ed.). Thousand Oaks, CA: Sage.

Jamil, H., Nassar-McMillan, S. C., & Lambert, R. G. (2007). Immigration and attendant psychological sequelae: A comparison of three waves of Iraqi immigrants. *Journal of Orthopsychiatry, 77,* 199–205.

Mruk, C. J. (2006). *Self-esteem research, theory, and practice: Toward a positive psychology of self-esteem* (3rd ed.). New York, NY: Springer.

Nassar-McMillan, S. C. (2010). *Counseling Arab Americans.* Boston, MA: Brooks-Cole/Cengage.

Nassar-McMillan, S. C., Ajrouch, K., & Hakim-Larson, J. (Eds.). (2013). *Biopsychosocial care of Arab Americans: Perspectives on culture, development, and health*. New York, NY: Springer.

Nassar-McMillan, S. C., Gonzalez, L. M., & Mohamed, R. H. (2013). Individuals and families of Arab descent. In D. Hays & B. Erford (Eds.), *Developing multicultural competency: A systems approach* (2nd ed., pp. 245–277). New York, NY: Pearson Merrill Prentice Hall.

Nassar-McMillan, S. C., Lambert, R. G., & Hakim-Larson, J. (2011). Discrimination history, backlash fear, and ethnic identity among Arab Americans: Post 9-11 snapshots. *Journal of Multicultural Counseling and Development, 39*(1), 38–47.

Nassar-McMillan, S. C., & Tovar, L. Z. (2012, Spring). Career counseling with Americans of Arab descent. *Career Planning and Adult Development, 28*(1), 72–87.

Nydell, M. K. (2006). *Understanding Arabs: A guide for modern times* (4th ed.). Boston, MA: Intercultural Press.

Shakir, E. (1997). *Bint Arab: Arab and Arab American women in the United States*. Westport, CT: Praeger.

Suleiman, M. W. (Ed.). (1999). *Arabs in America: Building a new future*. Philadelphia, PA: Temple Press.

Videos

Abi-Hashem, N. (2008). *Working with Arab Americans* [DVD]. Multicultural Counseling Video Series. Washington, DC: American Psychological Association.

Boulton, T., Egoyan, A., & Urdl, S. (Producers), & Nadda, R. (Director). (2005). *Sabah* [Motion picture]. Canada: T. L. Boulton Productions Limited.

Nassar-McMillan, S. C., & Hakim-Larson, J. (2008). *Counseling Arab Americans: Diversity, treatment goals, & interventions* [DVD]. Framingham, MA: Microtraining Associates.

Nassar-McMillan, S. C., Hakim-Larson, J., & Amen-Bryan, S. (2008). *Counseling Arab Americans II: Clinical Vignettes* [DVD]. Framingham, MA: Microtraining Associates.

Turner Classic Movies (Producer). (2011). *Race and Hollywood: Arab images on film* [Motion picture]. Atlanta, GA.: Turner Classic Movies.

Fiction Reading

Abu-Jaber, D. (2003). *Crescent*. New York, NY: Norton.

Abu-Jaber, D. (2005). *The language of baklava*. New York, NY: Pantheon.

Ellis, R. (2007). *Kisses from a distance: An immigrant family experience.* Seattle, WA: Cune Press.

Shaheen, J. (2001). *Reel bad Arabs: How Hollywood vilifies a people*. New York, NY: Olive Branch Press.

Assessments/Inventories

Amer, M. M., & Hood, R. W., Jr. (2008). Special issue: Part II. Islamic religiosity: Measures and mental health. *Journal of Muslim Mental Health, 3*, 1–5. doi:10.1080/15564900802156544

Amer, M. M., & Hovey, J. D. (2007). Socio-demographic differences in acculturation and mental health for a sample of 2nd generation/early immigrant Arab Americans. *Journal of Immigrant and Minority Health, 9*, 335–347. doi:10.1007/s10903-007-9045-y

Amer, M. M., Hovey, J. D., Fox, C. M., & Rezcallah, A. (2008). Initial development of the Brief Arab Religious Coping Scale (BARCS). *Journal of Muslim Mental Health, 3*, 69–88. doi:10.1080/15564900802156676

Barry, D., Elliott, R., Evans, E. M. (2000). Foreigners in a strange land: Self-construal and ethnic identity in male Arabic immigrants. *Journal of Immigrant Health, 2*, 133–144. doi: 10.1023/A:1009508919598 2008-10810-001

Britto, P. R., & Amer, M. M. (2007). An exploration of cultural identity patterns and the family context among Arab Muslim young adults in America. *Applied Developmental Science, 11*, 137–150. doi:10.1080/10888690701454633

Kira, I. A., Templin, T., Lewandowski, L., Ashby, J., Oladele, A., & Odenat, L. (2012). Cumulative Trauma Disorder scale (CTD): Two studies. *Psychology, 3*, 643–656. doi:10.4236/psych.2012.39099

Wrobel, N. H., & Farrag, M. F. (2008). Preliminary validation of an Arabic version of the MMSE in the elderly. *Clinical Gerontologist: The Journal of Aging and Mental Health, 31*, 75–93. doi: 10.1080/07317110802072223

Wrobel, N. H., Farrag, M. F., & Hymes, R. W. (2009). Acculturative stress and depression in an elderly Arabic sample. *Journal of Cross-Cultural Gerontology, 24*, 273–290. doi:10.1007/s10823-009-9096-8

6

Clinical Applications With Individuals of Multiracial Descent

Gregory J. Payton, Marie L. Miville, and Peggy Loo

"YOU JUST DON'T GET ME!": THE STORY OF ANITA

Case Description

Anita M. is a 26-year-old, first-year law student at a university located in the Midwest. Born and raised in New York City, Anita is an excellent student whose academic performance throughout elementary school, high school, and college was consistently outstanding. After graduating from college, Anita worked on the campaign of a congressional candidate and, after the candidate was elected to office, joined the congresswoman's staff in Washington, DC. There Anita worked in constituent relations and developed her passion for public interest law. Anita applied to several law schools and chose the university she currently attends due to the full scholarship she was awarded and the fact that her extended family resides in the area.

Anita identifies as biracial (her mother is African American and her father is White), although phenotypically presents as White, with a light skin tone and green eyes. Anita is frequently told that she could pass for

White, and many peers and adults are surprised to learn that Anita's mother is African American. She is the first female member of her family to attend college and law school. As a result of her identities, Anita feels a great responsibility to succeed in law school and impress her family, her peers, and the faculty. The summer before moving to the Midwest and starting law school, Anita came out to her friends as a lesbian and briefly dated a White female colleague working in the office of another congressperson. For Anita, her first experience of dating a woman was generally positive; however, her experiences within predominantly White lesbian, gay, bisexual, and transgendered (LGBT) social circles resulted in feelings of discomfort and isolation. As Anita explored the LGBT community of Washington, she became keenly aware of the racial segregation within the community and her girlfriend's unspoken preference to socialize with White lesbians. Moreover, Anita noticed that some straight friends of color reacted somewhat negatively to her girlfriend, and Anita wondered to what extent their reaction was affected by race or homophobia. Over time, Anita's girlfriend expressed disappointment that Anita was not out to her family, and she increasingly pressured Anita to disclose their relationship. Feeling reluctant to discuss her sexuality with her family and feeling anxious about moving away from Washington and starting law school, Anita decided to end the relationship.

For a time, Anita was excited by the move to the Midwest and the start of her legal studies. However, she became concerned by several developments over the course of the first semester. By the end of the October, Anita noticed she was having difficulty sleeping, was easily distracted and inattentive, frequently felt fatigued, and was increasingly disinterested in her studies. Moreover, her mood was low and she was having a difficult time making friends. After confiding in a faculty member about these struggles, Anita was referred to the Student Health Center on campus to explore counseling services.

At the Student Health Center, Anita requested a counselor who identified as lesbian and a woman of color. The current staff did not include a lesbian of color; moreover, the counseling staff was predominantly composed of White women who identified as heterosexual. In an effort to accommodate her request, Anita was assigned to a White, gay male therapist, Dr. Anderson. During the intake session, Anita minimized her concerns as well as her symptomatology, explaining, "I am okay. I think I'm just trying to adjust." When pressed to talk about her adjustment to law school, the campus, and the midwestern environment, Anita explained, "It's different, but I can manage." Anita then attributed her sleep problems, as well as her low energy and low mood, to the new demands of law school. Dr. Anderson attempted to normalize the adjustment by explaining "Everyone has a hard time their first semester. It sounds like you've been a successful student, and I'm sure that your work will improve." At the end of the intake, Dr. Anderson recommended that Anita join a law student support group that gathered once a week in the law library and meet for a follow-up appointment in one month to "reevaluate the situation." In Anita's file, Dr. Anderson recorded an "Adjustment Disorder, Depressed Mood" diagnosis and described the treatment plan as: "Referral to law student support group, follow-up appointment in one month."

Anita did not join the law student support group, and in the month that followed, her condition worsened. By December, Anita was frequently absent from classes and socially withdrawn. Her mood was generally depressed with frequent episodes of anxiety related to academic or social stressors. Family members living in the vicinity made efforts to reach out to Anita, but she declined their invitations. Anita's alcohol consumption increased significantly, and she increasingly worried that her decision to attend law school was a mistake. She missed her friends in Washington and her family in New York City. When she considered the impending final exams, her breathing became labored and she felt a tightness in her chest.

Reluctantly, Anita returned for her follow-up appointment with Dr. Anderson and explained that she was thinking of dropping out of law school. She reported that she had not attended the law student support group because she was no longer certain she wanted to remain in law school, and she believed her time would be better spent studying or evaluating other options. Dr. Anderson expressed disappointment in Anita's "rejection of help" and asked Anita if she had made efforts to get support in other ways. Specifically, Dr. Anderson asked Anita if she had attended law school mixers or other graduate student organization events. Anita reported that she has "not been feeling up to those kinds of things."

Dr. Anderson continued: "Anita, I also wonder if this is about your breakup over the summer and the fact that you are not out to your family."

At this, Anita became tearful and explained, "I don't think you have any idea what this is about."

Reflection and Discussion Questions

1. What are your clinical impressions of Anita? How would you characterize her presenting problem and diagnostic formulation? Contrast your impressions with Dr. Anderson's diagnosis and treatment recommendation.

2. What are your reactions to Dr. Anderson's efforts, during the intake interview, to normalize Anita's difficulty adjusting? How might these efforts demonstrate a lack of cultural competency?

3. How might Dr. Anderson's racial and gender identities impact his interactions with Anita? How do these identities shape his countertransferential reactions?

4. How might Anita's racial and gender identities impact her interactions with Dr. Anderson? How do these identities shape her transferential reactions?

5. In the follow-up appointment, Dr. Anderson described Anita's decision not to join the law student support group as "rejection of help." What do you believe led Dr. Anderson to make this judgment?

6. What are your impressions of Anita's behaviors between the intake and the follow-up appointment? How do you understand her decisions not to join the law student support group or participate in mixers or other student organizations on campus?

7. The conclusion of the case study involves an exchange between Dr. Anderson and Anita. In your opinion, what assumptions was Dr. Anderson working from in offering his intervention? What reactions did this invoke in Anita, and why?

8. What approach would you take in working with Anita? How would you conduct the intake appointment? What treatment recommendations would you have made, and how would you have followed up on these?

Brief Analysis of the Case

The preceding case illuminates the client's experience of multiple identities within new environments. Beginning to date women and attending law school at a midwestern university are significant developments that impacted Anita's perspective of herself and the world around her. In the following analysis, reflect on how Anita's perspective was shaped by her identities and how these identities informed her approach to counseling.

• Historically, mental health professionals have assumed universality of psychological functioning. This universal, or "culture-neutral," perspective was anything but; rather, this paradigm placed the White, middle-class, heterosexual male life experience as the reference point in evaluating mental health. Although there has been significant progress in understanding the saliency of cultural identities and how these identities shape individual experiences, the field remains biased, and cultural competency is often an addendum to diagnostic formulation. Dr. Anderson's efforts to normalize Anita's adjustment to law school by stating "Everyone has a hard time their first semester" epitomizes the universal perspective and ignores the impact of cultural identities in Anita's life.

• Cultural identities carry social meanings that result in social locations along a spectrum of privilege and power to marginalization and oppression. Because individuals hold multiple identities, the resulting matrix of social locations can create tension and discord. For instance, Anita holds and experiences several minority identities (e.g., biracial identity, African American identity, female identity, and lesbian identity) that likely result in multiple experiences of marginalization; however, she also holds and experiences a majority identity (White identity) that likely results in her experience of some racial privilege (e.g., passing as White). These identities are constantly operative and evoke different experiences based on the social context. In this case, Anita's experiences in a midwestern law school are likely to be different from her experiences in New York City, where she was raised.

• Racial identities are often viewed as singular racial categories (e.g., "African American," "Asian," "Latino," "White") that exclude biracial or multiracial identities. U.S. society tends to assume singularity of racial identity, expecting that individuals can be easily sorted by racial groups, such as those listed on the U.S. Census. People who identify as biracial or multiracial frequently experience tension between the sociocultural expectation of a single racial identity and their personal experience of race. This tension may result in feeling torn between two or more racial labels, two or more racial heritages, and two or more racial experiences or worldviews. In the preceding case, Anita encountered the racial assumptions of a singular racial identity (White), as indicated by the "surprised" reactions of others to her mother's African American identity and their assumption of Whiteness due to Anita's ability to pass. However, Anita's experiences of life are shaped by her biracial identity rather than a single racial identity. More specifically, Anita's experiences are shaped by holding two racial identities: one with privilege and one that is marginalized. This biracial identity is highly salient, as evidenced by her experiences among majority-White populations, sociocultural pulls to pass, and her encounters with racism.

♦ Racism is a pervasive force that affects all dimensions of society, including the LGBT community. Like the broader society, racial and gender privileges are operant and afford gay, White men power that other individuals within the LGBT community do not hold. This power often translates to visibility and presumed definitions of "normality"; as a result, people of color, lesbians, bisexual women, and transgender people are often marginalized within the LGBT community. In the case here, Dr. Anderson's reaction to Anita echoes the reactions of Anita's White girlfriend and, presumably, the dominant expectation of coming out as presumably the only healthy means toward resolving one's sexuality, thereby conforming to visibility norms that reflect gay, White male standards and privileged status.

♦ Historically, racial minority groups have been viewed by mental health practitioners as help rejecting or treatment avoidant. These labels, which pathologize racial minority groups, including biracial individuals, result from the disproportionately low percentages of racial minority group members who seek mental health services and the disproportionately high dropout/low treatment-retention rates among those who do seek services. However, these rates are less a reflection of an inherent aversion to mental health services and more a reflection of a field that has a racist history. Racial minorities may hold valid suspicions of mental health practitioners due to a legacy of racist abuses, including inaccessibility, pathologizing cultural values, cultural incompetency, and even experimentation. In the case described, Dr. Anderson's characterization of Anita as "help rejecting" echoes this history and ignores the sociocultural context of Anita's circumstances.

♦ Like other professions, the field of psychology historically has been dominated by the presence of White men. Although the diversity of the field is increasing—for instance, numbers of women entering the field frequently outpace men—many clinics, hospitals, and counseling centers remain predominantly White environments. As a result, racial and ethnic minority group members may be less likely to seek services. Moreover, if they seek services, they may feel discouraged by the lack of diversity among the staff and feel discouraged by treatment options. This is also true of other marginalized identities, such as LGBT people. The preceding case illustrates how the cultural identities of clinical staff members have meaning to clients, and this meaning should be explored.

Recommended Resources

Books and/or Articles

Ballou, M., & Brown, L. S. (Eds.). (2002). *Rethinking mental health and disorder: Feminist perspectives.* New York, NY: Guilford Press.

Childs, E. (2005). *Navigating interracial borders: Black-White couples and their social worlds.* New Brunswick, NJ: Rutgers University Press.

Daniel, G. R. (2001). *More than Black: Multiracial identity and the new racial order.* Philadelphia, PA: Temple University Press.

Root, M. P. (1995). *The multiracial experience: Racial borders as the new frontier.* Thousand Oaks, CA: Sage.

Root, M. P. (2003). Bill of rights for racially mixed people. In M. P. P Root & M. Kelly (Eds.), *The multiracial child resource book: Living complex identities* (p. 32). Seattle, WA: Mavin Foundation.

Steinbugler, A. (2012). *Beyond loving: Intimate racework in lesbian, gay, and straight interracial relationships.* New York, NY: Oxford University Press.

Fiction and Nonfiction Readings

Durrow, H. W. (2011). *The girl who fell from the sky.* New York, NY: Algonquin Books.

Prasad, C. (2006). *Mixed: An anthology of short fiction on the multiracial experience.* New York, NY: Norton.

Raboteau, E. (2005). *The professor's daughter.* New York, NY: Henry Holt.

Senna, D. (1999). *Caucasia.* New York, NY: Riverhead Books.

White, E. C. (2002). Foreword. In D. W. Carbado, D. McBride, & D. Weise (Eds.), *Black like us: A century of lesbian, gay, and bisexual African American fiction* (p. xii). San Francisco, CA: Cleis Press.

Videos

Chinhema, B. (Producer). (2010). *Multiracial identity* [Documentary]. United States: Abacus Production.

Espin, O. (2003). *Race, gender, and sexual orientation: Counseling people with multiple cultural identities* [Video]. Alexandria, VA: Microtraining and Associates/Alexander Street Press.

Haggis, P. (Producer), & Haggis, P. (Director). (2004). *Crash* [Motion picture]. United States: Bob Yan Productions.

Clinical Resources

Root, M. P., & Kelley, M. (Eds.). (2003). *The multiracial child resource book.* Seattle, WA: Mavin Foundation.

Shih, M., & Sanchez, D. T. (2009). When race becomes even more complex: Toward understanding the landscape of multiracial identity and experiences. *Journal of Social Issues, 65,* 1–11.

Thomas, V., Wetchler, J., & Karis, T. (Eds.). (2003). *Clinical issues with interracial couples: Theories and research.* Philadelphia, PA: Haworth Press.

Thompson, C., & Gillem, A. (2004). *Biracial women in therapy: Between the rock of gender and the hard place of race.* New York, NY: Routledge.

Websites/Blogs

Association of Multiethnic Americans: http://www.ameasite.org

Blended People of America: http://www.blendedpeopleofamerica.com

Family Diversity Projects: http://www.familydiv.org/ofmanycolors.php

InterracialFamily.org: http://interracialfamily.org

iPride: http://www.ipride.org

Loving Day: http://www.lovingday.org

MAVIN Foundation: http://www.mavinfoundation.org

Mixed Heritage Center: Information and Resources for People of Mixed Heritage: http://www.mixedheritagecenter.org

Mixed in Different Shades: http://www.mixedindifferentshades.net

Mixed Roots Movement: http://www.mixedroots.com/index2.php

Project RACE: Reclassify All Children Equally: http://www.projectrace.com

Swirl: http://www.swirlinc.org

Assessments/Inventories

Salahuddin, N. M., & O'Brien, K. M. (2011). Challenges and resilience in
the lives of urban, multiracial adults: An instrument development study.
Journal of Counseling Psychology, 58, 494–507.

"I CAN MAKE IT ON MY OWN": THE STORY OF DAVID J.

Case Description

David J. is a 42-year-old small business owner living in Phoenix, Arizona;
he is married and the father of three children, ages 13, 8, and 5. David was
referred to counseling by his primary care physician after his most recent
medical appointment. In the course of routine evaluation, David reported
occasional chest pains, difficulty breathing, and fatigue. After describing
these symptoms, David noted that he was "under a lot of stress at work and
home." Specifically, David explained that his business—a local restaurant—
was struggling financially and that his father, living in New Mexico, had
recently been diagnosed with lung cancer. David told his physician that he
was worried about providing for his family and taking care of his father as
he physically declines. David was reluctant to follow up on the referral for
counseling, but, at the encouragement of his wife, he contacted a local community clinic and met for an initial evaluation with Dr. Navarro.

In the course of the intake appointment, David stated that his primary
concern was his family's financial stability, explaining: "My restaurant is losing money, I'm working 80 hours a week just to stay afloat, and I'm having
a hard time making ends meet. I can barely find the time to come in for this
appointment, but my wife insisted that I see someone. She's worried about
me." As David described his concerns, he also stated, "I won't end up like
my dad . . . broke and desperate and a burden to everyone."

Dr. Navarro inquired about David's father and family history.
David explained that his mother—a Latina woman who immigrated to the
United States from Mexico—fell in love with his father—a Native American
(Navajo) living in New Mexico—and they married at a young age. David's
mother died in childbirth, and he was raised by his father on a reservation in
New Mexico. David described his childhood as "miserable," explaining: "My
father was a violent drunk, couldn't hold down a job or provide for us, and
I was always looking after him. His family were all the same as him. I left
the reservation at 16 to find work in Phoenix, and I've been here ever since."

In the course of the intake interview, it became clear that David has resented his father for many years; moreover, David currently felt that his father's decline in health is one more burden David must carry. Although biracial, David rejected his Native American heritage, explaining: "I didn't know my mother or much about her family, but I know my father and his family . . . and I don't want anything to do with them. They're all . . . all those people . . . they're all lazy, ignorant drunks who haven't done anything with their lives and probably won't. I couldn't wait to get away from that reservation."

At that moment, David became aware of Dr. Navarro's presence and apologized. "I'm sorry. I don't mean to offend you."

Dr. Navarro responded: "You're concerned you offended me?"

David explained, "Yeah . . . uh, I mean, I don't know much about you, but you sort of look like a lot of kids I grew up with on the reservation. I don't mean that all Native Americans are lazy drunks, but, you know . . . I was just talking about my experience."

Dr. Navarro replied, "I understand," and continued with the intake assessment. However, David's comment had unsettled the doctor, who also identifies as biracial. In fact, Dr. Navarro and David share a somewhat similar racial heritage in that Dr. Navarro's father, now deceased, was Latino and her mother, also deceased, was of the Apache tribe. Over the course of Dr. Navarro's life, she has struggled against the stereotypes David used to characterize his father's family and the Native Americans living on the reservation where he spent his childhood. Although Dr. Navarro could empathize with David's difficulty coping with his father's physical decline, she noticed negative, countertransference reactions to David's depiction of his childhood and his antipathy toward his father's family and the population of the reservation of his childhood.

Toward the end of the intake appointment, Dr. Navarro asked David to identify his goals for counseling. "To be honest, I don't think counseling is going to help. My stress is about my business. If you want to offer some business advice . . . some practical advice, please do. But I have rent to pay and a restaurant to run. I'm here because my wife asked me to make an appointment, but I don't see how me talking about this will really help."

Dr. Navarro replied, "I can understand how difficult this is and how much your business means to you."

David interrupted, "No offense, Doc, but I don't think that you do. My guess is that you don't worry about these things. So, I'm just going to do what I gotta do to get to the other side of this, but I don't think counseling is a part of that."

Dr. Navarro replied, "But I do believe that counseling can be helpful in getting you to the other side of these challenges. And I do believe that there are some goals that we can create to help you through this time."

At this, David stood, extended his hand to Dr. Navarro, and said, "I appreciate you wanting to help, but I can make it on my own. Thanks for your time."

Reflection and Discussion Questions

1. What are your reactions to David's presenting concerns, his description of his family background, and his approach to counseling? How would you respond to his priorities and impressions of counseling? Contrast your responses to the interventions of Dr. Navarro.

2. How does David's biracial identity affect his impressions of his father, his family history, and his current stressors? How does David's biracial identity affect his impressions of Dr. Navarro?

3. How do you understand Dr. Navarro's reactions to David's statements about his experience of life with his father and growing up on a reservation? Although Dr. Navarro shares David's racial heritage, how might their identities differ in terms of racial identity development and internalized racism?

4. David emphasizes his financial concerns throughout the appointment and presents significant doubts about the need for or value of counseling to address these concerns. What role does social class additionally play in David's life, and how does this intersect with his biracial identity? How does David's social class identity also affect his impressions of Dr. Navarro?

5. What approach would you take in working with David? How would you have conducted the intake? What recommendations would you have made and how would you have followed up on these?

Brief Analysis of the Case

The preceding case illuminates both the client's experience of multiple identities as well as the therapist's experience of multiple identities. Dr. Navarro's biracial identity was a salient force in her reactions to David; similarly,

David's biracial identity affected his interaction with Dr. Navarro. In the next analysis, reflect on how Dr. Navarro's perspective is shaped by her identities and how these identities inform her reactions to David and their counseling relationship.

• In research and counselor training, cultural identities are frequently dichotomized into binary, either/or categories (White/person of color, gay/straight) and are often viewed in isolation from other identities. However, our cultural identities overlap and are interconnected in complex ways that may result in conflicting thoughts, feelings, and experiences of the world. For people who identify as biracial, there may be a sense of existing "between two worlds" or holding two racial identities while feeling distinct from both; moreover, there may be a pull to identify with one racial identity over another, due to cultural stereotypes and stigmas associated with one group. In the preceding case, David seems to distance himself from his Native American identity due to negative stereotypes that he attributes to his childhood but that also abound in U.S. culture regarding both Native Americans and men of color in general. In working with clients, we must listen for the interactions of identities and their potential impact on presenting problems, encourage clients' capacities to resist dichotomization, and support client abilities to healthily navigate multiple identities at once.

• Cultural identities carry social meanings that impact both external and internal understandings of self. The internalization of these social meanings affects psychological functioning and global well-being; these internalized messages fundamentally shape our understanding of who we are, our place in the world, and the life we should lead. When oppressive or discriminatory messages are internalized, the negative effects are profound. For instance, internalized racism results from taking racist messages that abound in society and directing those attitudes toward oneself. Similarly, internalized classism results from taking classist cultural messages and directing them toward the self. In the preceding case study, David is distressed by the possibility of fulfilling racist and classist stereotypes of Native Americans; as a result, he is working tirelessly and distancing himself from his family so that he "won't end up like [his] dad." In contrast, David may idealize his mother's racial identity and associate himself with positive stereotypes about this heritage.

• In the United States, racial and social class identities are highly related; racial and ethnic minorities tend to hold lower positions within the social class strata while Whites tend to hold higher positions. As a result, classist stereotypes are frequently interchanged racist stereotypes, such as "lazy," "ignorant," or "violent." In the case study, David characterized his father, his family, and the population of the reservation with these stereotypes that hold both racist and classist meanings. David is distressed by the potential of fitting these stereotypes, as evidenced by his determination to leave his childhood reservation, distance himself from his family, and achieve financial success at all costs. Moreover, David's impressions of Dr. Navarro and the efficacy of counseling may reflect classist stereotypes—perhaps that counseling is a luxury and ineffective at addressing "practical" problems.

• In our work, we must continually be aware of how our cultural identities may be perceived by and interact with our clients. In the case, David makes assumptions about the racial identity of his therapist. Because he attaches such strong meanings to this identity, it can be inferred that David may associate Dr. Navarro with these stereotypes. Furthermore, Dr. Navarro was unsettled by David's use of these stereotypes to characterize his family, and she had difficulty summoning an empathic stance with him as a result. We must expect that clients will reveal their biases or stereotypes about cultural identities and prepare ourselves to respond in a therapeutic manner; however, we also must expect that these biases or stereotypes will interact with our personal experiences as members of cultural groups and evoke strong emotions. Reflection, exploration, and self-awareness of our cultural identities are essential tools in culturally competent practice. This case illustrates how essential it is to understand our cultural selves, anticipate how others perceive our identities, and constantly evaluate our reactions so as to provide culturally competent care.

Recommended Resources

Books and/or Articles

Meléndez, A. G., Young, M. J., Moore, P., & Pynes, P. (2001). *The multicultural Southwest: A reader.* Tucson, AZ: University of Arizona Press.

Menchaca, M. (2002). *Recovering history, constructing race: The Indian, Black, and White roots of Mexican Americans.* Austin, TX: University of Texas Press.

Root, M. P. P. (1995). *The multiracial experience: Racial borders as the new frontier.* Thousand Oaks, CA: Sage.

Root, M. P. P. (2003). Bill of rights for racially mixed people. In M. P. P. Root & M. Kelly (Eds.), *The multiracial child resource book: Living complex identities* (p. 32). Seattle, WA: Mavin Foundation.

Tayac, G. (2009). *IndiVisible: African-Native American lives in the Americas.* Washington, DC: Smithsonian Books.

Fiction and Nonfiction Readings

Halaas, D., & Masich, A. (2004). *Halfbreed: The remarkable true story of George Bent—Caught between the worlds of the Indian and the White man.* Cambridge, MA: Da Capo Press.

Johnson, K. (1999). *How did you get to be Mexican?* Philadelphia, PA: Temple University Press.

O'Hearn, C. C. (1998). *Half and half: Writers on growing up biracial and bicultural.* New York, NY: Pantheon.

Peterson, N. M. (2006). *Walking in two worlds: Mixed-blood Indian women seeking their path.* Caldwell, ID: Caxton Press.

Prasad, C. (2006). *Mixed: An anthology of short fiction on the multiracial experience.* New York, NY: Norton.

Videos

Chinhema, B. (Producer). (2010). *Multiracial identity* [Documentary]. United States: An Abacus Production.

Chip, R. (Director). (2001). *Black Indians* [Documentary]. United States: Rich-Heape Films.

Espin, O. (2003). *Race, gender, and sexual orientation: Counseling people with multiple cultural identities* [Video]. Alexandria, VA: Microtraining and Associates/Alexander Street Press.

Clinical Literature

Duran, E. (2006). *Healing the soul wound: Counseling with American Indians and other Native peoples.* New York, NY: Teachers College Press.

Good, G. E., & Brooks, G. R. (2005). *The new handbook of psychotherapy and counseling with men: A comprehensive guide to settings, problems, and treatment approaches* (rev. ed.). San Francisco, CA: Jossey-Bass.

Pedrotti, J. T., Edwards, L. M., & Lopez, S. J. (2008). Working with multiracial clients in therapy: Bridging theory, research, and practice. *Professional Psychology: Research and Practice, 39*(2), 192.

Websites/Blogs

Association of Multiethnic Americans: http://www.ameasite.org

Blended People of America: http://www.blendedpeopleofamerica.com

Family Diversity Projects: http://www.familydiv.org/ofmanycolors.php

InterracialFamily.org: http://interracialfamily.org

iPride: http://www.ipride.org

Loving Day: http://www.lovingday.org

MAVIN Foundation: http://www.mavinfoundation.org

Mixed Heritage Center: Information and Resources for People of Mixed Heritage: http://www.mixedheritagecenter.org

Mixed in Different Shades: http://www.mixedindifferentshades.net

Mixed Roots Movement: http://www.mixedroots.com/index2.php

Project RACE: Reclassify All Children Equally: http://www.projectrace.com

Swirl: http://www.swirlinc.org

7

Clinical Applications of a White Therapist Working With People of Color

Julie R. Ancis and Nicholas Ladany

TWO WORLDS: THE STORY OF MARCOS

Case Description

Dr. Frieden, a White, Jewish therapist, presented a case in which she expressed feelings of "frustration," "helplessness," and "sadness." She described working with a client by the name of Marcos, an 18-year-old Hispanic[1] student from New York City attending a predominantly White, Christian college in upstate New York. Marcos was a first-generation college student. His parents were born and raised in Puerto Rico, had not completed high school, and spoke limited English. His younger sister, Lita, enrolled in fourth grade in a public school in New York, was having academic difficulties. She was accustomed to her older brother walking her to and from school and helping her with her homework. Now that he was away at

---

[1] *Hispanic* is a term that is more typically used on the East Coast of the United States but may not necessarily reflect different geographic areas across the country.

college, she found it difficult to stay motivated. As the eldest child, and boy, Marcos served as a language and cultural broker for his parents in a variety of situations, including hospitals, schools, and government agencies. He had assumed this role from a young age. In this capacity, he was thrust into a role typically reserved for adults, which produced conflicting feelings for Marcos. On one hand, he felt smart and "in charge." At the same time, he often felt that he was in over his head, such as when translating diagnoses and treatment options for his parents in medical settings if a Spanish-speaking professional was not available.

This was Marcos's first time away from home. He described cultural differences, as most of the other students were White, non-Hispanic, and from upper-middle to upper-class New England backgrounds. Marcos described himself as social and extroverted, and the therapist perceived him as extremely likable, skills that helped to mitigate the challenges of adjusting socially. He seemed to have a diverse friendship network but at the same time described having difficulty relating to the experiences of his classmates (e.g., summer vacations in Europe, entertainment choices, etc.). He felt pressure to conform but struggled with what that would mean in terms of his cultural identity. Moreover, he was not sure that he could in fact pull it off. Marcos felt like he was an imposter when he tried to engage in conversations on topics outside of his experience, such as visiting museums in Europe. The more he tried, the more like an outsider he felt. In addition, Marcos struggled academically because he did not enter college as prepared as the other students. Although he was obviously bright and described doing well in high school, he expressed a lack of confidence in his ability to compete academically on the college level and perceived faculty expectations that he would not succeed.

A constant strain on Marcos related to familial pressures and obligations. Family members asked him, in his role as the language and cultural broker, to make regular trips home in order to help his parents navigate various institutions and their daughter's school, in particular. Marcos often found himself covering for his sister. On one occasion, for example, her parents were called in to the principal's office for her frequent use of profanity. Marcos convinced his parents that this was merely a misunderstanding. Familial and cultural expectations resulted in a great deal of psychological strain for Marcos, interfering with his academic success as well as his feeling completely integrated socially. He started to experience headaches and anxiety attacks when the phone rang. Casual conversations with family became less frequent as they pressed him for advice and urged that he make more frequent visits home to NYC. Visits home left him feeling drained by family obligations. In addition, his friends back home taunted him about his college attendance and acting "too White" as he described concepts and used language to which they could not relate. Friends ridiculed him for scheduling time to write a paper or study for an exam.

Marcos frequently entertained the notion of dropping out of college. He described cultural pulls and a primary duty to be responsible as the older child and son. Dr. Frieden felt frustrated every time the client brought this up. She perceived a great deal of potential in Marcos and was concerned about how dropping out would impact his future success. She did her best to try to encourage him to stay in school but was often at a loss in terms of guiding him in his conversations with his parents and offering "solutions." Dr. Frieden relied on encouraging statements related to Marcos's intelligence and potential. Her focus on his future achievements and potential success often fell flat as Marcos focused on his current stressors. The potential role of support networks was absent from their conversations. Dr. Frieden felt that Marcos's lack of access to transportation at this relatively rural college prevented him from participating in supportive networks and communities. She believed that applying the values that she internalized as a student, such as delaying gratification and focusing on career goals, would be enough and seemed to lack a deep understanding of the cultural stressors he faced.

Many counseling discussions revolved around negotiating the two worlds of home and family versus the academic environment. Dr. Frieden attempted to explore ways in which Marcos could continue to be successful and still retain his cultural and familial obligations. She often felt uncertain as to the best ways to help Marcos negotiate the challenges he experienced. Although Dr. Frieden also had been raised in New York City, she was brought up in a different economic and cultural context from Marcos. More specifically, the therapist grew up in an upper-middle-class setting and attended a predominantly White, non-Hispanic private high school and predominantly White university. She was certainly sympathetic but could not relate on a personal level. Dr. Frieden tended to emphasize individuation, independence, and personal choice, believing that this would lead to less frustration, greater academic and career success, and overall satisfaction.

Dr. Frieden felt that she and Marcos bonded as New York City residents as the therapist herself felt a bit out of place in a Christian college in upstate New York. Although she felt a certain kinship with the client, given their New York City connection and the relative ease with which they communicated, they were raised in different cultural and economic settings. Cultural differences between the therapist and client along the lines of race, ethnicity, gender, and socioeconomic status (SES) were not discussed. Dr. Frieden felt that such a conversation was unnecessary, given the ease with which they communicated. Marcos felt pulled in the direction of greater independence but also felt that he could not abandon his familial obligations. Marcos was on the verge of dropping out of school when counseling was terminated due to reaching a limit on the number of sessions allowable at the center.

Reflection and Discussion Questions

1. How can a therapist best help clients negotiate environments that may be in conflict with cultural and familial expectations?
2. How can the therapist best help the client facilitate a solution that is culturally responsive and consistent even though she cannot personally relate to the client's experience?
3. What are some approaches for helping therapists connect with clients whose cultural backgrounds differ from their own?
4. How can the counselor capitalize on Marcos's strengths? What are these strengths that could be brought to bear in this situation?
5. Should the therapist have initiated a discussion of cultural differences between herself and Marcos? What would be the potential clinical benefit of such a discussion?
6. How do you think a counselor brought up in similar environment as Marcos may have responded in sessions? What factors may have influenced a helpful versus unhelpful response?

Brief Analysis of the Case

• The case of Marcos highlights the role of Latino cultural values, broadly described. Moreover, it demonstrates the potential disconnect with a White therapist who does not have a Latino/a cultural background or awareness of traditional Latino/a values. Therapists working with Latino/a clients must consider the role of family structure, educational characteristics, and culturally influenced expressions of distress while acknowledging within-group differences.

• Marcos faces challenges balancing academic expectations with family obligations. The conflict between *familismo* (family cohesiveness, interdependence, and loyalty) and the demands of academic life is a source of stress. Familial differences in acculturation and conflicting views of roles and obligations present as challenges for Marcos. As a first-generation college student, Marcos feels pressure to achieve and bring pride to his family. At the same time, cultural and familial obligations make this challenging.

• The therapist encouraged Marcos to separate from his familial responsibilities. She has a limited understanding of traditional Latina/o cultural values and familial expectations, especially in regard to eldest sons. She has good intentions but misses the cultural context. As a result, she risks alienating the client. Negotiating the roles of independence and familial connection requires support and patience on the part of both the therapist and the client. The therapist must be cautious around this conflict, as she does not want to risk alienating the client by communicating a lack of understanding and empathy around these seemingly divergent pulls. It is curious that the therapist chooses to move ahead when she is out of her comfort zone rather than seek consultation for her work. Therapists faced with similar situations would do well to seek relevant consultation as well as demonstrate therapeutic flexibility. In the case of Marcos, doing this may entail serving as a mentor, coach, guide, and consultant as he attempts to negotiate different expectations and roles.

• Similarly, the therapist may have considered openly asking Marcos how he felt about obvious cultural differences between her and himself in regard to ethnicity, gender, and SES. Their cultural similarities as New Yorkers who both felt a bit disconnected from the cultural environment of college could have served as an entry to such a discussion. Not acknowledging the obvious and how it may be impacting the counseling relationship and process may limit the extent to which counseling is helpful. For example, the client may get the impression that the therapist is "not ready" for more difficult dialogues about being a minority, which may then stifle the conversation. Open dialogue may provide an opportunity to further explore how the client is responding to academic and familial challenges. Increased cultural empathy on the part of the therapist via the active examination of her worldview would facilitate this process.

◆ Marcos lacks a social support system integral to his academic success and retention. Mental health professionals may consider the importance of facilitating external supports as opposed to relying solely on individual counseling. Mentoring relationships and supportive role models may be found outside the university environment. As ethnic identity is associated with overall adjustment among Hispanic students, the counselor may want to explore community cultural resources and encourage the client's participation. Strategies for navigating the dominant culture of the college may also prove helpful. Similarly, assistance with transitioning to and navigating the college environment may be particularly useful, especially for a first-generation college student.

◆ Among Latina/o clients, psychological distress may be expressed via somatic symptoms. This may be the result of stigma associated with perceptions of mental illness and treatment as well as cultural idioms of distress. Marcos's somatic complains may be a manifestation of psychological stress, although this interpretation must be approached cautiously. The resultant headaches and anxiety attacks may be addressed with relaxation training and/or mind–body therapy. Exercise of the client's choice could prove helpful, as could yoga and meditation practice.

◆ Mental health professionals often focus on client limitations, as opposed to strengths, particularly when they work with clients of color. For Marcos, challenging his low academic self-efficacy and discussing how it contrasts with his actual abilities as evidenced by his high school grades and test scores may be useful. This also would be useful for many clients whose perception is inconsistent with their actual performance. In this regard, the therapist may help Marcos critically examine messages that he may have received about his academic ability from parents and teachers. The therapist should be attuned to biased assumptions and related messages that Marcos receives as a Puerto Rican student, particularly as a minority in a predominantly White institution.

◆ Similarly, Marcos evidences useful social and communication skills, which can be used to negotiate with parents. His cultural attachment to his parents, consistent with the value of *familismo*, may also be used to involve them in college life, rather than to push them away. Mental health professionals can connect with student affairs personnel to assist parents when they have questions about a student's college experience and provide them with related literature, including information about the cultural environment of a predominantly White, non-Hispanic college.

Recommended Resources

Books and/or Articles

Ancis, J. R. (Ed.). (2004). *Culturally responsive interventions: Innovative approaches to working with diverse populations.* New York, NY: Brunner-Routledge.

Barajas, H. L., & Pierce, J. L. (2001). The significance of race and gender in school success among Latinas and Latinos in college. *Gender & Society, 15*(6), 859–878.

Comas-Díaz, L. (2010). On being a Latina healer: Voice, consciousness, and identity. *Psychotherapy: Theory, Research, Practice, Training, 47*(2), 162–168. doi:10.1037/a0019758

Dennis, J. M., Phinney, J. S., & Chuateco, L. I. (2005). The role of motivation, parental support, and peer support in the academic success of ethnic minority first-generation college students. *Journal of College Student Development, 46*(3), 223–236.

Garrod, A., Kilkenny, R., & Gómez, C. (Eds.). (2007). *Mi voz, Mi vida: Latino college students tell their life stories.* Ithaca, NY: Cornell University Press.

Harrell, P. E., & Forney, W. S. (2003). Ready or not, here we come: Retaining Hispanic and first-generation students in postsecondary education. *Community College Journal of Research and Practice, 27*(2), 147–156.

Kalsner, L., & Pistole, M. C. (2003). College adjustment in a multiethnic sample: Attachment, separation-individuation, and ethnic identity. *Journal of College Student Development, 44*(1), 92–109.

Riehl, R. (1994). The academic preparation, aspiration, and first-year performance of first-generation students. *College and University, 70*, 14–19.

Wallace, D., Abel, R., & Ropers-Huilman, B. (2000). Clearing a path for success: Deconstructing borders through mentoring in higher education. *Review of Higher Education, 24*(1), 87–102.

Yazedjian, A., & Toews, M. L. (2006). Predictors of college adjustment among Hispanic students. *Journal of the First-Year Experience & Students in Transition, 18*(2), 9–29.

Videos

Arévalo, R. (2010). *Latinos on campus: A documentary* [DVD]. (Beyond Documentary, Tufts University, Latino Center, Decatur, GA)

Hispanic Scholarship Fund. (2011). *Hija, debes ir a la universidad/Hija, you must go to college* [DVD]. United States: Target.

Assessments/Inventories

Marín, G., Sabogal, F., Marín, B. V., & Otero-Sabogal, R. (1987). Development of a short acculturation scale for Hispanics. *Journal of Behavioral Sciences, 9*(2), 183–205.

Steidel, A. G., & Contreras, J. M. (2003). A new familism scale for use with Latino populations. *Hispanic Journal of Behavioral Sciences, 25*(3), 312–330.

Zea, M. C., Asner-Self, K. K., Birman, D., & Buki, L. P. (2003). The abbreviated Multidimensional Acculturation Scale: Empirical validation with two Latino/Latina samples. *Cultural Diversity and Ethnic Minority Psychology, 9*(2), 107–126.

MY WAR PARENTS FOUND MY GAY BOX: THE STORY OF BENJAMIN

Nicolas Ladany and Julie R. Ancis

Case Description

Benjamin was a 20-year-old biracial (Vietnamese–African American) college student at a small mid-Atlantic college. He sought help at the college counseling center and presented with two primary concerns: (1) chronic frustration with his family's insistence that he change his gay sexual orientation and (2) anxiety about choosing an academic major. He was encouraged to go to the counseling center by his boyfriend, who was concerned with Benjamin's "obsessive thinking and constant worry." For example, Benjamin would discuss with his boyfriend his frustration with his parents and his worry about choosing the right major to the point that his boyfriend couldn't listen to it any more.

Jessica was a 30-year-old White counselor who had just received her psychologist license. She attended a graduate program that, according to the website, integrated multiculturalism throughout the curriculum. However, to her disappointment, the website was both more diverse and more multiculturally sensitive than her professors. She left the program feeling undertrained in a variety of multicultural concepts, even though she did her best to supplement her training with attendance at multicultural talks, conferences, and student professional organizations.

Benjamin and Jessica worked together for seven sessions. Their work concluded at the end of the semester when Benjamin went home during the summer break. They began their time together discussing Benjamin's family history and background. They spent the bulk of their time addressing his two primary presenting concerns.

In terms of family history and background, Benjamin's mother was Vietnamese and his father was African American. They met toward the end of the Vietnam War and, soon afterward, moved to the United States. Benjamin was a "surprise-gift" baby. He had three older siblings, the youngest of whom is 8 years older than he. His mother worked as an English teacher for honors students in a high school. His father was a commercial airline pilot. By all accounts, his parents demonstrated love toward Benjamin, and the conflicts they had were of the mild sort and were developmentally appropriate. However, while Benjamin was at college, his parents stumbled across a box in his closet at home that contained a variety of pictures and memorabilia from boyfriends, a box that Benjamin referred to as his "gay box." His parents were quite distraught. His mother, in particular, while seeming to understand him, strongly encouraged him to go to a urologist to fix the problem (i.e., so Benjamin would no longer be interested in men). She made many appointments, all of which Benjamin canceled. She could not understand his refusal to "get cured." His father was more accepting of his sexual orientation and indicated to Benjamin that he "kind of knew" as he was a bit "funny" throughout his life (e.g., his father noted his own discomfort with his son's effeminate manners and his disinterest in sports). However, he too encouraged Benjamin to look into getting himself "fixed" as his mother had requested.

In relation to the frustrations that resulted from his parents' requests to change his gay sexual orientation, Jessica primarily relied on her basic helping skills of listening, reflections, and empathizing as best she could (i.e., her Rogerian hat). Her self-doubt heightened when their discussions led them into areas with which she was less familiar. For example, she was very curious about the suggestion to go to a urologist but did not ask for clarification until two sessions after Benjamin brought it up. Upon reflection, she was worried about looking stupid but, of course, felt relieved once she realized that the suggestion, according to Benjamin, was a common one in his mother's culture. At other times, Jessica also felt emboldened and, upon reflection, overly confident in her approach. She found herself having a strong desire to "cause" Benjamin to have "insight" into what was happening culturally. For example, once in response to Benjamin's expression of frustration about his parents' beliefs, Jessica replied, "Well, it makes sense that they feel that way because of the cultures that they come from. They are still very early in their identity development."

During their discussions about his "constant worries" about his academic major, Jessica initially believed she was on more solid footing from a theoretical approach perspective, until she realized that none of the manualized treatments she learned about really fit the situation at hand. She ended up again spending a great deal of time learning about Benjamin's particular experience of worries and how cultural elements were integrated in these worries. For example, Benjamin physically had more Asian features than African American features. As a result, his peers, teachers, and academic advisors would respond mostly to his "Asian side." He was chronically encouraged to take science and math courses and was rebuffed when he let these folks know that he really hated science and math and would rather do something in the arts. In one instance, his academic advisor, without Benjamin's consent or knowledge, scheduled him for an advanced math course because he believed that if only Benjamin was exposed to math more, he would naturally take to it. As a result of all of these pressures, Benjamin developed a great deal of anxiety and worry about how he could respond to these suggestions and stay true to his career interests.

By the end of their work together, Benjamin had made some gains in managing and decreasing his worrisome outlook on life. Initially his frustrations about his parents decreased; however, they became heightened by the end of their work as he got closer to going home for the summer. Jessica and Benjamin strategized some options, including seeing a urologist as a way to appease his parents. In addition, part of the strategy involved finding a urologist who would be sensitive to his concerns and would agree to a meeting with his parents with the goal of convincing them that sexual orientation cannot be changed. Having a plan seemed to help him, albeit it was not a plan in which he had great confidence. Jessica felt energized by the case and came to appreciate Benjamin's struggles. She maintained a great deal of self-doubt about her multicultural skills but vowed to do her best to learn from her mistakes.

Reflection and Discussion Questions

1. In what ways has your current training program prepared you (or not prepared you) to deal with this case?

2. Assume Jessica is heterosexual. What are the implications of her racial identity and sexual orientation identity in relation to this case?

3. What thoughts, feelings, and behaviors of Benjamin reflect reactions that are culturally healthy versus culturally unhealthy?

4. What personal thoughts and feelings arose in you as you read the case? Be sure to identify feelings that fall into at least one of the six feeling clusters (anxiety/fear; depression/sadness; shame/humiliation; frustration; anger; and/or happiness/joy) (Ladany, Walker, Pate-Carolan, & Gray Evans, 2008).

5. Which aspects of the case attend to race/ethnicity only, sexual orientation only, and an integration of race/ethnicity and sexual orientation?

6. Was Jessica practicing outside of her competence area?

7. What are Benjamin's strengths?

8. How would Jessica's strengths and growth edges be assessed in this case?

Brief Analysis of the Case

• The case analysis begins with an understanding of the assumptions of one's personal counseling and therapy model. One can begin with practice background experiences that include settings and types of clients. A second set of assumptions is how to conceptualize the client in terms of two primary areas: (1) the etiology of the concerns and (2) the treatment of the concerns, both in the moment and projected future treatment. There are four foundations to this model:

1. It is integrative and pantheoretical in nature.
2. It attends to a multiculturally based working alliance.
3. It is strengths-based.
4. It is ever-evolving.

• The model we are presenting includes four components:

1. Client
2. Process and outcome

3. Counselor
4. Multicultural environments

In relation to the client component, there are four subcomponents to consider:

1. Identity
2. Presenting concerns
3. Interpersonal style/personality (i.e., patterns of feeling, thinking, and behaving)
4. Life-shaping events (big "T" and little "t" traumas).

Benjamin's identity, particularly his gender, racial, ethnic, and sexual orientation identities, all seem to be developing and may be characterized as an advanced stage of identity development (i.e., at least in the exploration stage) (see Ancis & Ladany, 2010, for more information). For example, Benjamin seems comfortable with his sexual orientation, as evidenced by his willingness to bring it up in therapy. However, it clearly brings distress in discussions and interactions with his parents. His frustration about his major is directly connected with his racial identity, as people attempt to put him in the Asian box, as well as theoretically the cultural and environmental oppression (from feminist and multicultural approaches to therapy).

• In terms of the process and outcome component, three subcomponents include:
1. The multiculturally based working alliance (i.e., mutual agreement on the goals and tasks, and an emotional bond built via empathy about his specific cultural circumstance).
2. Response modes and responsiveness (e.g., in-the-moment counselor skills and client reactions).
3. Counseling outcome or change in presenting concerns and associated concerns.

It seems that Jessica was able to build the alliance by empathizing and learning about Benjamin's concerns, particularly around his sexual orientation and race/ethnicity. Her Rogerian approach, in particular the skills necessary to develop an emotional bond with Benjamin, were essential.

Although these basic skills do not seem like much, these basic helping skills are the primary mechanism for change in this case. Related to outcome, Benjamin seemed to gain from their work together, and his concerns became heightened only when he was going to move back with his parents for summer break.

- In relation to the counselor component, there are three primary subcomponents to consider:
  1. Self-awareness (e.g., multicultural identities, multiculturally based countertransference)
  2. Knowledge (e.g., multicultural understanding from relevant literature, experience)
  3. Skills (i.e., helping skills and theoretically based interventions, such as discussing gender or racial differences and similarities, environmental interventions, etc.)

Jessica's self-awareness seemed to evolve in the case; however, it seemed as if she, like Benjamin, had advanced stages of multicultural identity development, particularly around race/ethnicity and sexual orientation. Hence, together, their racial/ethnic and sexual orientation identity interaction would be noted as parallel-advanced (see Ancis & Ladany, 2010, for more information). A fair question is how well can someone from one multicultural background work with a client from another multicultural background, as in this case, for example, sexual orientation and race. The answer to this question is that there is no correct way, and little help comes out of stereotyping cultural groups. Rather, by attending to identity variables, which are more relevant and psychologically meaningful than simple nominal or demographic variables, the counseling work can be analyzed in a more meaningful way. To that extent, it is clear that Jessica does well in many ways (e.g., addressing the racial difficulties that Benjamin faces on campus) but also has challenges in other ways (e.g., limited connection with Benjamin in relation to previously unheard of idea of seeing a urologist to adjust sexual orientation or making assumptions about Benjamin's parents' beliefs).

- The final component of the model pertains to multicultural environments that influence both the client and the counselor. These multicultural environments, from largest to smallest, include the world, nation, region, community (e.g., work, religious, school, etc.), family, and clinical setting. In addition, each level of the multicultural environment contains aspects of cultural health and cultural pathology, as defined by the extent to which social justice and human rights are present. In the case of the culture of Benjamin's family, the cultural pathology (e.g., disrespect for his sexual orientation) could be viewed as oppression about his sexual orientation. Alternatively, there seemed to be cultural health in the family in relation to the acceptance of him as a biracial person (e.g., his biracial self was accepted by his parents).

◆ In sum, Jessica and Benjamin's work together seemed to be fruitful because of some key multicultural factors. These factors included their respective multicultural identities, Jessica's multiculturally sensitive interventions, and the clinical setting's multicultural health, all of which offered more acceptance than oppression toward Benjamin.

Recommended Resources

Books and/or Articles

Ancis, J. R. (2004). (Ed.). *Culturally responsive interventions: Innovative approaches to working with diverse populations.* New York, NY: Brunner-Routledge.

Chase, C. (1999). *Queer 13: Lesbian and gay writers recall seventh grade.* New York, NY: William Morrow.

Helms, J. E. (1992). *A race is a nice thing to have. A guide to being a White person or understanding the White persons in your life.* Topeka, KS: Content Communications.

Inman, A. G., & Ladany, N. (in press). Multicultural competencies in psychotherapy supervision. In F. T. L. Leong (Ed.-in-Chief), L. Comas-Díaz, V. C. McLoyd, G. C. N. Hall, & J. E. Trimble (Assoc. Eds.), *APA handbooks in psychology: APA handbook of multicultural psychology: Vol. 2. Applications and training.* Washington, DC: American Psychological Association.

Kerwin, C., & Ponterotto, J. (1995). Biracial identity development. In J. Ponterotto, J. M. Casas, L. A. Suzuki, & C. M. Alexander (Eds.), *Handbook of multicultural counseling* (pp. 199–217). Thousand Oaks, CA: Sage.

Ladany, N. (2010). Learning what not to do: Lessons from lousy educators and supervisors. In M. Trotter, J. Koch, & T. Skovholt (Eds.), *Voices from the field: Defining moments in counselor and therapist development.* (pp.98–100). New York, NY: Routledge.

Ladany, N. (in press). Conducting effective clinical supervision. In G. P. Koocher, J. C. Norcross, & S. S. Hill, *Psychologists' desk reference* (3rd ed.). New York, NY: Oxford University Press.

Ladany, N., & Inman, A. G. (2012). Training and supervision. In E. M. Altmaier & J. C. Hansen (Eds.), *The Oxford handbook of counseling psychology* (pp. 179–207). New York, NY: Oxford University Press.

Steele, C. M. (1999, August). Thin ice: Stereotype threat and Black college students. *Atlantic Monthly Online*, 1–10. Retrieved from http://www .theatlantic.com/magazine/archive/1999/08/thin-ice-stereotype-threat-and-black-college-students/4663/

Wu, F. H. (2002). The model minority: Asian American "success" as a race relations failure. In F. H. Wu, *Yellow: Race in America beyond Black and White* (pp. 39–77). New York, NY: Basic Books.

Yoo, H. C., & Lee, R. M. (2008). Does ethnic identity buffer or exacerbate the effects of frequent racial discrimination on situational well-being of Asian Americans? *Journal of Counseling Psychology, 55,* 63–74.

Fiction Reading

Brown, Rita Mae. (1983). *Rubyfruit jungle.* New York, NY: Bantam.

Melville, H. (1853). "Bartleby, the Scrivener. A Story of Wall-Street." *Putnam's Monthly Magazine,* 546–557.

Videos

Costas, C. D. (Producer), & Nichols, M. (Director). (2004). *Angels in America* [Television miniseries]. United States: HBO Home Video.

Kane, M. (Producer), & Anderson, J., Coolidge, M., & Heche, A. (Directors). (2000). *If these walls could talk 2* [Television film]. United States: HBO Home Video.

Pillsbury, S., & Sanford, M. (Producers), & Spottiswoode, R. (Director). (2001). *And the band played on* [Television docudrama]. United States: HBO Home Video.

REFERENCES

Ancis, J., & Ladany, N. (2010). A multicultural framework for counselor supervision: Knowledge and skills. In N. Ladany & L. Bradley (Eds.), *Counselor supervision* (4th ed., pp. 53–95). New York, NY: Routledge.

Ladany, N., Walker, J. A., Pate-Carolan, L., & Gray Evans, L. (2008). *Practicing counseling and psychotherapy: Insights from trainees, clients, and supervisors.* New York, NY: Routledge.

PART II
Case Studies Involving Special Circumstances With Ethnic Populations

8

Clinical Applications With American Jews

Daniel C. Rosen and Ora Nakash

L'DOR V'DOR, OR FROM GENERATION TO GENERATION: THE STORY OF SCOTT

Case Description

Scott, a 33-year-old White, heterosexual American Jew presented in therapy reporting concerns regarding anxiety, difficulty with decision making, and problems in his current intimate relationship. He described his life as being "really great" in a lot of ways, though often feeling as though he could not "actually enjoy" himself. Scott expressed his concern that his early experiences at home with his family may be getting in the way of his ability to live a fulfilling life as an adult, stating that "I still haven't figured out how to live on my own terms and leave my parents' ways of doing things behind."

In describing his experience of anxiety, Scott stated that he tends to be a "very analytical" thinker, often creating major distress out of "minor" decisions. He recounted a recent experience attempting to purchase a pair of concert tickets and finding himself nearly unable to make a decision. He explained that such experiences of "overthinking" all of his options often result in making the "wrong" choices, in both minor decisions (e.g., what to order at a restaurant) as well as more important areas of his life (e.g., deciding where to live). He expressed concern related to both his career choice in law and with his choice to remain in his current intimate relationship of four years. He explained that he had a difficult time knowing what he wanted or how he felt about things.

Scott also disclosed his concerns about his growing discomfort and worry in social situations involving more than small groups of people and his distractedness in "high-pressure" situations. To manage his discomfort, Scott explained that he often turned to "somewhat ritualized" behaviors, including particular systems around eating healthy, sleeping, and exercise. He explained that none of these behaviors prevented him from functioning at a high level at work, although he has been criticized for his way of "doing things" by his current partner. "She suggested I come to therapy to loosen up and figure out my issues," he explained.

Scott became noticeably more distressed when speaking about his family of origin, which included his mother, father, and younger brother. He stated that his parents had been "very involved" in his life, although since he had become an adult they had vacillated between periods of close communication and months where he rarely returned calls. He recalled their involvement in his activities and schooling throughout his childhood, saying that he appreciated a lot of their love and attention, although it sometimes was "overboard." Particular memories that stood out in this regard included his mother's involvement in his extracurricular activities and desire to know details of his social events as he grew older and the way both of his parents "micromanaged" his academic progress and success. "They showered me with so much attention," he explained, "as well as expectations that I still feel pressured by today." Conversely, he expressed his appreciation for the high value his family placed on education and their care and love for one another.

He went on explain that three of his four grandparents, now deceased, were survivors of the Holocaust, and that memories of the Holocaust have continued to hang over his family like a "dark cloud." He wondered out loud how this might have impacted him, although stated he had not been able to figure it out on his own. Growing up, he recalled that his family rarely acknowledged the Holocaust or his grandparents' experiences directly. He could, however, recall messages from his parents that Jews were unsafe. When the country was at war during his elementary school years, he was frightened by overhearing his parents discuss whether Jews would need to leave the country. He remembered other events in which his parents warned him about others' dislike of Jews, were more restrictive than his friends' parents regarding participation in social events, and expressed general feelings of concern and worry about openly identifying as Jewish.

As he became older, Scott acknowledged that most of his major life decisions were made in accordance with his parents' wishes. "Where I went to college, what I studied—I still don't know if these were things I wanted or if I was just trying to please my family," he explained. In his current intimate relationship, Scott acknowledged largely deferring to his partner to make day-to-day decisions and her annoyance at his inability to identify his emotions and preferences.

When asked about his relationship to being Jewish, Scott explained that it was a source of confusion. He explained that its importance in his life had ebbed and flowed and that he currently identified only as a "cultural Jew." He explained that while he planned to potentially one day raise Jewish children, he did not participate in religious observance beyond the High Holidays and resented the pressure he felt from his parents to "be more engaged" in his local Jewish community. Scott acknowledged being uncomfortable talking about the subject, although he stated it was probably something he needed to "sort out."

When asked about his hopes and expectations during therapy, Scott stated that he would like to be more comfortable in his "own skin" and figure out how to make decisions that reflect who he is and who he wants to be. "I love my family," he explained. "I just need to find a way to live my own life."

Reflection and Discussion Questions

1. What stereotypes do you have about American Jewish clients? How does Scott conform to and/or differ from your general expectations of someone from this cultural group?
2. What would a therapist need to know/understand about Jewish culture and history in order to work effectively with Scott? Would it be possible for a non-Jew to do this work effectively?
3. If Scott's therapist was Jewish, would it be useful for her or him to disclose this to Scott? What might be the advantages and disadvantages of doing so?

4. In what ways do you imagine Scott's grandparents' experiences in the Holocaust impacted his family of origin? What additional questions, if any, would you have for him to assess this area of family history/dynamics?

5. To what extent does anti-Semitism still exist in the United States? In what ways, if any, do you imagine that such experiences impact the psychological well-being of American Jews? Do you think anti-Semitism has played a role in Scott's experiences? Explain.

6. In what ways do you think Scott's relationship to his Jewish identity may be relevant to his treatment goals? What other factors may be equally or more relevant?

7. What do you envision as your own treatment goals in working with Scott? How might these be congruent or incongruent with his cultural background?

Brief Analysis of the Case

• Understanding the intersection of cultural, social, biological, and psychological variables within an individual client is a complex process and requires us to be aware of both the relevance of Scott's American Jewish identity while not relying solely on this variable to conceptualize his psychological functioning. Understanding how, if at all, Scott's challenges are related to his being Jewish is at the heart of practicing from a place of cultural awareness and competence.

• American Jewish identity is a dynamic and multidimensional construct, rarely a single social identity. Jewish identity has been said to encompass one's religion, ethnicity, and, historically, one's race. Other intersecting factors, such as language (Hebrew, Ladino, and Yiddish); diet; political orientation; interest in literature, art, food, music; and relationship to the United States and to Israel have also been proposed as aspects of Jewish identity. For any American Jewish client, a combination of these dimensions may comprise their American Jewish identity. Scott has acknowledged his uncertainty and ambivalence related to his own Jewish identity, which may prove useful for further exploration.

• The degree to which any of the previously listed dimensions of Jewish identity are salient for an individual at any given time is best viewed as a dynamic and multidirectional process. The complexity of American Jewish identity at the individual level necessitates an understanding of how each Jew relates to these dimensions in the broader context of her or his life as well as recognizing this may not predict past or future importance of these dimensions. Additionally, understanding how Jewish identity intersects with other social identities (e.g., gender, social class, race) is essential to seeing the whole person.

♦ The Holocaust (Shoah) remains psychologically significant for many Jews, regardless of whether they experienced it directly or not. Research on the intergenerational transmission of trauma offers differing conclusions as to the ultimate impact of these experiences. Empirical findings generally acknowledge the Shoah's potential impact on family communication style, the process of individuation, parenting style, and traumatic stress, including the transmission of fear and mistrust. In Scott's case, it appears that his parents' experiences as children of Holocaust survivors may prove relevant to their parenting style and his current challenges in identifying his own needs and feelings.

♦ Distinguishing healthy paranoia or cultural mistrust from clinical paranoia may be a relevant aspect of treatment, as Scott may still be attempting to make sense of his parents' fears of anti-Semitism. Determining whether a client's fear is grounded in reality or symptomatic of an underlying pathology necessitates recognition of cultural factors, including historical oppression and one's lived experience. For some Jewish clients, a struggle exists between holding a relatively privileged status in the United States yet still feeling the discomfort of being marginalized through historical experiences of oppression, current manifestations of anti-Semitism, and concern for the future safety of oneself and the American Jewish community. Therapists who have an historical understanding of the Jewish people and experiences of oppression may help to facilitate inquiry into a client's own sense of safety and well-being in this broader context.

♦ The "pressure" that Scott experiences from his parents' expectations may be understood, in part, within the context of his grandparents' experiences as Holocaust survivors. For some families, being survivors of an event where so many died has placed an increased sense of responsibility and related survivor's guilt for those still living to continue the family's lineage in the greater community.

♦ Clients may have varying levels of comfort in disclosing their identities as Jews. Therapists may do best to follow a client's lead in this regard, neither assuming that one does nor does not wish to address this aspect of identity. Likewise, assumptions surrounding the importance any individual of Jewish descent gives to this aspect of identity are best left behind. Internalized anti-Semitism has led some Jews to reject this identity completely, while others simply may value alternate social identities to a greater extent in making sense of their lives. If one's Jewish identity is a relevant treatment variable, allowing a client to discuss its import (or lack thereof) in a self-directed way may prove beneficial. For Scott, this would include respecting his comfort in discussing the silence surrounding his grandparents' Holocaust experience. Additional areas of assessment may include one's relationship to other Jews and general relationship with members of the dominant culture.

• Largely missing from the case description is a focus on the strengths that many American Jews attribute to their cultural heritage and religion. In addition to the values of learning, education, and family that Scott alluded to in the case, many Jews may find a sense of meaning and purpose within this aspect of their identities. Values associated with Jewish identity may include social justice and equality, *Tikkun Olam*, a Hebrew phrase that translates to "healing the world" through caring for others and the greater environment.

THE "OTHER" IN US: THE STORY OF GABRIELLA

Case Description

"Hell is other people" (*l'enfer, c'est les autres*)—this is what Garcin, one of the main characters in the play *No Exit* by Sartre, says to Estelle when they find themselves locked in a drawing room. This utterance is, in the briefest form possible, Sartre's definition of fundamental sin. In social situations we play a part that is not ourselves, according to Sartre. If we passively become that part, we avoid the important decisions and choices by which our personality in interplay with our environment is shaped. I (Ora Nakash) often thought of this definition of hell by Sartre while sitting with Gabriella. For her, otherness was a major theme in therapy. What does it mean to really know another? What makes "another" an other? These are questions that stood at the center of her therapy.

Gabriella presented to treatment with symptoms of depression and confusion about her professional path and personal difficulties with intimate relationships. Gabriella, a 27-year-old single woman, grew up in a Jewish

Orthodox family. She described her father, a rabbi of a small congregation, as a charismatic and dominant man who has little capacity to tolerate differences. One of the most important messages her father conveyed to Gabriella throughout her childhood and adult life is that she cannot be different: "Being Jewish is what defines her and she can never escape it." Gabriella's mother, now retired, worked as a kindergarten teacher for more than 30 years and was described as highly anxious. Her mother's continual message was that the world is a dangerous place for Jews, and Gabriella should be wary of it. Gabriella recalled daily conversation at the dinner table in which her mother would "complain about being persecuted by peers and supervisors at her work." Gabriella's parents divorced five years ago. Their divorce was quite shameful in the closed community where they lived.

Gabriella's sister, four years her junior, lives in Israel. She moved to Israel to follow her husband and reside in an ultra-Orthodox community there. Gabriella painfully mourns the growing distance between the sisters. She struggles with her ambivalent wish to visit her sister in Israel. On one hand, it is her only opportunity to see her sister and nephews, yet on the other hand when she visits, she "has to be someone else." She is "forced" to follow the rules of her sister's Orthodox way of living.

As her sister became more observant, Gabriella became more secular over the past several years. This process has been a particular source of conflict for Gabriella, as she could not share her experiences and ambivalence around her choice to become secular with members of her family for fear of their banning her new way of life. When talking about her decision to "leave religion," she described that it was actually decided for her: "Religion rejected me—I had no place there because I was not married and had no children."

Gabriella graduated from a prestigious college, and despite doing very well in school, she has had great difficulty finding jobs and a "career path." She described feeling helpless and powerless in searching for a job. Her father's relentless pressure around this issue added to her conflicted feelings about searching for a job or applying to graduate school. He constantly reminded her that "everyone has a calling" and she is wasting her talent not pursuing hers. However, at the same time, he insisted that her "fate is in the hands of the one above" and that she "just needs to let it happen."

In one session while discussing her conflict around looking for a job, she made reference to her father's work: "I am so embarrassed to talk about it," she said. "Embarrassed?" I inquired. "He is involved in so much politics."

"Politics?" I inquired again. "I don't want you to judge him or think bad things about him . . . I'm really so confused, I remember going to so many protests with him feeling proud of him giving speeches and organizing all these people talking in public." "What kind of politics is he involved in?" I asked curiously. "Jewish politics, well, he is a conservative right-wing . . ." She hesitated, looking for signs of disapproval. "It sounds like it is hard to talk about it," I said. "Yes," she replied. "I feel very self-conscious."

Gabriella described having several good friendships. However, she has not been able to keep in touch with her childhood friends as they drifted apart over the years, particularly since she became more secular. Gabriella painfully recalled the longing for an intimate relationship during her adolescence and young adulthood. This was partly motivated by feelings of loneliness, but perhaps more important it was the expectation that through marriage and bearing children she could fulfill her destiny as a Jewish woman. She recalls nights of praying to God to send her someone to be with—believing that it was God's doing that would make it happen. She would lie in bed wondering what she had done wrong not to have that wish granted.

Her struggle to find her voice and navigate her path through the religious world she grew up in became more apparent recently as she started dating Dave, who grew up in a Catholic family. In one session, Gabriella tearfully started describing how hard it was for her to speak her mind. Fears of being ridiculed often contribute to her shame. When I asked for an example for these difficulties, she described how Dave never told his mother about her. Once, while spending time in his apartment, Dave's mother called. He picked up the phone and signaled to her to keep quiet. It deeply offended her, but she could not bring herself to ask him why he does not mention her to his mother. She kept feeling bothered by not knowing, until one day he referred to her as "my Jewish girlfriend." She then thought that it may be his Catholic upbringing that may have led him to keep their relationship a secret from his mother, who is a devout Catholic. Gabriella was not able to directly discuss her concerns with Dave. Upon exploration of her fears, it became clear that she again found herself facing a very painful dilemma. Not only was she reluctant to ask the questions for fear of being humiliated or dominated, but she could not afford to hear the answers. "What if he indeed says that he cannot be with me because I'm Jewish?" she fearfully asked. "What if my parents tell me that they cannot have a relationship with me if I'm with someone who's not Jewish?"

Reflection and Discussion Questions

1. What makes it hard to talk about religion and culture in the therapy room? What biases/assumptions might you have when working with someone like Gabriella?

2. What differences are most comfortable/safe for you to talk about in the context of this case? What differences are most difficult/threatening to talk about?

3. When/how does working with the "other"—namely clients who are culturally different from us—facilitate treatment, and when/how may such differences impede treatment? Could you imagine yourself working effectively with Gabriella?

4. How can we negotiate a cultural clash of values (e.g., the definition of *well-being*)? For example, in this case, the clash between the Western secular values of choice, agency, and feminism versus a religious emphasis on collectivism, obedience, and acceptance of higher power appear relevant. Can a patient and a therapist who embrace such disparate value systems find a common ground for effective and tolerant communication?

5. What impact, if any, would the therapist's religious-cultural identity have on the therapeutic alliance and progress of Gabriella?

6. Should the therapist disclose her cultural heritage and religious values? Why or why not?

7. How do you understand Gabriella's conflict around becoming secular? What are the risks she is facing? How might you address this in therapy?

8. How do you understand the message Gabriella received from her mother of "not trusting the world" from a sociocultural perspective? Would you address this in therapy? If so, how?

9. How do you understand Gabriella's reported painful feelings of loneliness from a sociocultural perspective? In this context, what role, if any, does the rejection of the different emerging parts of her religious identity play in the social difficulties she experiences as an adolescent and young adult?

Brief Analysis of the Case

• The interplay of religious values, gender expectations, and therapeutic approaches exemplified in the reflection and discussion questions is challenging and complex. These complexities challenge us to constantly reflect on the cultural sensitivity of our therapeutic approaches as well as the explicit and implicit values that guide our work as therapists.

• For individuals who grow up in Jewish Orthodox communities, becoming secular is, under the best circumstances, a difficult and painful process. This process threatens not only one's existing relationships but also one's whole way of constructing reality and leading everyday life. Judaism is a comprehensive religion with over 300 rules (*mitzvoth*). These rules instruct on how to lead one's life and include rules regarding what can be eaten, when one can travel, and how one should relate to others. Stepping out of this world often leaves one in a state of fear and confusion. Similar to other struggles in her life of dealing with differences, Gabriella faces a grave dilemma when it comes to her decision to become secular: If she chooses to remain observant, she risks losing her own integrity and wish for a separate way of life; if she becomes different and "leaves religion," she risks losing the relationships that are so important to her. For her family, there was no room for negotiation. You are either Jewish or not. Validating this dilemma and helping Gabriella find a way to safely explore her values and negotiate them with her family is pivotal to the success of the therapeutic intervention.

• Promoting agency as part of a Western individual viewpoint that has traditionally dominated psychotherapeutic interventions may conflict with the religious demand to follow a higher power. A long list of questions emerges in this regard: Can Gabriella allow herself to want? Can she allow herself to know her interests? Desires? Should these be left to be determined by a higher power? Should the goals of therapy include enhancing her sense of agency? Are these really her wishes or wishes dictated by a secular therapist? Growing up in a world that cherishes communal values and where agency can be considered a sin, will therapy help her find her voice amid a history of oppression? Or are we creating a new one oppressor—a secular Western one? Can Gabriella be different from her parents? From her therapist? Who will she be betraying if she chooses to have a different way of living? These questions can be explicitly explored with Gabriella in the therapeutic context in order to facilitate open communication and foster a culturally humble stance toward these complex identity questions.

• Gabriella's conflict can be framed from both a relational/developmental perspective as well as sociocultural one. We can think of her struggle to develop a separate identity and the lack of tolerance of differences by those around her from a sociocultural context. For Gabriella, the price of claiming her mind as separate, of positioning herself as an agent in the world, is extremely high. The significant relationships she has with others around her cannot tolerate it. The price is often very concrete and viable—in the form of physical and emotional disconnection. They include the growing distance with her sister who will not come and visit her in her secular world and her father's threats that he will not know his grandchildren should she choose to marry someone who is not Jewish. The dilemma is painful: Gabriella can be in a relationship with members of her family only if she follows their rules, if she gives up her separate mind. Understanding that this may conflict with her religious values and empowering the client to find her path may come with significant challenges.

• Therapy that traditionally represented the Euro-American worldview may clash with the value system of religiously observant clients. Growing up, Gabriella's way of surviving conflict within her relationships with her parents was to isolate herself and minimize their importance in her life. The cost for this compromise solution was high—in the process of surviving, she had to renounce her own needs, disconnect from herself. Particularly painful was the demand to fulfill her role as a Jewish woman through marriage and childbearing. These values may conflict with the feminist values of women empowerment and self-actualization. Therapists should be wary of imposing values on clients instead of providing a facilitating environment to explore different value systems.

• Gabriella's mother's message that the "world is an unsafe place" (which in many ways contributed to Gabriella's difficulty trusting and allowing closeness with others) can have many causes. A sensitive cultural viewpoint will consider viewing this as part of an adequate "cultural mistrust" that is a result of past and present ethnic and religious oppression. It is possible that the mother's experience of being "persecuted at work" was a realistic perception of anti-Semitic attitudes. To provide culturally sensitive care, it is critical to consider the emotional impact of past and present discrimination and oppression on American Jews.

• Within Judaism, one's degree of observance may vary. Explicit assessment of the degree of adherence to religious traditions is important to avoid both stereotypes and ignorance of this topic. In addition, assessment of the prominence of religious fate in the client's identity and relationships with family and friends is important to evaluate. Gabriella did not explicitly present with her conflict around her religiosity; it is the responsibility of the culturally sensitive therapist to evaluate the role of religion and religiosity in the client's world. With Gabriella, for example, such an evaluation would start as early as the intake session with screening questions about her religious belief system and its importance both historically and in her current life.

Recommended Resources

Books and/or Articles

Beck, E. T., Goldberg, J. L., & Knefelkamp, L. L. (2003). Integrating Jewish issues into the teaching of psychology. In P. Bronstein & K. Quina (Eds.), *Teaching gender and multicultural awareness: Resources for the psychology classroom* (pp. 237–252). Washington, DC: American Psychological Association.

Bilu, Y., & Witztum, E. (1993). Working with Jewish ultra-Orthodox patients: guidelines for a culturally sensitive therapy. *Culture, Medicine and Psychiatry, 17*(2), 197–233.

Cohen, S. M., & Eisen, A. M. (2000). *The Jew within: Self, family, and community in America*. Bloomington, IN: Indiana University Press.

Friedman, M. L., Friedlander, M. L., & Blustein, D. L. (2005). Toward an understanding of Jewish identity: A phenomenological study. *Journal of Counseling Psychology, 52*(1), 77.

Goldenstein, E. L. (2006). *The price of Whiteness: Jews, race, and American identity*. Princeton, NJ: Princeton University Press.

Langman, P. (1999). *Jewish issues in multiculturalism: A handbook for educators and clinicians*. Northvale, NJ: Jason Aronson.

Sachar, H. M. (1993). *The history of Jews in America*. New York, NY: Vintage Books.

Sarna, J. D. (2004). *American Judaism: A history*. New Haven, CT: Yale University Press.

Schlosser, L. Z. (2006). Affirmative psychotherapy for American Jews. *Psychotherapy: Theory, Research, Practice, Training, 43*(4), 424–435.

Telushkin, J. (1991). *Jewish literacy: The most important things to know about the Jewish religion, its people, and its history*. New York, NY: Morrow.

Novels or Fictional/Nonfictional Readings

Brody, L. (1997). *Daughters of kings: Growing up as a Jewish woman in America*. Boston, MA: Faber & Faber.

Chabon, M. (2000). *The amazing adventures of Kavalier & Clay: A novel*. New York, NY: Random House.

Chametzky, J., Felstiner, J., Flanzbaum, H., & Hellerstein, K. (Eds.). (2001). *Jewish American literature: A Norton anthology*. New York, NY: W.W. Norton & Co.

Foer, J. S. (2003). *Everything is illuminated*. New York, NY: Perennial.

Goodman, A. (1996). *The family Markowitz*. New York, NY: Farrar, Straus and Giroux.

Krauss, N. (2005). *The history of love*. New York, NY: Norton.

Mirvis, T. (2000). *The ladies' auxiliary*. New York, NY: Ballantine.

Roth, P. (1997). *American pastoral*. Boston, MA: Houghton Mifflin Harcourt.

Videos

Daum, M., & Rudavsky, O. (Producers & Directors). (1997). *A life apart — Hasidism in America*. United States: EMI UNART.

Joffe, C. H. (Producer), & Allen, W. (Director). (1977). *Annie Hall* [Motion picture]. United States: United Artists.

Kagan, J. P. (Director). (1981). *The chosen* [Motion picture]. United States: Analysis Film Releasing Corp..

Landau, E., & Landau, E. A. (Producer) & Kagan, J. P. (Director). (1981). *The chosen* [Motion picture]. United States: Analysis Film.

Miller, R. A., Bloomberg, M. R., & Slavin, N. (Producers), & Slavin, N. (Director). (2001). *Focus* [Motion picture]. United States: Paramount Classics.

Rubin, D. (Director). (2008). *The Jewish Americans* [Documentary]. United States: JTN Productions, WETA Washington, DC, and David Grubin Productions in association with Thirteen/WNET New York.

9

Clinical Applications With Immigrants

Pratyusha Tummala-Narra and Diya Kallivayalil

NEGOTIATING CULTURAL CHANGE AND IDENTITY: THE STORY OF NADIA

Immigration entails adjustment to a new cultural context that challenges and transforms identity and relationships with others. The process of migration imposes loss and separation from one's loved ones and culture of origin. Further, immigrants face multiple stressors in the new cultural context, including discrimination, as they negotiate identity and life transitions (e.g., marriage, parenting). The following vignette illustrates how these processes are relevant to mental health and psychotherapy.

Case Description

Nadia is a 52-year-old woman who migrated with her husband to the United States from a large city in Pakistan in her early 20s. She sought psychotherapy to cope with anxious and depressed mood and headaches, which had been increasing in frequency over the course of several months. She was referred by a family physician who, after finding no physical basis for her headaches, recommended that she work with a psychotherapist to cope with her problems with mood. Nadia hoped to work with a South Asian therapist. When I (Pratyusha Tummala-Narra) first met her, she indicated that she was relieved to work with a therapist of a similar cultural background, although she noted my Asian Indian ancestry as different in some ways from her Pakistani background.

Nadia migrated to the United States when she was 22 years old, soon after her marriage to her husband, Javed, who worked as a technician in a research laboratory. Both Nadia and Javed are fluent in English, having been educated in English-language schools in Pakistan. Although Javed had obtained an advanced degree in Pakistan, he was unable to find work in the United States in his discipline. He decided to move to a suburban area of the Midwest to live near his two older brothers who had left Pakistan several years earlier. Nadia, while reluctant to leave her family in Pakistan, looked forward to beginning a new life with her husband in the United States. She had attended two years of college in Pakistan, and when she arrived in the United States, she worked part time in a grocery store, until the birth of her two daughters. She reported having a loving relationship with her husband, whom she described as supportive and kind. However, over the years, a major source of stress in their marriage has been her relationship with her in-laws, particularly with her husband's brothers, whom she describes as controlling and disrespectful to her and her husband. She worries that her brothers-in-law influence her husband's decisions regarding their personal matters, such as his approach to raising children and managing their finances.

Nadia recalled that when she first moved to the United States, she had felt alone, even though her in-laws lived nearby. She missed her family, and due to financial constraints, her visits to Pakistan were infrequent. She coped with her feelings of loss and isolation by investing her energy into her role as a mother and wife; she has a strong sense of pride in her ability to care for her daughters. Both of her daughters were successful academically, developed friendships, and remained close to both parents. Nadia also felt proud of her daughters' identification with Pakistani culture and with their Muslim heritage. Her ability to carry forth her cultural and religious traditions has been an important part of her mothering role. She was also invested in her daughters gaining more financial independence and self-reliance, an opportunity that was limited in her own experience as a young woman in Pakistan and in the United States. As her children have gotten older, she has experienced increasing anxiety about her physical distance from them; her daughters live in different parts of the United States.

Approximately one year prior to meeting with me, her younger daughter had come out to her and her husband as a lesbian. Nadia and Javed were shocked to learn about their daughter's sexual identity and have difficulty accepting her lesbian identity. Nadia stated, "Being from Pakistan, we never imagined anything like this would be possible. Sometimes I wonder if we should have moved here [to the United States]." She struggled with wanting to maintain a close, supportive relationship with her daughter and with her anxiety about others, particularly family members, reacting to her daughter's sexual orientation. She was also troubled by the possibility that her daughter will receive negative and discriminatory treatment due to homophobia both in the Pakistani and mainstream American communities. She was unsure about whether to talk with her in-laws and her family in Pakistan about her daughter's sexual identity.

Her primary care physician stated in his referral that he was concerned about Nadia experiencing a clinically significant depressive episode. Although Nadia experienced anxious and sad mood, her presenting issues (e.g., headaches, anxiety, sadness) did not meet criteria for a specific diagnosis in the *Diagnostic and Statistical Manual of Mental Disorders* (DSM-5) (American Psychiatric Association, 2013). Her distress was situated in the context of both long-standing issues of adjustment to a new cultural context and more recent developments in her family life that posed a threat to her sense of emotional and interpersonal connection with her daughter, her family of origin, and her in-laws. She felt torn about her sense of duty as a Pakistani, Muslim mother who could maintain her cultural heritage and about her wish to embrace her daughter's ability to come out to her.

Nadia's goals in psychotherapy were formulated not within a traditional diagnostic framework but rather from an understanding of acculturation, acculturation gaps between her and her children, and loss. Her own formulation of her distress involved a focus on her feelings of distance from her family members and a sense of isolation. When Nadia and I discussed her goals for psychotherapy, she expressed that her headaches were expressions of her body "feeling stressed out with all that is happening with the family." Her own conceptualization of her presenting issues and a growing recognition of the role of separation from her family and friends in Pakistan, experiences of discrimination against Muslims in the United States, and the transformation of identity as a result of immigration played a central role in framing the psychotherapy process. As her therapist, I felt it was important to recognize her unique experience of her social context in order to more fully understand her distress and to develop effective interventions.

Nadia perceived her decision to move to the United States as one that was more or less determined by her husband and her parents, who had arranged her marriage. In the initial years of her adjustment to living in the United States, she found her interactions with her in-laws to be challenging, as she felt that they excluded her and her husband from participating in decisions that affected the extended family. At work, she recalled feeling humiliated when she was called offensive names and when someone told her to "go back home." Over the years, Nadia made friends in a local Pakistani American community who have remained an important source of support to her. She and one of her friends began teaching Urdu, her heritage language, to children in her local community. Approximately 10 years after her migration to the United States, a mosque was constructed near her home, and she has regularly attended services since the mosque opened. Nadia met other Pakistani families there who became their extended family in the United States.

One of Nadia's greatest fears in learning about her daughter's sexual identity is that her friends would not understand her daughter's sexual orientation and condemn the family in some way, especially when her friends ask her when her daughters plan to get married. Although Nadia tried to keep silent about her concerns with her daughter, she noticed that she started to feel somewhat more distant from her. When her daughter asked that she and Javed meet her partner, Nadia explained to her that she was not ready to do so. Nadia felt ashamed of her inability to respond to her daughter in a supportive way.

Reflection and Discussion Questions

1. The therapist and the client in this vignette are from similar and yet different backgrounds, which the client referred to during therapy. What implication does this have for culturally responsive treatment?
2. How did the therapist find language that was personally meaningful for Nadia to discuss her symptoms and her conceptualization of these symptoms?

3. What implications does Nadia's migration to the United States and subsequent adjustment to living here have for her presenting concerns and her relationship with the therapist?
4. What can be understood of Nadia's thoughts that her daughter's sexual orientation was somehow a result of their migration to the United States?
5. How can the therapist approach Nadia's dilemma about whether to tell her close Pakistani and Muslim friends about her daughter's sexual orientation?
6. How can the therapist help Nadia draw on the strength she gains from her connection to her Pakistani and Muslim communities to help her cope with her stress and dilemmas concerning her relationship with her daughter?

Brief Analysis of the Case

Several issues in the therapeutic process require attention, particularly those related to immigration, acculturation, religion, gender socialization, sexual orientation, and discrimination.

♦ Nadia's feelings of loss and separation from family of origin and conflict with her extended family in the United States seemed to have heightened her fear of losing her connection with her children. She has been coping with separation from a familiar cultural environment and with ambivalence about acculturating to mainstream American culture. Immigration poses significant challenges with respect to changes in family structure, gender roles, and parenting. Nadia struggled with differences between her worldview and that of her daughters, reflecting an acculturation gap among various members of the family. She began to recognize that although she worked hard to teach her daughters about Pakistani and Muslim culture and spirituality, they had constructed their worldviews based on a blend of Pakistani, Muslim, and American values. In one session, she stated, "I feel like I cannot fully understand what it must be like for them [her daughters]. It's too hard sometimes because this is not what we expected it would be like, so hard to raise children here." Psychotherapy offered a space in which Nadia could discuss her identifications with her culture of origin and her apprehension about her daughters' adoption of mainstream American views.

For example, she could actively discuss both sides of her ambivalence about meeting her daughter's partner and reflect on how her role as a mother had transformed as a result of migration and acculturation.

• Nadia recognized the cultural similarities and differences between herself and her therapist. She felt connected to the therapist as they shared a common South Asian ancestry, and at the same time she was unsure of whether someone from a Hindu, Indian background would be able to understand her Pakistani, Muslim identity. In psychotherapy, we gradually discussed her concerns about working with a Hindu, Indian therapist and specifically about her concern that I would evaluate her as "too old-fashioned or backward." I too worried that at times she experienced me as an outsider, such as when she stated, "You grew up here, and I don't know if you can understand what it is like to be a woman from Pakistan or India." It was necessary for us to talk openly about her perceptions and apprehensions regarding my background and their implications for building trust in our relationship.

• Therapists conducting psychotherapy with immigrant clients should consider the role of various aspects of social context that influence cultural adjustment and psychological well-being. In Nadia's case, it was especially important to explore the development of her religious and cultural identity throughout her adjustment to living in the United States. Nadia's religious community is an important source of resilience in the face of acculturative stress. In fact, she had deeply invested in her relationships with her Pakistani friends when she began to teach Urdu in her community, which helped her to develop a sense of safety and belonging in the United States.

• As she faced her daughter's coming out as a lesbian, she began to question her beliefs concerning homosexuality. She felt torn about her commitment to her spiritual beliefs and her community and yet longed to remain connected with her daughter and be supportive of her. Her emotional distress manifested in somatic symptoms (e.g., headaches), a common experience particularly among first-generation immigrants (those born outside the United States), as this type of symptom presentation tends to be less stigmatized than verbal expression of distress (Foster, 2001). It is important, however, to note that in psychotherapy, Nadia became increasingly willing to talk about her conflicts within her family and her community and understood her headaches as a sign of stress resulting from these conflicts. Her concern about talking about her daughter's sexual orientation with others in the Pakistani and Muslim communities was a focal point of this tension. Nadia wished both to preserve her values of collectivism through her connection to her community and to cultivate a space for her daughter to experience acceptance within the community. Religious and cultural identity transform throughout the life span for immigrants, and critical moments such as her daughter's coming out place clients in a position to confront and reevaluate long-standing identifications with the culture of origin and the immigration process itself. For instance, at times, Nadia would wonder whether moving to the United States was related to her daughter's sexual orientation, and at other times, she felt grateful to live in the United States, where homosexuality is more accepted in broader society when compared with Pakistan.

♦ Nadia's sense of belonging in the United States has been influenced by experiences of discrimination. It is worth noting that although these experiences left a marked impression on her during her adjustment to living in the United States, she rarely discussed the problem of discrimination with her husband, children, extended family, or friends. She was most upset by incidents when her daughters felt different from other children at school. Because the dynamics of the psychotherapeutic relationship can reflect racial and intercultural relations in broader society, it was important that our discussion of cultural similarities and differences expanded to engagement with discrimination and prejudice. As she felt increasingly settled in her therapy, she began to talk about specific experiences of discrimination by White Americans and later about discrimination she experienced by Asian Indians. The recognition of the prejudice that many Hindu Indians and Muslim Pakistanis have toward each other was an important aspect of authentic engagement and honest dialogue in psychotherapy. Although we were both apprehensive in having such discussions, the ability to talk openly about these prejudices both validated Nadia's experiences and deepened our connection in the therapeutic dyad.

After her daughter came out as a lesbian, Nadia worried about her daughter's safety both within and outside of Pakistani and South Asian communities, due to homophobia and racism. Recent studies have demonstrated the negative effects of discrimination on mental health outcomes, such as depressive and anxiety symptoms, among South Asians in the United States and elsewhere (Tummala-Narra, Alegria, & Chen, 2012; Tummala-Narra, Inman, & Ettigi, 2011). It is critical that therapists attend to the cumulative effects of discrimination on physical and mental well-being. For Nadia, experiences of discrimination complicated her feelings of belonging and exacerbated her feelings of loss and separation from her family and friends in Pakistan. She struggled with a sense of home and whether she would be able to return home to Pakistan.

LOSS AND POLITICAL EXILE: THE STORY OF PAUL

Many immigrants experience traumatic events in their countries of origin, during their journey to the new country, and post-migration in the new country. The experience of political violence and exile poses unique vulnerability in the new cultural context, where individuals struggle with ongoing concerns about safety and trust. Psychotherapists working with immigrant clients with such histories are often faced with challenges to traditional diagnostic and treatment considerations. The following vignette illustrates these issues in psychotherapeutic work with a refugee client.

Case Description

Paul is a man in his 30s who fled his home country in East Africa. He arrived in the United States a year prior to my (Diya Kallivayalil) first meeting with him. Paul recounted growing up under an oppressive regime in his country, and he became politically active at a young age. He attended a deeply split and politicized high school and grew up in what he described as a relatively affluent and middle-class family. He also spoke of his belief that it was the role of the middle class in his country to work toward political change, even though political activity was deeply repressed and dangerous. He learned English in his secondary school and spoke it fluently. He reported having no psychiatric difficulties prior to the incidents leading to his fleeing his country.

In response to an upcoming local election, Paul began to increase his visible political activity. One night when he was returning home to his mother's house where he lived, he was ambushed and kidnapped. He was kept in confinement in a room for over two weeks and was interrogated and tortured. He was told by his captors that they would never let him go and that his family would be tortured as well. He was deprived of food, beaten into unconsciousness, forced into ice-cold water, given electric shocks, and forced to listen to the screams of other prisoners. He believed he would be killed. Eventually he was put into a van and dumped on the side of a road and warned that his life would continue to be in danger. He was hospitalized for over a month for his injuries. Realizing that he had no other option, he arranged to flee to the United States and apply for political asylum. His family continues to receive threatening phone calls demanding to know where he is. He was referred to treatment by his primary care physician whom he saw for continued pain related to his torture injuries. He lived in the basement of a house of a family from his home country whom he met at a religious function.

Paul received a diagnosis of posttraumatic stress disorder (PTSD) and major depressive disorder. He endorsed repetitive flashbacks of the traumatic events he experienced: "The thoughts of what has happened are always in my mind. The wounds are always there." He suffered with chronic insomnia and experienced nightmares and intrusive memories during the day. He developed a fear of the dark due to his confinement and could not take showers without the bathroom door open. He felt alternately overwhelmed and anxious and emotionally numb. He also felt irritable and angry when he was around others and would say, "I feel out of touch with other people." He lost interest in normal activities and experienced great fear and anxiety about the future: "How will my life be meaningful again? My dreams are crushed." He was extremely hypervigilant and was very fearful of the police: "When I see them, I hold my breath." He felt he would never call the police if he were in trouble. He worried about his family in his home country and felt guilty and responsible for the harassment they were suffering. He also felt guilty that he could not support them financially. He had depressed mood and his sleep and appetite were erratic. He reported low energy, anhedonia, and psychomotor retardation. He did not report suicidal thoughts, but he felt hopeless at times and felt an acute sense of loss, loneliness, and displacement.

Three treatment issues were identified:

1. *Trust.* Paul had a deep mistrust of authority figures in general and of health care providers. He was wary of providing information about himself and tended to experience questions about his history or symptoms as an interrogation. He would often say, "It is very difficult to open up—I feel bad and sick all over again." He lived with a pervasive sense of vulnerability and felt anxious when he saw security

officers at the clinic. The severity of his intrusive symptoms made it difficult for him to "forget" his torture experiences. He felt easily triggered and would often lose time, "coming to" with severe headaches. He avoided news about his home country and stayed away from members of his community for fear that there would be some reprisal against his family. As a result he felt very isolated and lonely.

2. *Stigma of mental illness.* Paul's difficulties were complicated by a fear of the label of mental illness and receiving psychiatric care. He found it difficult to understand the role of psychotherapy in his care; in his home country, there were few therapists and people who accessed psychiatrists tended to be severely mentally ill. His suffering was compounded by his shame about his psychological decline and his symptoms, and he felt angry and frustrated with himself for having emotional difficulties, which he interpreted as weakness. He would often say, "I've never felt like this before. What's wrong with me? Will I ever get back to who I was?" He worried that his difficulties were permanent.

3. *Dislocation and change in socioeconomic status.* As with many immigrants and with refugees, Paul experienced profound and sudden loss and displacement. It was never his intention to leave his home and his family and come to the United States. The decision was made under duress, and it forced him into a life of dislocation and poverty. This was in contrast to the life of relative comfort and status that he lived at home and made any kind of adjustment to the United States very difficult for him. He felt he was "begging" for help here, and this wounded his pride. He experienced various incidents of overt and systemic racism that made him feel unsafe and sometimes lost in understanding racial dynamics and hierarchies in the United States. He tended to idealize his home country and his life there and talked in negative terms about America: "In my country, everyone helps each other. No one goes hungry."

Reflection and Discussion Questions

1. How do you understand Paul's desire to educate his therapist about his home country and the political situation there?
2. How was his cultural identity an issue in treatment?

3. How would you think about Paul's diagnoses of both major depression and PTSD?
4. When considering the client's mistrust of authority figures, what are some ways that the therapist facilitated a safe therapeutic space? How would you address the issue of the client's mistrust in your work with Paul?
5. How did the therapist help the client manage his immediate post-traumatic stress symptoms and his concerns of safety for his family? If you were to work with Paul, how would you work address his PTSD symptoms?
6. What implications does the client's view of psychiatric illness and emotional problems have for diagnosis and treatment?
7. In what ways do you see psychotherapy helping clients in coping with the shifts in social identity that can occur as a result of migration, such as socioeconomic status, shifts in work and relationships, career aspirations, religious practice, and sense of place?
8. How would you address Paul's shame about his mental illness in treatment?

Brief Analysis of the Case

♦ There are several important and multifaceted issues to consider in providing culturally responsive therapy to refugees and asylum seekers. While recognizing the enormous variation in asylum seekers and refugees on a number of dimensions including country of origin, path to the United States, pre-immigration stressors, gender, and many others, some general points can be made to inform their care. Providing culturally informed treatment is important with all clients and populations but perhaps paramount in working with asylum seekers because the *basis* for a political asylum claim in the United States is a history or fear of persecution based on identity factors such as race, religion, membership in a social group, or political opinion. Therefore, identity or identification is generally the main reason for fleeing one's home country. In this way, cultural identity is both an "identity" and a lived reality. Further, refugees and asylum seekers frequently experience discrimination, language barriers, racism, and harassment in their journeys to their host country and once they arrive there (Pope & Garcia-Peltoniemi, 1991). These experiences are distressing and also disorienting because they often do not mirror the racial, gender, or class dynamics in their home countries.

◆ Further, because these clients have been targets based on some aspect of their identity, their relationship to this identity and the cultural group to which they belong is deeply complicated. Understanding their own construction of their multiple identities, both prior to and after migration, and how this may have changed can be central to proving culturally responsive care and provides a useful alternative to imposing our own notions or biases. This understanding can be particularly important when the therapist is from the client's home country or feels he or she has prior knowledge of it from study or travel. Attending to these issues may reduce the risk of misjudging the implications of cultural factors in treatment (Silove, Tarn, Bowles, & Reid, 1991). It is also important to be aware of assumptions about symptom presentation—such as assuming clients who are originally from other countries will show higher levels of somatization or somatic symptoms.

◆ It is also important not to consider working with refugees and asylum seekers as simply the treatment of the "cultural other" (Smith, 2007). This stance can prevent therapists and others from seeing the treatment as co-constructed, and they often undervalue the implications of their own cultural background and biases. There is also the danger of minimizing or distorting how the client relates to the therapist's background (although this is often assumed or a projection).

◆ Determining the goals of treatment was straightforward: Given that fear and trust were among the most salient issues that Paul presented with, working with these two issues was paramount. This work involved psychoeducation about PTSD and about psychotherapy, my role as a psychologist, confidentiality, my involvement in his legal case, the role of psychopharmacology, and concrete suggestions and resources around his immediate needs, such as food and housing. We worked together on developing skills to manage his posttraumatic response, including his intrusive symptoms, sleep strategies, follow-ups for medical care, referrals for medications, reducing avoidance, and managing his panic symptoms. In this way, there was an ongoing effort to communicate to Paul that trust in a relationship with an authority figure is something built over time and not assumed. We also talked openly about his issue regarding trust over the course of our work together.

◆ In Paul's case, the change in his class circumstances and his life in poverty in the United States was a significant issue in treatment. He struggled with the sense that he was receiving charity from others, including the family he lived with. Once he did receive his work papers, the idea of working, at least initially, in jobs that he considered low status was a blow to him. He began to feel that people felt he was not "being grateful" for the opportunities he did have and that they did not want him to aspire to more. He coped with this in part with fantasies of how he would "repay" the people who helped him when he rebuilt his life and became wealthy. As it is with all clients, it was important in therapy with Paul to be careful in the language used around these issues and the choices he made—that is, to not imply, overtly or covertly, that he was "better off" here or in his home country, that class was not an issue in the United States, to make assurances about his court case, to imply that he should settle for a certain job, and so on. Doing this would have been deeply disruptive to any tenuous trust that was being built in the relationship.

♦ Paul's case can be looked at through the lens of loss and shame. In addition to the detrimental view he held of mental illness before he himself became ill and the shame associated with seeing himself as a "mental patient," he also experienced his symptoms as another loss; he would often say, "I've lost everything, even my mind." He lived with the loss of his family and his community, with the painful knowledge that he could never regain his country and his old life, and often embodied this tenet that has been said of refugees: "Exile is the most painful form of torture" (Fischman & Ross, 1990, p. 139). He felt also acute loss and shame over his role as provider and protector of his family back home, something he at times discussed in terms of losing his masculine identity. The guilt and worthlessness he felt in the United States made him at times question whether he had made the right decision in coming here and wonder if he should return and risk his life: "At least I'll be facing things," he said. I understood his behavior of educating me about his country and his political life in part as a wish to feel less like a "patient" for some part of the session and became instead the expert. I also understood it as a way for him to work through validating his political activity for which he had taken such risks and that had cost him so much. This was an important component of treatment.

♦ In regard to the therapeutic relationship and transference/countertransference: Paul's reaction to me as the therapist was ambivalent. Although a part of him was comforted by my being an immigrant, the perception that I was an "immigrant by choice" was troubling to him and made him feel that we were psychologically fundamentally different. Therefore, he felt, could I truly understand his plight? He would devalue therapy and therefore me at times. My own countertransference was also mixed sometimes. His devaluing of therapy made me feel that perhaps therapy was not "enough" and feel guilty that I had not engaged in political activity. Sometimes I would worry about how to answer his questions about whether I liked my job and why I had chosen it or whether I regretted leaving my home country. This led to discussions with him around whether "sameness" was required for therapy to work and what level of it was required for the client to feel heard and understood. Paul was able to express that much of his wish for "sameness" was related to the deep shame and guilt he felt about his choices and his mental health problems and that devaluing treatment at times was a way to step away from these feelings. He was also able to hear my admiration for his political work and the personal risks he had taken.

Recommended Resources

Books and/or Articles

Ainslie, R. C. (1998). Cultural mourning, immigration, and engagement: Vignettes from the Mexican experience. In M. Suarez-Orozco (Ed.), *Crossings: Immigration and the sociocultural remaking of the North American space* (pp. 283–300). Cambridge, MA: Harvard University Press.

Akhtar, S. (1996). "Someday" and "if only" fantasies: Pathological optimism and inordinate nostalgia as related forms of idealization. *Journal of the American Psychoanalytic Association, 44,* 723–753.

Akhtar, S. (2011). *Immigration and acculturation: Mourning, adaptation, and the next generation.* New York, NY: Jason Aronson.

Blanche, M., & Endersby, C. (2004). Refugees. In D. Olivere and B. Monroe (Eds.), *Death, dying and social differences.* Oxford, England: Oxford University Press.

Comas-Diaz, L. (2006). Latino healing: The integration of ethnic psychology into psychotherapy. *Psychotherapy: Theory, Research, Practice, Training, 43,* 436–453.

Leary, K. (2000). Racial enactments in dynamic treatment. *Psychoanalytic Dialogues, 10,* 639–653.

Mahalingam, R., Balan, S., & Haritatos, J. (2008). Engendering immigrant psychology: An intersectionality perspective. *Sex Roles, 59*, 326–336.

Sirin, S. R., & Fine, M. (2008). *Muslim American youth: Understanding hyphenated identities through multiple methods.* New York, NY: New York University Press.

Suárez-Orozco, C., & Suárez-Orozco, M. M. (2010). *Learning a new land: Immigrant students in American society.* Cambridge, MA: Harvard University Press.

Turshen, M. (2001). The political economy of rape: An analysis of systematic rape and sexual abuse of women during armed conflict in Africa. In C. Moser & F. Clark (Eds.), *Victims, perpetrators or actors? Gender, armed conflict and political violence* (pp. 55–68). London, England: Zed Books.

Fiction Reading

Alexander, M. (1996). *The shock of arrival.* Boston, MA: South End Press.

Diaz, J. (2007). *The brief wondrous life of Oscar Wao.* New York, NY: Riverhead Books.

Eggers, D. (2007). *What is the what.* New York, NY: Vintage Press.

Fadiman, A. (1997). *The spirit catches you and you fall down: A Hmong child, her American doctors, and the collision of two cultures.* New York, NY: Farrar, Straus & Giroux.

Japin, A. (2000). *The Two hearts of Kwasi Boachi.* New York, NY: Knopf.

Lahiri, J. (1999). *Interpreter of maladies.* New York, NY: Houghton Mifflin.

Rushdie, S. (1995). *East, west.* London, England: Vintage Press

Tan, A. (1991). *The kitchen god's wife.* New York, NY: Penguin Books.

Videos

Coppola, F. F. (Executive producer), & Nava, G. (Director). (1995). *Mi familia (My family)* [Motion picture]. United States: New Line Cinema.

Golin, S., Kilik, J., & Gonzalez Inarritu, A. (Producers), & Gonzalez Inarritu, A. (Director). (2006). *Babel* [Motion picture]. United States: Summit Entertainment, Central Films, and Media Rights Capital.

Konwiser, K. (Producer), & Konwiser, K., & Ren, D. (Directors). (2007). *Shanghai kiss* [DVD]. United States: Anchor Bay Entertainment.

Nair, M. (Producer & Director). (2006). *The namesake* [Motion picture]. United States: Fox Searchlight Pictures.

Parkes, W., et al. (Producers), & Forster, M. (Director). (2007). *The kite runner* [Motion picture]. United States: DreamWorks Pictures.

Villalobos, L., & Barrera, G. (Producers), & Riggen, P. (Director). (2007). *Under the same moon (La misma luna)* [Motion picture]. United States: Fox Searchlight Pictures, The Weinstein Company.

Wang, W. (Producer), & Markey, P., Wang, W., Tan, A., & Bass, R. (Directors). (1993). Joy Luck Club [Motion picture]. United States: Hollywood Pictures.

REFERENCES

American Psychiatric Association. (2013). *Diagnostic and statistical manual of mental disorders* (5th ed.). Washington, DC: Author.

Fischman, Y., & Ross, J. (1990). Group treatment of exiled survivors of torture. *American Journal of Orthopsychiatry, 60*(1), 135–142.

Foster, R. P. (2001). When immigration is trauma: Guidelines for the individual and family clinician. *American Journal of Orthopsychiatry, 71*(2), 153–170.

Pope, K., & Garcia-Peltoniemi, R. (1991). Responding to victims of torture: Clinical issues, professional responsibilities, and useful resources. *Professional Psychology: Research and Practice, 22*(4), 269–276.

Silove, D., Tarn, R., Bowles, R., & Reid, J. (1991). Psychosocial needs of torture survivors. *Australian and New Zealand Journal of Psychiatry, 25,* 481–490

Smith, H. (2007). Multicultural issues in the treatment of survivors of torture and refugee trauma: Toward an interactive model. In H. E. Smith, A. S. Keller, & D. W. Lhewa, *". . . Like a refugee camp on First Avenue": Insights and experiences from the Bellevue/NYU Program for Survivors of Torture* (pp. 38–64). New York, NY: Bellevue/NYU Program for Survivors of Torture.

Tummala-Narra, P., Alegria, M., & Chen, C. (2012). Perceived discrimination, acculturative stress, and depression among South Asians: Mixed findings. *Asian American Journal of Psychology, Special Issue,* Secondary analysis of the National Latino Asian American Study (NLAAS) Dataset, Part I, *3*(1), 3–16.

Tummala-Narra, P., Inman, A. G., & Ettigi, S. (2011). Asian Indians' responses to discrimination: A mixed-method examination of identity, coping, and self-esteem. *Asian American Journal of Psychology, 2*(3), 205–218.

10

Clinical Applications With Refugees

Oksana Yakushko and Indhushree Rajan

FLEEING RELIGIOUS PERSECUTION: THE STORY OF LARISSA

The following case focuses on the experience of a religious refugee from Eastern Europe. The case highlights distinct challenges faced by refugees based on their religious affiliation, national origin, and refugee background.

Case Description

Larissa is a Russian refugee woman in her late 40s. She moved to the United States with her husband and six children during the early 1990s under the religious refugee relocation program. Prior to migration, Larissa, a member of conservative evangelical Baptist church, experienced numerous instances of prejudice and discrimination. She was denied access to higher education and fired from her jobs because of her religious affiliation. Her children reported bullying at schools and their community. Similarly, her husband was allowed to hold only menial jobs. He was also imprisoned for several months for his participation in "religious proselyting," illegal under Soviet laws. When her oldest son was hospitalized after being physically attacked on his way back from a church function, Larissa actively pursued relocation options she knew were available to religious minorities.

Since moving to the United States, Larissa struggled further with feelings of discrimination and prejudice. Her appearance made her stand out from others; because of her religious convictions, she did not cut her hair or use makeup. She always wore long skirts. Although she has been in the United States for several decades, she was never able to learn English. She resided in a community with other Russian-speaking Baptists. She worked alongside her husband and others from her community at a meat-packing plant. She devoted much of her time to her church: She sang in a choir during several weekly services, made meals for the needy in the community, and led her women's prayer group.

Larissa was referred to counseling at the employee assistance program counseling by her supervisor at work. She initially refused to speak with a counselor, stating that "only God and her church" can help her. Fearing she would lose her job, she decided to "try it" for only few sessions. Her supervisor noticed that Larissa appeared sad, numb, and confused when spoken to. During conversations at his workplace, her husband explained to the supervisor that he believed that Larissa was "falling into sin" by "not praying enough and letting God heal her."

During the initial session, the counselor, working through an interpreter, learned that Larissa's difficulties began when her oldest son announced that he was moving away to live on his own. The counselor also learned that the son began to abuse alcohol. Larissa stated that it was "all her fault," because she did not do her duties as a Christian mother. She expressed an intense worry over decisions made by her other children. Although they attended a church-based school, she was aware that they had access to other "ungodly" influences. Having her children "leave God for Satan" felt devastating to her. She experienced her husband as frequently angry with her for not doing well her "wifely duties."

During counseling, Larissa shared that she has unusual physical sensations in her abdomen. She prayed about them and sought "prayer help" from her church members, but these sensations seemed to intensify over the past several months. She expressed reluctance to seek medical help because she believed that "God alone" can heal and that doctors "should not take God's place." However, she felt physically uncomfortable most of the time and was worried that her declining health would influence her ability to be with her family or serve her church.

Larissa initially refused to sign a consent form. In several discussions with her counselor and interpreter, she disclosed that as a religious minority in the former Soviet Union and now a religious refugee in the United States, she felt tremendous distrust of all authorities. She especially doubted that information in the counseling sessions will remain confidential. After several discussions regarding a rationale for the consent form and reassurance about confidentiality in treatment, she agreed to fill out and sign documentation. However, she felt that multiple assessments as part of the initial paperwork were designed to confuse her and to expose her to others. She also shared that it was difficult for her to answer questions "not as God wants her to think" but as she "sometimes feels."

During the initial sessions, Larissa was reluctant to open up. She trusted her counselor and her interpreter only when she perceived that they were supportive rather than judgmental of her religious beliefs. During a therapeutic intervention that focused on rapport building, the counselor and interpreter processed with Larissa her fear that counseling is intended to "Americanize and secularize" her. She was reticent to speak about her past or current experiences as a religious minority. However, she appeared relieved to discuss her relationship with her son and other family members, a topic she felt ashamed to bring up with others in her community. A family session was offered. She refused such a session because she did not want her children or her husband to hear about her "struggles." She did agree to receive a medical screening with a local medical provider who was a member of an English-speaking Baptist church. The medical provider requested that the counselor attend with her.

Reflection and Discussion Questions

1. What further information about Larissa's case as a religious refugee would you need in order to proceed with therapy?
2. What rapport-building strategies would you use with Larissa, given that she is both unfamiliar with the process of counseling and reluctant to engage in treatment? How could the intersection of Larissa's cultural values and religious influence the rapport building?
3. What challenges may arise in working with an interpreter? What ethical considerations could emerge with using an interpreter?

4. What would be your approach to dealing with cultural or religious views and experiences that may be drastically different from your own (e.g., patriarchal norms, abusive partner relations)?

5. What do you believe are the key factors influencing Larissa's presenting concerns? How would you address the presenting concerns in therapy?

6. How would you manage the conflict with Larissa about seeking urgent medical care?

Brief Analysis of the Case

• Although popular media have highlighted certain aspects of the refugee experience (i.e., torture or war survivors), other categories of refugees typically are unknown to many U.S. individuals. One such example is religious refugees. One of the first waves of religious refugees began in the 1970s with Soviet-born individuals of Jewish descent. These individuals experienced tremendous prejudice and discrimination not only because of their ethnicity but also because of their religious practices. Larissa's case exemplifies many of these struggles.

• In their homeland, religious minorities typically are denied educational and work opportunities and are continually harassed by state authorities. Some individuals experience direct violence because of their religious affiliation. Religious refugees come from many countries where religious diversity is not tolerated, such as those dominated by communist ideals (e.g., China, North Korea) or those with state-supported dominant religions (e.g., Pakistan, Sudan).

• A culturally responsive counselor may wish to engage in self-education about the ways in which refugee status is assigned. In the case of Larissa, a counselor may wish to understand the differences between a U.S.-based image of a "Baptist" church member versus the "Baptist" affiliated religious person from another country, such as Larissa (i.e., small and culturally marginalized).

• Larissa represents a person with very traditional beliefs and practices. It may be helpful to read information about conservative and ultraconservative religious communities in the United States to understand how their religion defines their worldview and dictates their life choices.

• Among key challenges in working with religious refugees like Larissa is building rapport. In fact, because of faith beliefs, Larissa, like most religious refugees, is unlikely to seek counseling services and may view them as contrary to her faith. She may see her agreement to seek counseling as a sign of "sinful weakness" related to her inability to "trust God" or "be healed through prayer." In addition, if others within Larissa's refugee community learned about her participation in counseling, she may be ostracized and judged.

• In addition, many individuals who experienced governmental persecution are likely to distrust assurances of confidentiality. Like Larissa, they may refuse to sign a consent form. Because of legal and ethical responsibilities, counselors may be at difficult crossroads in approaching documentation with such clients.

• Another challenge of working with religious minority clients may be in understanding the strict gender and family roles to which they adhere. What U.S. counselors view as emotionally or physically abusive relational practices may be seen as normal and divinely ordained within Larissa's community. Although counselors must follow their commitment to supporting the safety and well-being of their clients, they may also seek to understand how to do so in the most culturally sensitive manner.

• Larissa's challenging relationship with her children is typical for most immigrant and refugee families. Intergenerational conflict can contribute to significant distress among refugee parents. Often this distress is especially profound because many refugee adults opt for relocation to a foreign country primarily for the benefit of their children.

• For Larissa and other religious refugees, such conflicts often exceed the typical cultural rifts between generations: Conservative religious parents view their children's loss of culture and faith as a sign of their children's condemnation (e.g., their "going to hell"). Thus, her fears may be traumatically disturbing for her.

• The case of religious refugees such as Larissa also highlights the realities experienced by racially White immigrant individuals. Larissa reports experiencing xenophobia and discrimination. Although she may assign such prejudice to her religious minority status, it is likely that negative attitudes may be also related to her linguistic difference, cultural practices, and immigrant status.

• Larissa's case points to the vital importance of collaborative work with an interpreter. A counselor who has access to a trained and experienced interpreter is more likely to create a culturally safe and therapeutically successful experience for the client.

• Larissa's case points to the importance of flexibility in approaching assessment and treatment, including a multidisciplinary approach that may include medical or pastoral care. In addition, the counselor and interpreter may choose to forgo the use of the formal assessments and include relevant questions as part of the sessions (e.g., suicide assessment, domestic violence assessment, trauma assessment).

Recommended Resources

Books and/or Articles

Brody, E. (1994). The mental health and well-being of refugees: Issues and directions. In A. J. Marsella, T. H. Bornemann, S. Ekblad, & J. Orley (Eds.), *Amidst peril and pain: The mental health and well-being of the world's refugees* (pp. 57–68). Washington, DC: American Psychological Association.

Hill, P., & Pargament, K. (2003). Advances in the conceptualization and measurement of religion and spirituality implications for physical and mental health research. *American Psychologist, 58*, 64–74.

Koenig, H. G., McCullough, M., & Larson, D. B. (2001). *Handbook of religion and health: A century of research reviewed*. New York, NY: Oxford University Press.

Levitt, P. (2007). *God needs no passports: Immigrants and the changing American religious landscape*. New York, NY: New Press.

McCullough, M. E. (1999). Research on religion-accommodative counseling: Review and meta-analysis. *Journal of Counseling Psychology, 46*, 92–98.

Miller, A. M., Birman, D., Zenk, S., Wang, E., Sorokin, O., & Connor, J. (2009). Neighborhood immigrant concentration, acculturation, and cultural alienation in former Soviet immigrant women. *Journal of Community Psychology, 37*, 88–105. doi:10.1002/jcop.20272

Miller, A. M., Sorokin, O., Wang, E., Feetham, S., Choi, M., & Wilbur, J. (2006). Acculturation, social alienation and depressed mood in midlife women from the former Soviet Union. *Research in Nursing & Health, 29*, 134–146. doi:10.1002/nur.20125

Miller, W. R., & Thoresen, C. E. (2003). Spirituality, religion, and health. An emerging research field. *American Psychologist, 58*(1), 24–35.

Salsman, J. M., Brown, T. L., Brechting, E. H., & Carlson, C. R. (2005). The link between religion and spirituality and psychological adjustment:

The mediating role of optimism and social support. *Personality and Social Psychology Bulletin, 31*(4), 522–535.

Yakushko, O. (2007). Career development in the former USSR. *Journal of Career Development, 33,* 299–315.

Websites/Blogs

Beeman, W. O. (2001). *Fundamentalism.* Retrieved from http://www.brown .edu/Departments/Anthropology/publications/FUNDMNTALISM.htm

BibleBelievers. (2012). Collection of writings and links on fundamentalist Christian traditions in U.S. and around the world. Retrieved from http://web.archive.org/web/20060614220715/http://www.biblebelievers .com/

University of Chicago. (2004). *The Fundamentalism Project.* Retrieved from http://web.archive.org/web/20060713060632/http://www.press .uchicago.edu/Complete/Series/FP.html

Videos

Ewing, H., & Grady, R. (Producers & directors). (2006). *The Jesus camp* [Documentary]. United States: Magnolia Pictures.

Documentary about conservative religious teachings and practices.

Robertson, S., & Camerini, M. (Producers & directors). (2000). *The well-founded fear* [Documentary]. United States: The Epidavros Project.

About asylum cases in the United States, including religious refugee cases. More cases can be found at http://www.pbs.org/pov/archive/ wellfoundedfear/frameset.php3?section=waitingroom

Wang, W. (Producer), & Markey, P., et al. (Directors). (1993). *Joy Luck Club* [Motion picture]. United States: Hollywood Pictures.

Film exploring generational impact of immigration.

Assessments/Inventories

Centers for Disease Control and Prevention. (2013). *Guidelines for Mental Health Screening for Newly Arrived Refugees.* Retrieved from http://www .cdc.gov/immigrantrefugeehealth/guidelines/domestic/mental-health-screening-guidelines.html

Measures of religion and spirituality. (2010). Religions (Special Issue). Retrieved from http://www.mdpi.com/journal/ religions/special_issues/ measures_spiritual.

AFTERMATH OF TRAFFICKING: THE STORY OF KAMALA

The following case highlights the traumatic aftermath of human trafficking and its effects on refugees, especially women and girls. The case describes challenges faced by these groups of refugees as well as clinicians who work with them.

Case Description

Kamala was a sex trafficking survivor who was forcibly trafficked from her native home of Nepal at the age of 16. In the five years of her enslavement, she was sold numerous times to brothels in Thailand, Bangladesh, and India. She was finally rescued and brought to a shelter, where after seven years of trial proceedings she was selected for a refugee relocation program to the United States through a Catholic refugee agency. Kamala is now 28 years old.

Prior to being trafficked, Kamala was married for three years, had a two-year-old daughter with her husband, and lived on a farm with her immediate family and her in-laws. Kamala shared that she is a Hindu, her native language is Nepalese (though she learned to speak a little bit of Hindi and Thai over the course of her enslavement), and that she discontinued her schooling at the age of 6 to begin working because her family was extremely poor.

Kamala reported that she was abducted by a man on her way to a marketplace in a neighboring town. Following her capture, Kamala says that she was regularly drugged, kept isolated in a large crate, and starved during travel. At the first brothel to which Kamala was sold, she refused to have sex with clients. Every time she refused, the madam at the shelter would beat her and several times she arranged for men to rape and burn Kamala with cigarettes until she lost consciousness. Finally, unable to endure the repeated bouts of physical, sexual, and psychological torture, Kamala began to comply with the madam's orders. She had sex with as many as 10 clients per day. Kamala tried to hang herself twice during her enslavement. Her body was discovered and cut down both times. Each time she was beaten for her actions and held in isolation for weeks at a time. Kamala was finally rescued at the age of 21 during a police raid on a brothel in India. At the time of her rescue, Kamala had not eaten for days and had fresh bruises and scratches on her body.

During her first four months at the rescue shelter, Kamala shared that she had terrible nightmares from which she would wake up screaming and physically striking out at anyone around her. She would also defy daily living directives given by shelter staff, such as taking a bath or going to sleep; she cried nearly every day. She reported that she was afraid of eating and as a result lost a considerable amount of weight.

Following her relocation to the United States, Kamala's symptoms temporarily improved. She was placed to live with an Indian family who were distant relatives of Kamala's family. During this time, she developed closer relationships with caseworkers at the Catholic Refugee Relocation Agency. After living in the United States for about a year, Kamala's symptomology returned. It included hypersensitivity to her environment (e.g., noises and smells, the proximity of others to her person, or human touch), a heightened startle response, emotional numbing, difficulty eating, inability to make eye contact, occasional disorientation to her surroundings, and marked insomnia. Kamala was referred for psychiatric evaluation as well as treatment at a local domestic violence shelter. In addition to medical help, she received individual and group counseling services as well as opportunities to participate in variety of skill training classes (e.g., English, computing, cooking, academic success skills).

Initially, Kamala refused individual and group counseling sessions. However, after six months of participating in other domestic shelter's classes, she agreed to "try" counseling. Both individual and group counseling sessions were conducted with a female interpreter of Nepalese background, who was consistently present during treatment. In her group, Kamala was one of several refugees who survived trafficking, but the majority of women in the group were native-born Americans who were there to receive services after experiencing domestic violence or sexual abuse.

After several months of individual and group counseling, Kamala reported that hearing the other women share their stories helped her to process, face, and eventually share her own experiences. She also reported that the willingness of staff members to accept her even though she did not initially trust or overtly respond to them helped her feel safe. It is clear that Kamala's trust has been fostered by openness, unconditional acceptance, and flexibility in the counseling process. Kamala's counselor was sensitive to her needs in the moment (e.g., shortened sessions or outdoor sessions), and Kamala was given the freedom to choose what questions she would answer.

Choices like this provided her an opportunity to finally experience some measure of control and authorship over her painful past. Kamala's initial rejection of counseling and, more generally, of being in the presence of others has given way to a willingness to speak out about her pain and explore relationships and vocational opportunities within her new community.

Kamala's long tenure at the domestic violence shelter has slowly, over the course of years, grown into her rediscovery of trust and an ability to build relationships, learn new skills, and embark on a journey of emotional healing. Kamala admitted that she still experiences a deep sense of shame and fear that is rooted in her trafficking experiences. The pain of losing all contact with her daughter, husband, and family is one challenge she cannot yet face, but she also stated that individual counseling and her friendships with other women have helped give her hope for the future. Kamala shared that her desire for life is finally eclipsing her desire to die.

Reflection and Discussion Questions

1. What therapeutic modalities or approaches would be appropriate to work with Kamala? Explain.

2. What evidence-based clinical interventions could be taken to address the severity of Kamala's symptoms and extensive trauma history, given the very limited resources available at the domestic violence shelter?

3. How would issues of trauma, language, cultural intertextuality, and sociocultural identity impact the formation of a treatment alliance with Kamala?

4. How would work with aspects of transference and countertransference prove to be clinically significant in treating trafficking survivors?

5. Discuss the importance of physical and space dynamics in the treatment of formerly trafficked women and girls. How would Kamala's somaticized symptoms of trauma impact the therapist's use of the therapy room or physical treatment space? What about the formulation of a treatment plan? Would certain activities offered at a counseling office be of greater benefit to Kamala, given her trauma history?

6. Would assessment of suicidal and homicidal ideation be important in treating trafficking survivors? If Kamala exhibited symptoms of active suicidal or homicidal ideation, describe the most prudent clinical course to follow in each instance.

Brief Analysis of the Case

• Kamala's experience, although extreme, is quite typical of girls and women who are trafficked into sexual slavery worldwide. Because the highest incidence of sex trafficking occurs in the poorest communities in developing nations, trafficked populations suffer dangers related to multiple sociocultural factors and stigmas that impact the treatment of women and girls in the best of circumstances. Indeed, in many communities, girls who are identified as sex workers are at risk of honor killings. Thus, often refugee relocation is the only opportunity for girls and women to find safety and receive help.

• Many girls are trafficked and enslaved at very young ages, sometimes as young as 5 or 6 years old. Most trafficked girls are forcibly relocated, resold, and made to perpetually adapt to new conditions, suffer prolonged exposure to severe trauma and various forms of torture, and live under the constant threat of death.

• Owing to their extreme experiences of trauma, most trafficking survivors, after rescue, struggle with adjustment to new environments and experience great difficulties forming or sustaining relationships and acquiring new skills. A number of studies have identified the serious and often complex mental health needs of victims of human trafficking like Kamala. The majority of research related to the mental health needs of this population focuses on the significant levels of posttraumatic stress disorder (PTSD). In addition to PTSD, victims of human trafficking have been found to experience other anxiety and mood disorders, including panic attacks, obsessive-compulsive disorder, generalized anxiety disorder, and major depressive disorder.

• Further, it is important to note that psychological treatment of trafficked populations is fraught with unique challenges, in part because it is a relatively newly studied phenomenon. In this regard, having a clinical understanding of evidence-based therapeutic interventions in work with formerly trafficked women and children such as Kamala is critical.

• Empirical evidence on the treatment of PTSD increasingly supports the use of cognitive-behavioral therapy that incorporates cognitive restructuring and exposure therapy. Such treatment techniques are especially effective when they include behavioral interventions, such as exposure therapy, thought stopping, and breathing techniques.

• Complete psychiatric and psychological evaluations are preferable when working with victims of human trafficking. However, in cases like

Kamala's, which involve survivors of trafficking from developing countries, culturally sensitive assessments may be unavailable. Adaptations can be made to assess Kamala's physical, psychological, and neurological functioning while continually seeking consultations with those familiar with her cultural background.

• In Kamala's case, a culturally sensitive diagnosis and treatment plan may include focused processing of ethnic conflicts involving cross-racial issues, since relocated trafficking survivors may struggle with added anxiety stemming from xenophobia and discrimination in their host countries.

• In order to establish a positive therapeutic alliance, it would be essential that the counseling process be one that effectively addresses linguistic differences, varying cultural practices, and sensitivity to immigrant status. For women and girls like Kamala, who have endured and now seek recovery from extensive physical and psychological torture and abuse, the widely espoused sociocultural narratives that originate from their countries of birth often define their views of themselves.

• Perhaps the most important aspect of moving clinical work with trafficking survivors forward is cultivating a sensitivity to and awareness of the client's own perspective of her symptoms and experiences.

• In addition, many sex trafficking survivors have difficulties adjusting to life after rescue because their core identity formation has occurred during enslavement. In most cases, girls who are trafficked and sexually enslaved have lived under the perpetual threat of torture and death if they refuse any aspect of life as a sex worker. In Kamala's case, for example, a shift from being a sex worker to working in an regular occupation may carry the simultaneous impact of positively influencing her morale and self-esteem while, at a different level, creating a sense of loss or displacement.

• Another aspect to consider in working with trafficking survivors concerns the pace and process of treatment. Although many books on trauma work offer specific models and treatment plans, counselors who plan on working with trafficked populations may be more effective in forming therapeutic alliances by adopting a culturally responsive perspective. Such a perspective does not privilege Western-developed models, even if supported by research or endorsed in clinical circles. For example, in Kamala's case, biases and abuses that are layered in the Asian sociocultural landscape and economic class structure may confuse and complicate definitions that would help to contextualize how she has internalized her traumas.

◆ Western methods of trauma therapy, if culturally insensitive, may create pressure to share sensitive information before a client is ready and perhaps impel her to reject treatment altogether.

◆ It is also important to note that in treating trafficking survivors, the presence of a trained multilingual interpreter is essential to creating an atmosphere that is culturally sensitive and safe. This would ensure accuracy in communication and assist in building trust and rapport between client and clinician.

Recommended Resources

Books and/or Articles

Antonopoulou, C. (2006). Symptoms of posttraumatic stress disorder in victims of sex related trafficking. *International Psychology Bulletin, 10*(4), 32–37.

Bales, K. (2004). *Disposable people: New slavery in the global economy.* Berkeley, CA: University of California Press.

Bales, K. (2005). *Understanding global slavery: A reader.* Berkeley, CA: University of California Press.

Barry, K. (1979). *Female sexual slavery.* New York, NY: New York University Press.

Beyrer, C., & Stachowiak, J. (2003). Health consequences of trafficking of women and girls in Southeast Asia. *Brown Journal of World Affairs, 10*(1), 105–117.

Breslau, N., Kessler, R. C., Chilcoat, H. D., Schultz, L. R., Davis, G. C., & Andreski, P. (1998). Trauma and post-traumatic stress disorder in the community: The 1996 Detroit area survey of trauma. *Archives of General Psychiatry, 55,* 626–632.

Bryant-Davis, T., & Moon, N. (2010). Child trafficking: Risk factors and developmental considerations. In K. London (Ed.), *The Advocate, 33*(3), 6–8.

Hughes, D. M. (1999). Introduction. In D. M. Hughes & C. Roche (Eds.), *Making the harm visible: Global sexual exploitation of women and girls* (pp. 23–31). Kingston, RI: Coalition Against Trafficking in Women.

Human Rights Watch, Asia. (1995). *Rape for profit.* New York, NY: Author.

International Organization for Migration. (2006). *Breaking the cycle of vulnerability: Responding to the heath needs of trafficked women in east and southern Africa.* Pretoria, South Africa: Author.

Isaac, R., Solak, J., & Giardino, A. (2011). Health care providers' training needs related to human trafficking: Maximizing the opportunity to effectively screen and intervene. *Journal of Applied Research on Children: Informing Policy for Children at Risk, 2*(8), 1–16.

Pico-Alfonso, M. A. (2005). Psychological intimate partner violence: The major predictor of posttraumatic stress disorder in abused women. *Neuroscience and Biobehavioral Reviews, 29,* 181–193.

Rajan, I. (2011). Voices from the void: A depth psychological reconceptualization of sex trafficking in modern-day India. *Psychotherapy and Politics International, 9,* 97–102. doi:10.1002/ppi.238

Rauch, S. A., & Cahill, S. P. (2003). Treatment and prevention of posttraumatic stress disorder. *Primary Psychiatry, 10*(8), 60–65.

Seedat, S., Stein, D. J., & Carey, P. D. (2005). Post-traumatic stress disorder in women. *CNS Drugs, 19*(5), 411–427.

Yakushko, O. (2009). Human trafficking: A review for mental health professionals. *International Journal for the Advancement of Counseling, 31,* 158–167, doi:10.1007/s10447-009-9075-3

Zimmerman, C., Hossain, M., Yun, K., Roche, B., Morison, L., & Watts, C. (2006). *Stolen smiles: A summary report on the physical and psychological health consequences of women and adolescents trafficked in Europe.* London, England: London School of Hygiene & Tropical Medicine.

Websites/Blogs

Hughes, D. M. (2003, October). *Hiding in plain sight: A practical guide to identifying victims of trafficking in the U.S.* Retrieved from http://www .uri.edu/artsci/wms/hughes/hiding_in_plain_sight.pdf

Hundal, S. (2013, January). *India's bitter culture of rape and violence.* Retrieved from http://www.guardian.co.uk/commentisfree/2013/jan/03/india-rape-violence-culture

Mitchels, B. (2004). *Developing effective communication with children victims of violence and trafficking. Practical handbook for social workers, police, and other professionals.* UNICEF and UNMIK/Government of Kosovo Ministry of Labour and Social Welfare. Retrieved from http://www .childtrafficking.org/pdf/user/handbook_lets_talk_a5_eng.pdf

United States Department of State. (2009, June 16). *Trafficking in persons report 2009—India.* Retrieved from http://www.unhcr.org/refworld/docid/4a4214b4c.html

Williamson, E., Dutch, N., & Clawson, H. C. (2010). Evidence-based mental health treatment for victims of human trafficking. Study of Department of Health and Human Services programs serving human trafficking victims. Retrieved from http://aspe.hhs.gov/hsp/07/HumanTrafficking/MentalHealth/index.shtml

Videos

Bilheimer, R. (Director). (2010). *Not my life* [Documentary].
Filmed over 4-year period detailing human trafficking of children around the globe. Retrieved from http://notmylife.org/about-film
Kreuzpaintner, M. (Director). (2007). *Trade* [Motion picture]. United States: Lions Gate Films.
Discusses trafficking and slavery of Mexican children for the purpose of selling children for sexual exploitation in the United States.
Duguay, C. (Director). (2005). *Human trafficking* [Documentary]. United States: Lifetime TV.
Discusses human slavery and trafficking around the world and the struggles to end it and to rehabilitate the victims.

Assessments/Inventories

Courtois, C. A. (2004). Complex trauma, complex reactions: Assessment and treatment. *Psychotherapy: Theory, Practice, Research, Training, 41,* 412–425.
Mollica, R. F., Cardozo, B. L., Osofsky, H. J., Raphael, B., Ager, A., & Salama, P. (2004). Mental health in complex emergencies. *Lancet, 364*(9450), 2058–2067.
Van der Kolk, B. A. (2001). The assessment and treatment of complex PTSD. In R. Yehuda (Ed.), *Traumatic stress* (pp. 127–156). Washington, DC: American Psychiatric Association Press.

PART III
Case Studies With Other
Multicultural Populations

11

Clinical Applications With Women

Christina M. Capodilupo

LIVING IN THE SHADOWS: THE STORY OF MONIQUE

Case Description

Monique was a 26-year-old biracial woman. Her mother was a White European American and her father was a Haitian American who immigrated to the United States in his early 20s. Monique self-identified as biracial but felt that she was received by society at large as a Black woman due to her phenotype: She had short, tightly curled kinky black hair and mocha-colored skin. At five foot five inches and 156 pounds, she was slightly overweight.

Monique played a musical instrument and provided backup vocals in a small jazz band. There were three other members of the band: a White female lead singer, a Black male drum player, and a Black male saxophone player. The band was fairly successful, having recorded several CDs and being booked frequently for live performances.

Monique was seeking therapy to talk about her fluctuating weight, feelings of unhappiness, late-night eating episodes, and low self-esteem. She reported that her body image and weight had been an issue for her since she was a teenage girl. She said she felt pulled between feeling "beautiful" and feeling like an "absolute beast." She worried aloud that she might not be making sense to me, her White female therapist. In her previous therapy, her therapist suggested that she had binge eating disorder and wanted the two of them to collaboratively devise a healthy plan to lose weight. Although Monique sometimes felt that losing weight would make her happier and improve her self-image, she did not agree that becoming thin was a solution to her problems. In fact, she had a nagging sense inside her that the very *last* thing she wanted to do was become thin. She was not completely clear on why she felt this way.

I had a sense that, as a biracial woman, Monique could be struggling with conflicting body ideals between her White and Black cultures. When I asked Monique about this, she began to talk about how her larger body size was considered beautiful among her father's family and within the Black community where she lived. But when she was around her mother's family and in mainstream society, she felt very overweight and unattractive. Monique struggled to feel like she fit into either of these communities and never quite felt comfortable "in her skin." She further talked about how she did not have "good hair," and she wrestled with the decision to get a weave. On one hand, she believed that with longer, straighter hair she would feel more confident and attractive. On the other hand, she felt like getting a weave was "selling out" and accepting that White beauty features were superior to Afrocentric beauty features.

Monique often spoke about her desire for a healthy romantic relationship, and she lamented her inability to "find a man." She felt plagued by her position in the band of being a backup singer, as if it were a metaphor for her life: never being center stage. After performances, she would come to therapy sessions talking about how everyone "swooned" over their lead singer and how invisible she felt. The lead singer was attractive and svelte, and Monique felt very much in her shadow. Further compounding these feelings was the romantic relationship that existed between the lead singer and the drum player, a man whom Monique had been pining after for years. She felt "desperate" to be seen as a sexual, desirable woman by him but instead felt that he only saw her as a good friend. They were very close and shared many confidences but never had a sexual encounter.

Being thin and White, I wondered aloud how Monique experienced me as her therapist. Although she initially seemed surprised by my question, Monique revealed that she figured I viewed her as "unattractive" and "lazy."

As we continued to explore the racial dynamic between us, Monique went on to experience feelings of anger and resentment toward me that she recognized were directed at the lead singer in her band and the larger White culture. She felt disappointed in her Black band mate for choosing a White woman and felt it was a reflection of mainstream society's preference for White women and White features. Monique identified this preference as racism and reached an insight that not only did it depress her, but it also contributed to her overeating behaviors in that she was actively (if not unconsciously) resisting the pursuit of a thin physique.

Monique stated that when she experienced overeating episodes late at night, it was often after her live performances with the band. She was not ashamed of her eating behavior; rather, she found it to be comforting. She usually chose foods like brownies or cookies, which she made herself. The process was slow and deliberate, not rushed and impulsive. She joked that the food was her "substitute man." I recognized that there were positive aspects associated with this eating behavior and validated Monique's related feelings. However, I also wanted Monique to explore the idea that this eating behavior served to isolate her in some ways and might be eclipsing deeper feelings about herself and her experiences in the world.

Reflection and Discussion Questions

1. If you were privy just to Monique's presenting concerns, what might your thoughts be about diagnosis and treatment considerations?
2. Monique's previous therapist diagnosed her with binge eating disorder and identified weight loss as a goal for treatment. What assumptions underlie this formulation? What are the implications for treatment?
3. What are your reactions to the current therapist bringing her own race and appearance into the treatment room?
4. How might experiences of oppression be contributing to Monique's presenting concerns?
5. How is Monique's biracial identity related to her body image and self-concept?
6. How do you understand Monique's overeating behavior? How might you address it in treatment?

Brief Analysis of the Case

Monique's presenting concerns are fairly common among female clients (i.e., body image, self-esteem, weight issues) and yet treating these issues according to the traditional literature would not be culturally competent practice.

• The majority of theories and assessments related to body image centralize the thin ideal. In fact, two of the major eating disorder diagnoses in the fifth edition of the *Diagnostic and Statistical Manual of Mental Disorders* require a preoccupation with weight and shape (bulimia nervosa) and/or fear of becoming fat (anorexia nervosa) in order for a person to meet criteria. However, for some groups of color (e.g., Black Americans, some Latinas), a thin physique is not important or relevant. Multiple studies have demonstrated that African American males and females prefer a larger, more curvaceous body size than their White peers.

• Focusing on the thin ideal as if it were a universal ideal among women represents ethnocentric monoculturalism. Monique's previous therapist assumed that she has a desire to lose weight. By making this the focus of treatment, she missed crucial exploration of other aspects of Monique's body image, such as her feelings about her hair. Just because hair texture and length are not traditionally recognized as an important element of body image (and perhaps are not relevant to the therapist) does not mean that this is not an important area of inquiry.

• In fact, among Black women, issues related to hair length and texture are crucial elements of body image, perhaps even more important to appearance satisfaction than body shape and size. Therefore, therapists should be mindful of including appearance characteristics other than weight and shape in conversations about body image.

• Overeating behavior traditionally is pathologized and seen as an impulsive, secretive action associated with feelings of shame and disgust. Rather than label this behavior as binge eating disorder, the therapist should have considered the purpose it might serve for Monique. For example, feminist scholars have contended that women of color often use food and eating as a mechanism for coping with multiple oppressions. In this case, Monique reported that her eating behavior is comforting and, notably, frequently takes place after performances during which she feels invisible.

• Thus, including experiences of racism and sexism as potential causes for or contributors to symptoms is important when working with Monique.

Does she turn to food as a means for dealing with race-related and gender-related stress? Overeating could be a coping mechanism for difficult feelings. However, this behavior can also have larger sociocultural meaning. As we see in this case, Monique reached an insight that her overeating may have been an active resistance to the dominant culture's emphasis on thinness.

♦ Monique's feelings that she is invisible are indicative of feeling undervalued and underappreciated by society. This is a common experience among oppressed groups in the United States. In fact, many women of color have reported daily experiences of racism (i.e., microaggressions) related to being looked over, avoided, and ignored. In Monique's case, exploring these feelings of invisibility is likely crucial to understanding her presenting concerns. However, traditional models of psychotherapy would focus on internal conflicts and dynamics that have contributed to her low self-esteem or depressed mood.

♦ Working toward understanding the racial dynamic between Monique and myself meant being open to the idea that my presence as a White woman exacerbated her feelings of invisibility and unattractiveness. Not acknowledging my Whiteness and my appearance would be sending the message that I believed my race did not matter and thus had no social significance in the helping relationship. This is similar to the idea of colorblindness, which people of color generally experience as subtle racism or microaggression, given that it negates the social meaning that race has in the United States. In this case, talking openly and directly about my Whiteness created an opportunity for Monique to explore how racism and resultant feelings affected her eating behavior.

♦ Being biracial, Monique is affected by stereotyped societal messages about both Black and White women's beauty. It is imperative to consider that her phenotype creates a unique social experience for her regardless of how she personally identifies (and feels). Monique has a White mother and embraces a biracial identity and yet does not "look White." Exploring how she understands her body and self-image as a biracial woman (and not as a White or Black woman) is crucial.

♦ Further, Monique is consistently exposed to mass media, which suggests that White features are synonymous with beauty. She is part of a Black community that embraces her larger body size as being beautiful; however, this same community sends her conflicting messages by also prizing White features such as long, straight hair. What effect does this have on Monique's body and self-image? Consider the case of the drummer in her band who enjoys Monique's companionship but does not see her as a sexually attractive partner. This Black man's preference for the White woman in the band takes on social meaning beyond rejection at the personal level.

• Monique's feelings of anger and resentment about the racism she experiences need to be validated and encouraged by the therapist. This can be difficult for some White therapists who shy away from or discourage these feelings out of their own fears of facing an "angry Black woman." They may be afraid that the client is going to direct their anger at them and accuse them of being racist. However, closing this door prevents meaningful exchange that can foster the therapeutic relationship.

• Compounding this racial stereotype is the gendered assumption that anger is a negative, unproductive emotion for women. Due to their own socialization to see women as caretakers and nurturers, therapists may (unconsciously) avoid questions and/or discussions that explore feelings of anger and resentment.

• From a relational feminist perspective, a goal of treatment with Monique is to help her establish meaningful, mutual relationships (both with the therapist and socially). In this case, although Monique reported experiencing comfort from her overeating episodes and the behavior seemed like a coping mechanism for daily experiences of racism, the therapist recognized that overeating was also an obstacle to connecting with others. It isolated Monique and was a way of cutting herself off not only from others but also from her own feelings.

Recommended Resources

Books and/or Articles

Ballou, M., & Brown, L. S. (Eds.). (2002). *Rethinking mental health & disorder: Feminist perspectives.* New York, NY: Guilford Press.

Boston Women's Health Book Collective & Norsigan, J. (2011). *Our bodies, ourselves.* New York, NY: Touchstone, Simon & Schuster.

Gillem, A. R., & Thompson, C. A. (2004). *Biracial women in therapy: Between the rock of gender and the hard place of race.* New York, NY: Routledge.

hooks, b. (2000). *Feminism is for everybody: Passionate politics.* Cambridge, MA: South End Press.

Johnson, D. (2009). Hairitage: Women writing race in children's literature. *Tulsa Studies in Women's Literature, 28*(2), 337–355.

Thompson, B. (1996). *A hunger so wide and so deep: A multiracial view of women's eating problems.* Minneapolis, MN: University of Minnesota Press.

Novels or Fictional/Nonfictional Readings

Byrd, A., & Solomon, A. (2005). *Naked: Black women bare all about their skin, hair, hips, lips and other parts.* New York, NY: Perigee Trade.

Durrow, H. W. (2010). *The girl who fell from the sky.* New York, NY: Algonquin Books.

Videos

Hunter, J., & O'Donnell, K. (Producers), & Stilsen, J. (Director). (2009). *Good hair* [DVD]. United States: HBO Films/LD Entertainment/Chris Rock Productions.

Espin, O. (Writer). (2003) *Race, gender, and sexual orientation: Counseling people with multiple cultural identities.* [DVD] United States: Microtraining, An Imprint of Alexander Street Press. http://www.emicrotraining.com/product_info.php?products_id=129

Assessments/Inventories

Cash, T. F. (2008). *The body image workbook* (2nd ed.). Oakland, CA: New Harbinger.

Garaulet, M., Canteras, M., Morales, E., Lopez-Guimera, G., Sanchez-Carracedo, & Corbalon-Tutau. (2012). Validation of a questionnaire on emotional eating for use in cases of obesity: The Emotional Eater Questionnaire (EEQ). *Nutrición Hospitalaria, 27*(2), 645–651.

I'M A MOTHER FIRST! THE STORY OF SIMONE

Case Description

Simone was a 39-year-old African American woman who identified strongly as an Evangelical Christian. On the day of her first appointment, she arrived carrying a bag inscribed with the words "God is Faith." Simone attended a local Bible institute once weekly where she took classes about preaching. She dreamed that one day she might be a preacher in the church.

Simone was seeking services to talk about her 7-year-old son's death nearly six years earlier. She reported feelings of depression, apathy, difficulty sleeping, and difficulty bonding with her other children. Simone's son died of complications while being treated for asthma in the hospital. She reported that after he died, she ran out of the hospital and never returned. She did not attend his funeral and blamed herself for his passing. Simone had attended an intake session with a different therapist who gave her a provisional diagnosis of major depressive disorder with psychotic symptoms. The therapist ruled out a diagnosis of borderline personality disorder.

Simone had five children, three of whom shared a father who was killed on the street by someone who was asking for directions. This was also the father of her deceased son. Her eldest daughter was the result of a rape when she was 15 years old. She was married to the father of her youngest child. In our initial sessions, Simone expressed an interest in working on and strengthening her relationship with her husband. She mentioned that he had wanted to attend our sessions (he was currently out of work), but Simone felt that she needed her own space in therapy.

Simone reported that she believed she had a prophetic gift and that God spoke to her. She stated that she could often see things before they happened and frequently had visions of the deceased. For example, she told me that before her son died, God had said to her, "I am going to take the important thing away from you. Will you trust me?" She said she was sobbing when she heard this, overcome with fear and pain. Simone felt that she had a calling to "heal the world." When speaking to me about her gift, I could feel a heightened sense of mistrust between Simone and myself. She would maintain strong eye contact during these conversations as if to read my reactions to what she was saying. She would often state her position with conviction. Once during session, she was telling me about a young girl who sat across from her in a doctor's waiting room. She could sense the girl's sadness and pain, and stated, "I could feel it. No, I *know* it. I don't just feel it."

Several weeks into treatment, Simone missed an appointment. Later that day, I received a voicemail message from her that she had been having stomach cramps and spent the day at the hospital. After several ultrasounds, she was informed that she was pregnant with twins. Her initial response was, "What am I going to do with twins?" To which the doctors responded with laughter, telling her, "You will buy two of everything!" Simone confided in me that what she had meant was, "How am I going to bond with two babies?" She reported that her husband was "over the moon" and wanted her to drop out of Bible school. Her children were also very excited. One of her sisters told her, "God took one and gave you back two." Simone, however, seemed to have conflicted feelings. She told me that as soon as she heard the news, she went straight to the hospital chapel and prayed. "It's sad," she said, "and I can't even focus. I'm trying to vent to God." She went on to tell me that her due date was in May and graduation was meant to be in June. With a sigh she stated, "I won't be able to graduate anyway."

Around this time, Simone began reporting increasingly negative feelings toward her husband. She stated that she told him he had one more month to get a job or "he's got to go." He responded that it was the "pregnancy hormones talking" and thus she did not mean it. However, Simone insisted in session that she "just didn't like him." She said she didn't want him touching her or even looking at her.

For several sessions, Simone seemed noticeably on edge. She would nervously bring up her intentions with school, often laughing while making statements such as "I have to quit, it's too much, right?" and "I'm a mother first!" She was also distressed over recent hospital appointments that felt invasive and anxiety-producing. Because it was a teaching hospital, there were often several people in the room for Simone's exams. Simone was very uncomfortable with this, even nearly passing out during one ultrasound. She stated that she asked the doctors, "Is this *Candid Camera*?" because of all the onlookers, to which several people laughed. She did not find it funny. The following exchange was from a session during this time:

Simone: I keep having thoughts—headaches—a lot of them are negative.
Therapist: It sounds like you are feeling stressed.
Simone: Everyone says "Smile!" The nutritionist was so happy.
Therapist: But you feel . . . ?
Simone: Worried. What if one of them doesn't live, or is sick? Is this normal?
Therapist: Given all they have told you about it being a high-risk pregnancy and your needing an amnio[centisis], it seems natural.
Simone: But do you think I'm right for feeling like this? Would you feel like this?
Therapist: There is so much on your plate, Simone. You're trying to balance the life you have with your family now, work

through your feelings about your husband, and now this unexpected news! It's a lot.

In our next session, Simone came in telling me she had "lots of stories." Over the weekend, she had experienced vaginal bleeding and was hospitalized. Simone had difficulty relaying all the details, but after she left the hospital that day, she was no longer pregnant. She seemed confused by what had happened and said it was "keeping her up at night, wondering if she murdered her babies." She reported that on several nights, she had woken up around 2:00 a.m. because she felt something on her shoulder, but nothing was there.

Reflection and Discussion Questions

1. What are your thoughts about the diagnosis given to Simone by the intake therapist?
2. What could explain the feelings of mistrust between Simone and the therapist during discussions of her prophetic gift?
3. How might you incorporate spirituality into your treatment plan with Simone?
4. What cultural and/or sociopolitical factors might contribute to Simone's presenting concerns?
5. How do you understand Simone's report that she is no longer pregnant? What sociocultural issues might arise for you and Simone when discussing this loss?
6. What treatment approach would you use when working with Simone?

Brief Analysis of the Case

• The case of Simone calls for a careful consideration of the multiple intersections of identity. On the surface, her symptoms would suggest depression, anxiety, and even psychosis. Traditional models of psychotherapy locate these problems within the individual and point to internal dynamics as the cause. However, a closer look at the sociocultural issues in this case is helpful in understanding Simone's presenting concerns.

• The intake therapist diagnosed Simone as having psychotic symptoms. Taken out of context, it is understandable that reports of having visions and being able to see the future sound like magical thinking or psychosis. However, Simone's visions and associated symptoms were always closely linked to her spirituality. She believed very deeply in God and felt that her visions were messages from Him regarding how to best live her life. From a feminist perspective, Simone's faith and her belief in her gift can be seen as adaptive strengths.

♦ Simone is most likely aware that talking about her prophetic gift with her therapist might cause her to be pathologized and seen as unstable (i.e., diagnosis of psychosis). The therapist is in a position of power to diagnose and label Simone's problems. Black women, in particular, are disproportionately diagnosed with borderline personality disorder and disorders involving psychosis. The therapist needs to consider that behaviors and affect expressions can be culturally (and in this case, spiritually) normative.

♦ When working with Simone, it is important to consider her feelings about being a caregiver and a wife. Is she resentful or conflicted about these roles? If so, she might believe that these feelings are socially unacceptable and, as a result, internalize negative and critical beliefs about herself. Rather than stemming from a chemical imbalance or internal dynamics, her feelings of depression and anxiety may be related to her roles as a mother and wife. In particular, Simone may be experiencing role overload due to her multiple responsibilities in her household. Not only was she a mother to multiple children, but her husband was also out of work.

♦ We are all socialized to see females as natural nurturers and caregivers, and as a result, we have our own biases about what constitutes a "good mother." It is imperative for therapists to reflect on their own beliefs and assumptions about women's roles. In the case of Simone, might the therapist reinforce societal expectations by assuming that the client is content in her role as mother and wife and thus avoid questions in this area?

♦ Further, women are expected to feel thrilled and overjoyed at the prospect of being pregnant. Simone experienced multiple messages from doctors, friends, and family that her pregnancy was a "blessing" and even a way of healing from the loss of her deceased child. How does the therapist receive the news that the client is pregnant? Does the therapist unknowingly engage in subtle messages that the client should feel happy to be pregnant and should embrace the role of motherhood? Does the therapist explore all options with a conflicted client, including abortion, regardless of personal beliefs?

♦ In this case, Simone was overwhelmed and anxious by the prospect of being pregnant, and she did not feel that there was any room for her feelings in her household or out in the world. Instead of the therapy room being a microcosm for society at large, the therapist should create space for Simone to experience the entire spectrum of her feelings.

♦ Simone could benefit from more encouragement and support to create spaces for self-growth. There is plenty of evidence to suggest that attending Bible school and becoming a preacher were salient for her. Her pregnancy became an instant reason for her to quit these activities, a literal expression of traditional roles eclipsing her own interests and pursuits.

♦ Simone could also benefit from advocacy on the part of the therapist. In this case, it would include providing her with her rights as a patient and empowering her to speak up for herself in scenarios such as the hospital room where she felt uncomfortable by the number of attending physicians. Not only acknowledging Simone's feelings of unease but validating them is essential.

♦ Discussion around the loss of Simone's twins must be handled with delicacy and tact so as not to cause a rupture in treatment. The therapist would not want to directly ask or confront Simone about what transpired at the hospital until Simone herself brought the issue up. She was unclear and vague in her description, most likely because she was conflicted about what had occurred at the hospital. Her spirituality (which was extremely important to her) specifically prohibits abortion. Yet she clearly felt that the pregnancy was going to come at a great personal cost. These feelings were most likely frightening and overwhelming for her, and denying that they existed might be imperative for self-preservation.

♦ Therapies that embrace the feminist and multicultural movements in psychology will be beneficial for Simone. Relational-cultural therapy, as an example, helps clients to create and maintain mutually growth-fostering relationships. When Simone started therapy, she indicated that she would like to work on her relationship with her husband. Once she became pregnant, however, her negative feelings toward her husband intensified and she wanted him to move out. Simone's husband wanted her to drop out of school because she was pregnant and was not supportive of her goal of becoming a preacher. It would be useful for Simone to explore ways that this relationship could become more mutual and growth fostering for both parties. Aiding Simone in developing and maintaining strong social support networks is essential.

♦ Finally, Simone contends with a plethora of stressors on a daily basis. Use of a therapeutic approach such as relational-cultural therapy or feminist relational advocacy recognizes that oppression can cause emotional distress such as anxiety and depression. The therapist should consider the role of racism, sexism, and classism in her presenting problems.

Recommended Resources

Books and/or Articles

Boyd-Franklin, N. (2010). Incorporating spirituality and religion into the treatment of African American clients. *Counseling Psychologist, 40*(8), 976–1000.

Jordan, J. (Ed.). (1997). *Women's growth in diversity*. New York, NY: Guilford Press.

Jordan, J. V. (2009). *Relational-cultural therapy*. Washington, DC: American Psychological Association.

Miller, J. B., & Stiver, I. (1997). *The healing connection: How women form relationships in therapy and in life*. Boston, MA: Beacon Press.

Owen, J., Tao, K., & Rodolfa, E. (2010). Microaggressions and women in short-term therapy: Initial evidence. *Counseling Psychologist, 38*(7), 923–946.

Singleton, D. K. (2003). *Broken silence: Opening your heart and mind to therapy, a Black women's recovery guide*. New York, NY: One World/ Ballantine.

Sullivan, S. C. (2012). *Living faith: Everyday religion and mothers in poverty*. Chicago, IL: University of Chicago Press.

Worell, J., & Remer, P. (2002). *Feminist perspectives in therapy: Empowering diverse women*. Hoboken, NJ: Wiley.

Videos

Ballou, M., La Roche, M.J., & Tabol, C. (Writers). (2008) *Feminist counseling and cultural therapy: Two demonstrations.* United States: Microtraining, An Imprint of Alexander Street Press.

Jordan, J.V. (Writer). (2008) *Relational-cultural therapy.* (2008). Systems of Psychotherapy Video Series. United States: American Psychological Association Videos.

Kielty Briggs, M., & Gladding, S. (Writers). (2009) *Spirituality in counseling.* United States: Microtraining, An Imprint of Alexander Street Press. http://www.emicrotraining.com/product_info.php?products_id=401

12

Clinical Applications With Men

Mark A. Stevens and Jose Montes

MULTIPLE STORIES OF HENRY

Case Description

Henry is a 57-year-old male, born in Chicago and the oldest son of Greek immigrant parents. He is college educated, runs his own investment company, and has been making approximately $250,000 a year for more than a decade. Married at age 21 and divorced at 24, he did not have children with his first wife. He remarried at age 39 and has a 16-year-old son with his second wife, Ana. She moved out of their home two months ago, and they have made arrangements for their son to share time between the two residences. Henry's mother died recently, but his father died more than 20 years ago. The client has a history of alcohol and substance abuse starting in college. He struggles with health issues, such as hypertension and diabetes. Upon the recommendation of Ana's therapist, they were referred to a male counselor for couples therapy. This was the first time Henry had been in counseling. Ana complained that he was too controlling in the relationship and did not show her enough affection. Henry believed he was quite generous and accommodating to his wife's needs and wanted her to understand the pressures of his business. He wanted the relationship to work and did not want his son to be from a divorced family. Henry did not want another failed relationship and wanted the childhood and family life he never had while growing up. After two months of couples therapy, Ana made it clear she wanted a separation and divorce. This news was difficult for Henry, and he decided he wanted to try one-on-one therapy. Henry had felt understood by his therapist, a Caucasian male, also in his 50s.

Friendly and engaging, Henry was well read and had a gift for gab. Being successful in the business world was a huge accomplishment for Henry, and he wore it proudly. His main self-indulgent pleasures were reading and music. Most of his waking hours were spent in the "doing" mode and taking care of multiple business and family tasks. In many respects he was a self-made man. Through hard work, persistence, and intelligence, he thought he had built his dream life: a beautiful wife, adoring son, luxurious home, vacation getaways, and many future business opportunities. Henry had been sober for almost a decade, doing so by sheer willpower and a strong desire to be available for his son.

Although Henry wanted desperately to save the marriage, he was unaware that Ana had made up her mind to end the relationship. The couples counseling was a charade for Ana to break the news to Henry that she wanted a divorce. Issues of trust, resentment, accusations, and fear had taken over the relationship. From Ana's perspective, Henry saw their marriage as a business enterprise. He used denial and rationalization to avoid thinking about the quality of their relationship, the unhappiness of his wife, and his feeling of loneliness in order for his son to grow up in a two-parent household. His bitterness and mistrust, however, crept through and was felt by Ana. They attempted to create potential solutions to getting a divorce: separate bedrooms, rotating parental living arrangements, an open marriage, and financial incentives. Despite these accommodations, Ana still decided to move out and live her own life. Henry was devastated, angry, and started drinking again. It was the emotional turmoil that motivated Henry to continue therapy. He had a huge capacity to stuff his feelings and absorb relationship discontent. He felt scared, angry, alone, and foolish. Although he was a pro at getting what he wanted in business, he failed at this "relationship business." As hard as he tried, he could not control the perceived outcome of failure. Henry was uncomfortable with his emotional pain and had difficulty expressing it. He knew, however, that he wanted it to go away, so he could move on with his life. Like many other men, Henry was embarrassed to cry in sessions. In a half-joking manner, he blamed the therapist for his crying, noting that he rarely cried outside of the session. He later clarified that was a "crybaby" while watching movies.

Henry: Here you go again making me cry. I don't like to cry. I am not that weak.

Therapist: I can see how difficult it is for you to cry in front of me, particularly—another man.

Henry: Can I pay you more if you don't make me cry?

Therapist: Henry, I don't think you will be able to buy your way out this one. I see how much you want to feel your emotional pain and at the same time how ashamed you are of your emotional pain. Tell me more about how you were taught or shamed into not sharing yourself.

Henry tried hard to control his tears. When asked what his crying in session meant to him, he stated that he "felt weak." Henry hated feeling weak and experienced crying as being out of control and a indication of his lack of manhood. During sessions when he did not cry, he noted to the therapist, "I must be getting better, I did not cry today." Interestingly, though, after teary sessions, he usually felt better as he "got a lot off my chest." Over time, Henry responded well to the therapist's statements that he respected him for allowing himself to be vulnerable in sessions and understood how important it was for him to not feel weak or out of control. Crying in session became more comfortable for Henry, particularly when he was able to save face. Often he would save face by making a joke such as "Here you go again, Doc, making me cry." Acceptance of Henry's "masculinity face-saving" gestures was an important therapeutic consideration, as it is with many men in therapy.

Henry described his therapist as his friend and therapy as a place he could let down his business defenses. Much of the world, except for the therapist, did not know the intense pressure and pain Henry was experiencing. The client was very much like what David and Brannon (1976) label the "Sturdy Oak." He was deeply caring and empathic man who had a difficult time being vulnerable and asking for help. Henry described himself as someone who others came to lean on. His ability and willingness to lean on the therapist without shame eventually transferred to outside the therapy room. He joined a men's group and started to open up more about his drinking and fears of early death through self-care neglect and alcohol abuse. Henry's discussions with other men who had similar experiences were quite helpful to him. He found it both surprising and reinforcing when other men he opened up with shared similar stories of fear and anxiety. Eventually he decided to stop drinking and face the pain by sharing with others.

Another significant aspect of gender-sensitive counseling issues that became a focus of treatment was his transitioning role as a "single father." Woven into this transition were issues of physical health and his relationship with his own father. Henry's desire to be such an integral part of his son's life was not congruent with how he physically took care of himself. Knowing his father died from diabetic complications created an internal nagging level of tension and fear within Henry. He had been diagnosed with high blood pressure and blood sugar problems more than 10 years ago. Told to lose weight for many years, Henry was quite open to discussing a lifelong pattern of soothing from food. What appeared to have the most impact in treatment in terms of creating sustained "self-care" patterns was Henry's willingness to vividly share his dreams about being present with his son as they both grew older. Sessions slowed down as Henry described his feelings and images of being at his son's college graduation, his wedding, and being a grandfather. Tears rolled down his face as he experienced what he described as the joy of sharing and the fear of not sharing in these future celebrations.

This therapeutic breakthrough led to more intimate conversations and insights for Henry. As a young child, he was overweight and frequently teased by being called "fat Henry." For many men, boyhood stories of "masculinity shame" are often kept secret yet never really forgotten and often are a source of acting out in nonauthentic or unhealthy ways. The conversations can touch on culture, loss, and shame. Power and control for who can be "more masculine" is often a dynamic in the room when two men are together. Often this shows up as subconscious homophobic and hypermasculine types of subtle and not-so-subtle behaviors. For example, Henry would make "gay" jokes and deny any homophobic meaning.

Henry: [Tells a gay joke.]

Therapist: Wondering why you decided to tell me that joke now.

Henry: You are too serious; sometimes a joke is just a joke. I have no problem with gay people.

As our relationship became more trusting and Henry was more comfortable sharing nuanced psychological material, he revealed that, as a teenager, he was always afraid that others would think he was gay and intentionally told gay jokes to try to fend off his anxiety about what others thought of his masculinity.

For many men, fathers and father loss also offers a deep well of emotionally charged material often accompanied by untold stories. With tears, Henry shared his regrets and how much he missed his father. With some role-playing he recognized that while he had his father on a pedestal, he also was holding onto a good deal of anger and resentment. Henry became aware of the anger that he felt toward his father for not taking better care of himself and subsequently dying at an early age. His pain and anger toward his father opened up awareness that he did not want his own son to feel the same type of pain and anger. His increased empathy for his son and wanting to be a "good" father by protecting him from future pain had a tremendous impact on his motivation and ability to change some lifelong poor lifestyle habits.

Often in session, Henry would ask questions about raising a son. His concern for him and anxiety about doing the "wrong thing" as a parent showed his vulnerable and courageous Henry. He shared stories of his son's successes and struggles with the gleam of an engaged and proud parent. His time with his son became sacred time. Henry worked through some of the rejection he felt when his son became upset about leaving his mother and having an extended stay with him. He came to trust that, over time, the day-to-day interactions would serve as the glue to their relationship for now and the future. Henry was open to better understanding the developmental needs of children his son's age. Over time, Henry became more trusting of his abilities as a single father. The opportunities of the crisis became more apparent and served as a chance to reevaluate his priorities and gain a type of nurturing and self-efficacy as a parent that he had never experienced before. Henry continues to seek support for the ongoing struggles with health concerns, raising a teenage son, and getting involved in a new romantic relationship.

Reflection and Discussion Questions

1. How might your own gender role socialization process and experiences influence your work with men? What were you taught about the roles of boys and girls and men and women? Make a list and discuss their impact on your own gender role relationships.

2. What stereotypes are you aware of when counseling men? How might this show up in your therapeutic work?

3. What dynamics might show in the room with a male client and a female therapist? Do you believe, for example, that Henry's crying or showing emotions would have been harder or easier with a female therapist? Explain your answer.

4. How would you help men who are struggling with self-care issues?

5. How might issues of homophobia show up in the room with a male client and male therapist?

6. Why did Henry want to continue therapy after his wife decided to separate? What did Henry appreciate about coming to therapy? What were his stated goals? His unstated goals?

7. Identify some of Henry's "rules of masculinity" or cultural role scripts by which he lived. How might these impact the way he "did" therapy?

8. How might men's ambivalence about being in therapy show up?

9. One of the salient features of this case is unresolved loss. How do men like Henry tend to deal with issues of loss?

10. How did Henry's paradigm for doing business impact the way he ran his life?

11. How does substance abuse factor into the therapy process?

12. How did Henry's cultural background show up in the therapy room and impact his way of seeing the world?

13. What types of gender role conflict issues might men bring to therapy?

Brief Analysis of the Case

In analyzing the case of Henry, it may be helpful to apply three basic principles in working with men and some specific guidelines in regard to gender-sensitive counseling.

1. Principle 1. Men have (often unstated) strong desires and longings for deeper, more intimate, satisfying, trusting, safe, noncompetitive,

heartfelt connections yet are often too scared or lack the knowledge about how to attain such connections.

2. Principle 2. Men do have a full range of feelings and often are able to sort out what the feelings are and how they may impact their relationships, although this may take some extra time and coaching.

3. Principle 3. When in pain and wanting relief, men are often conflicted about acknowledging their need for help for fear of appearing weak and vulnerable.

There are seven guidelines for providing gender-sensitive counseling interventions with male clients:

• Guideline 1. Recognize, acknowledge, and affirm gently the difficulty that men have for entering and being in counseling. Relationship building and trust took time with Henry. Henry and many men often objectify relationships through a lens of power and control. Asking for help implies weakness and failure to be self-sufficient. Men do not want to feel dependent on therapy or the therapist.

• Guideline 2. Help the client save "masculine face." It is important for counselors to communicate their genuine respect for their male client coming into therapy. Contextualizing coming to therapy as a brave, courageous, and honorable behavior is congruent with traditional male socialization. Many male clients need acceptance as a man before progressing with treatment. There were many instances where Henry was fearful of being seen as weak. This fear is deeply rooted and socialized for many men.

• Guideline 3. Educate men up front about the process of therapy. Check out a man's assumptions of what will be expected of him as a client. Clarify your role as the therapist. Explain how you practice psychotherapy. For example, most men do not know how the therapy process works and worry that the therapist will be judgmental or discover their weaknesses. Male clients often have fears of not being "good enough" clients. Men perceive therapy as a place where they will need to become emotional. Men often don't feel ready or equipped in what they believe will be asked of them in a traditional therapy setting. Although the mystery and fear of what happens in therapy is potentially present for all clients, it is often a more salient issue for male clients. Because of male gender role socialization messages, men are often quite uncomfortable with "just being" with a problem. Often male clients expect and hope for immediate results from therapy. This was quite true for Henry. His discomfort with the unknown process of therapy and wanting solutions paralleled how he did relationships. This therapist finds it useful to be aware of the positive impact that selective and intentional transparency has on the therapeutic relationship.

• Guideline 4. Be patient. To build a strong therapeutic alliance, it is important for counselors to be patient and understand the walls men have erected. Men may slam their emotional doors and leave therapy prematurely if they are not given enough time build a feeling of safety. Men often need to start therapy slowly and may resist sharing intimate personal details and feelings up front. Often rituals of initial engagement through more traditional masculine means are needed. The therapist carefully understood Henry's defensive structure and well-developed ability to intellectualize and rationalize his behaviors. Confrontation of his defensive structures could not have been successful without a thick foundation of knowing that the therapist valued and respected Henry.

• Guideline 5. Use therapy language and approaches that are congruent with your client's gender role identity. Using words to substitute for *psychotherapy*, such as *consultation*, *meeting*, or *discussion*, may be more consistent with providing meaning for how male clients may want to view their involvement in the process. Male clients often resist feeling words and other types of relational language that counselors typically are trained to use. Creating a male-friendly psychotherapeutic process is critical to the success of treatment. Henry made certain to shake my hand when saying hello and good-bye. This was an important ritual for him. He also called me Doc. Although I (Mark Stevens) am not enamored by this greeting, I think in his own way it was an affectionate way to express his masculinity to me. Allowing Henry to express his traditional masculinity without judgment was an important part of sustaining a male-friendly environment.

• Guideline 6. Be genuine. Male clients may want to be treated in ways that feel congruent with their masculine socialization. This can be accomplished by listening carefully, projecting warmth without appearing overly sympathetic. Male clients often trust and are more engaged in treatment when they experience their counselor as a "real human" being. Conveying masculinity type warmth was important to Henry. As with many male clients, Henry did not want to be pitied, yet he very much desired to be understood both on a cognitive and feeling level. Cognitive empathy goes a long way with male clients. Additionally, being frank with invitations, such as "Like to know what I think about what you just said?" or "Would you like some coaching on this?" offered a type of casual confrontation that seemed to lower Henry's defensives.

◆ Guideline 7. Tell stories. It is much easier for males to tell a story than to communicate how they feel. Entwined in these stories are layers of feelings and emotions that are expressed as the story unfolds. Henry had many stories that were untold. He had stuffed them away for years. They included stories about his father's infidelity, stories about drugs and alcohol, stories about growing up overweight, and stories about rejection. The telling of untold stories by male clients often leads to more self-compassion. Men hold onto lots of inner world secrets. The vulnerability of the stories allows men to do some outside-of-the-box or nontraditional masculinity by revealing themselves in front of another person.

Recommended Resources

Books and/or Articles

Constructs of Masculinities: Cultural Considerations

Caldwell, L. D., & White, J. L. (2001). African-centered therapeutic and counseling interventions for African American males. In G. Brooks & G. Good (Eds.), *The handbook of counseling and psychotherapy approaches for men* (pp. 737–753). San Francisco, CA: Jossey-Bass.

Casas, J. M., Turner, J. A., & Ruiz de Esparza, C. A. (2001). Machismo revisited in a time of crisis: Implications for understanding and counseling Hispanic men. In G. Brooks & G. Good (Eds.), *The handbook of counseling and psychotherapy approaches for men* (pp. 754–779). San Francisco, CA: Jossey-Bass.

Franklin, A. J. (1999). Invisibility syndrome and racial identity development in psychotherapy and counseling African American men. *Counseling Psychologist, 27,* 761–793.

Haldeman, D. C. (2006). Queer eye on the straight guy: A case of gay male heterophobia. In M. Englar-Carlson & M. Stevens (Eds.), *In the room with men: A casebook of therapeutic change* (pp. 301–318). Washington, DC: American Psychological Association.

Hammond, W. P., & Mattis, J. S. (2005). Being a man about it: Manhood meaning among African American men. *Psychology of Men and Masculinity, 6,* 114–126.

Johnson, P. D. (2006). Counseling African American men: A contextualized humanistic perspective. *Counseling and Values, 50,* 187–196.

Liu, W. M. (2002). Exploring the lives of Asian American men: Racial identity, male role norms, gender role conflict, and prejudicial attitudes. *Psychology of Men & Masculinity, 3,* 107–118.

Liu, W. M., & Chang, T. (2007). Asian American masculinities. In F. T. L. Leong, A. Ebero, L. Kinoshita, A. G. Arpana, & L. H. Yang (Eds.), *Handbook of Asian American psychology* (2nd ed., pp. 197–211). Thousand Oaks, CA: Sage.

Wester, S. R. (2007). Male gender role conflict and multiculturalism: Implications for counseling psychology. *Counseling Psychologist, 36,* 294–324.

Male-Sensitive Therapy

Brooks, G. R. (1998). *A new psychotherapy for traditional men.* San Francisco, CA: Jossey-Bass.

Englar-Carlson, M., & Shepard, D. S. (2005). Engaging men in couples counseling: Strategies for overcoming ambivalence and inexpressiveness. *Family Journal, 13,* 383–391.

Englar-Carlson, M., & Stevens, M. (Eds.). (2006). *In the room with men: A casebook of therapeutic change.* Washington, DC: American Psychological Association.

Good, G. E., Gilbert, L. A., & Scher, M. (1990). Gender aware therapy: A synthesis of feminist therapy and knowledge about gender. *Journal of Counseling and Development, 68,* 376–380.

Meth, R. L., & Pasick, R. S. (1990). *Men in therapy: The challenge of change.* New York, NY: Guilford Press.

Pollack, W. S., & Levant, R. F. (1998). *New psychotherapy for men.* New York, NY: Wiley.

Scher, M., Stevens, M., Good, G., & Eichenfield, E. (1987). *Handbook of psychotherapy with men.* Thousand Oaks, CA: Sage.

Men and Depression

Addis, M. E. (2008). Gender and depression in men. *Clinical Psychology: Science and Practice, 15,* 153–168.

Cochran, S. V., & Rabinowitz, F. E. (2000). *Men and depression: Clinical and empirical perspectives.* San Diego, CA: Academic Press.

Real, T. (1997). *I don't want to talk about it: Overcoming the secret legacy of male depression.* New York, NY: Fireside Press.

Men and Loss

Cochran, S. V., & Rabinowitz, F. E. (1996). Men, loss and psychotherapy. *Psychotherapy, 33,* 593–600.

Martin, T. L., & Doka, K. J. (2000). *Men don't cry . . . women do: Transcending gender stereotypes of grief.* Philadelphia, PA: Brunner/ Mazel.

Men's Health

Courtenay, W. H. (1998). College men's health: An overview and a call to action. *Journal of American College Health, 46,* 279–290.

Courtenay, W. H. (2000). Engendering health: A social constructionist examination of men's health beliefs and behaviors. *Psychology of Men & Masculinity, 1,* 4–15.

Sandman, D., Simantov, E., & An, C. (2000). *Out of touch: American men and the healthcare system.* New York, NY: Commonwealth Fund.

Men and Substance Abuse

Hanna, E., & Grant, B. (1997). Gender differences in DSM-IV alcohol use disorders and major depression as distributed in the general population: Clinical implications. *Comprehensive Psychiatry, 38,* 202–212.

Lemle, E., & Mishkind, M. E. (1989). Alcohol and masculinity. *Journal of Substance Abuse Treatment, 6,* 213–222.

Fiction Reading

Beatty, P. (1996). *The White boy shuffle.* New York, NY: Houghton Mifflin.

Bezos, M. (2006). *The testing of Luther Albright.* New York, NY: Harper.

Ford, R. (1995). *The sportswriter.* New York, NY: Vintage.

Iida, D. (1996). *Middle son.* New York, NY: Algonquin.

Wolff, T. (1989). *This boy's life.* New York, NY: Atlantic Monthly Press.

Videos

American Psychological Association Psychotherapy Series: http://www.apa.org/videos/

Brown, L. S. (2005). *Working with male survivors of trauma and abuse.* Washington, DC: American Psychological Association.

Englar-Carlson, M. (2009). *Engaging men in psychotherapy.* Washington, DC: American Psychological Association.

Kiselica, M. S. (2009). *Positive psychology interventions with men.* Washington, DC: American Psychological Association.

Stevens, M. A. (2006). *Psychotherapy with men.* Washington, DC: American Psychological Association.

Films

Allen, L. M. (Producer), & Brook, P. (Director). (1963). *Lord of the flies* [Motion picture]. United Kingdom: British Lion.

Bender, L. (Producer), & Van Sant, G. (Director). (1997). *Good Will Hunting* [Motion picture]. United States: A Band Apart, Lawrence Bender Productions.

Black, T., Haines, R., & Washington, D. (Producers), & Washington, D. (Director). (2002). *Antwone Fisher* [Motion picture]. United States: Fox Searchlight Pictures.

Cohen, B., & Jinks, D. (Producers), & Mendes, S. (Director). (1999). *American beauty* [Motion picture]. United States: DreamWorks Pictures.

Pratt, C. A. (Producer), & Carlino, L. (Director). (1979). *The great Santini* [Motion picture]. United States: Warner Bros. and Orion Pictures.

Websites/Blogs

American Psychological Association Division 51: Society for the Psychological Study of Men and Masculinity, http://www.apa.org/divisions/div51/

Men's Health Network: http://www.menshealthnetwork.org

Men's Issues page: http://menstuff.org/mensissues/current.html

National Organization for Men Against Sexism: www.nomas.org

Real Men Real Depression Campaign: http://www.wellnessproposals.com/mental-health/handouts/nimh/real-men-real-depression.pdf

REFERENCE

David, D. S., & Brannon, R. (1976). The forty nine percent majority: The male sex role. Reading, MA: Addison-Wesley

WHY AM I HERE? THE STORY OF MARTIN

Martin is a 22-year-old Chicano male who pronounces his name with an emphasis on the "i," Mart–in. He comes from an intact family of Mexican origin where his father emigrated from Michoacán, Mexico, as a teenager and now works as a mechanic. Martin's mother came from the state of Jalisco, Mexico, when she was about 22 years old and currently works at a garment factory. Martin's parents met at a regional Mexican music nightclub and have been married for twenty-four years. He spent most of his early years living in a largely Mexican barrio in Los Angeles but is currently attending a prestigious university and pursing an undergraduate degree.

When I (Jose Montes) saw Martin at the counseling center, he was less than a year away from getting his degree. Standing 6 foot 3 inches tall and weighing about 230 pounds, Martin was an imposing figure. Phenotypically, he is dark skinned with dark brown eyes, has straight very short buzzed hair, and is direct, but soft spoken. Although a little older than Martin, I shared a similar background. I am Chicano, bilingual, grew up in Los Angeles, and our skin color and hair tone was about the same.

Martin was referred to counseling for "anger management issues." The intake interview was conducted by another provider, but when I first saw him he lightly tipped his head backward as he softly but firmly uttered, "What's up?" Martin looked around my office, stopping briefly at certain objects, briefly making eye contact, and said "Why am I here?" Martin was under the impression that he was mandated to attend therapy and expressed his resentment at being coerced to do so. When asked about his willingness to share his thoughts about his interactions or events that may have led him to my office, he shut down. He slouched down in the sofa, fixed his gaze around different parts in my office, and remained relatively silent. I began to get a sense that Martin may have perceived me as one more authority figure, imposed on him against his wishes. In effect, he perceived me as "the man" (arm of the law). Very little happened during that first meeting, and I informed him that he was not mandated to come for therapy. I would, however, be making another appointment to see him, but it was his choice whether he came. I did reiterate that I would be there and ready to see him.

After Martin left my office, I took a moment to reflect on my interaction with him. I must admit that I felt a bit intimidated and fearful that he might act out his "anger." His towering and imposing figure, along with some visible tattoos, dark skin, and "anger issues" was a representative heuristic of the "angry brown male." I concluded that I was not the only one on that campus having the same reaction to Martin. Given his lack of therapeutic interest, I was not so sure if I wanted to see him again, although part of me was intrigued. I just felt that he would not come back to see me. Why did I feel this way? Was I making an assumption based on his ethnic and cultural background that he would not find value in counseling? Was I projecting my feelings if I was in Martin's shoes? Not aware at the time, I think I underestimated the connection we made.

Martin did return, and the same thing happened during our second session. He was mostly quiet, reserved; perhaps suspicious? I did my best to convey unconditional acceptance and support of him being there even when we were mostly in silence. This happened repeatedly until the fourth session. By then, I decided to self-disclose in a chitchat fashion (mostly one way) about my day. I talked about an interesting headline in the newspaper, being cut off on the freeway, and so on. At the end of the fourth session, as I opened the door for him, we shook hands. However, the way this handshaking occurred was unusual in this type of setting. We both locked hands and leaned in shoulder to shoulder. This greeting gesture is the way I interact with my family and friends around my neighborhood, but I never thought it could happen in a therapeutic room. I am very glad it happened.

Next session, he was a completely different person. He began to share and trust the process. We know that for many men, verbal communication can be a challenge, especially if it involves vulnerability. Later on in our work, Martin shared that he was "sizing me up" trying to determine if I too would be another judgmental figure on this campus. He talked about how he learned to survive in the street by first observing his environment and trying to determine if it was safe or not.

Martin shared his frustration about the campus climate. He felt discriminated against by professors, peers, and just about everyone. He felt out of place and judged by his appearance. When walking at night around campus, he would be stopped by campus police as a suspicious person, and when he did well in exams, his professors would question whether he achieved them fairly. He had tried joining student groups but found that even those that were similar (ethnically) were judgmental and entitled. When he shared his background story with others, particularly "White" people, he felt that they would pity him, use him as an "ethnic token" to boast about campus student diversity. When he would speak his mind, he was labeled as angry.

Martin was an ex-gang member and had been shot twice in a leg and torso area. He was lured to "bangin" (gangs) around the ninth or tenth grade. Both parents were working hard to provide for four siblings. He had lost some friends, and his parents feared that he too would perish in their community. Given that he had a 4.0 grade point average in high school, he received multiple college invitations. His parents were more than happy that he would be out of their community into a safer one. During high school, Martin had to keep his grades a secret from his friends and family members. He would be called names and ridiculed for having good grades: "smarty pants," "too good for us," "nerd." This, he explained, posed a challenge for him. Having good grades and doing well academically diminished his masculinity status with his male friends as it made him look "weak." He could not be both, a man's man and getting perfect grades. However, he also noted that getting good grades allowed him to gain status with women and ample opportunities to date. This seemed to change in college. He felt that other male students would "mad-dog" him (to stare and show hostility or disdain) and that most females would avoid him. This contributed to Martin feeling rejected, unwelcomed, and quite isolated. Not belonging is often a common perception and feeling for individuals like Martin, who have made such a dramatic demographic transition.

Martin had no problem with self-assertiveness. He described his parents as passive and soft spoken; he credits his outspokeness to time spent in the gang. He had opened up to a couple of roommates about his situation but felt that they were dismissive. Indeed, he felt very lonely, distant, and removed from his immediate environment. He later indicated that our interactions were the first ones on campus where he could "just be," meaning that he felt completely safe and accepted. When I explored with him what it was like for him to be working with another Chicano male (me), he talked about family dynamics. He felt that it would be easier for him to open up to a woman as he felt emotionally closer to his mother. Indeed, for him, women seemed safer, less critical, and more accepting than most men he had encountered. However, he remembers his dad saying "*Mijo* [son], if you need to cry, go ahead and cry . . . just not in front of others." Eventually, Martin did allow himself to be whatever he needed to be in any setting. Indeed, in later sessions, Martin began to make changes, both internally and externally. Internally, he explored other meanings to many perceived situations:

Martin: Lot of guys around here just mad-dog me.

Therapist: I wonder what that is all about.

Martin: I don't know . . . they just don't like me . . . they probably think, "What this Mexican doing here?"

Therapist: Back in L.A, while you were gang bangin', did you ever mad-dog anyone?

Martin: Yeah . . . a lot. . . . Mostly people I didn't know.

Therapist: So you mad-dog anyone that came into your neighborhood whom you didn't know. I imagine they can pose a threat.

Martin: I see. . . . You mean I am a threat to these people?

Therapist: Not sure. . . . Maybe they fear you. Maybe they fear you will change their world.

Martin: Umm. Never saw it that way, well, that is their problem.

Martin also made external changes. He became socially more active on campus, carefully choosing and picking his battles. Was it worth it to him to argue with a professor when questioned about perfect grades? Since he strongly believed that his campus lacked multicultural awareness/sensitivity, would he stay idle or rock the boat? He decided that this fight was worth fighting. He created his own student organization challenging the campus stand on multicultural issues. Internal and external activism provided Martin with a sense of purpose, empowerment, and direction. I am happy to announce that Martin is now enrolled in a PhD program in medical engineering.

Reflection and Discussion Questions

1. Given the initial presentation by Martin, what may you have done differently or similarly?
2. How do you define therapeutic progress? Would the first four sessions, which were spent mostly in silence, be considered progress?
3. What was the significance of the handshake from a cultural perspective?
4. In what way would Chicano culture impact gender role relationships? How might this be played out in the therapeutic session with a male therapist? With a female therapist?
5. In the absence of any other symptoms, what *Diagnostic and Statistical Manual* diagnosis would you consider?

6. If indeed, there was widespread institutional and individual prejudice and/or discrimination in this college, how would your theoretical orientation address it?

7. If indeed much of Martin's problems are caused externally and not due primarily to intrapsychic reasons, what recommendations or actions might be taken to help the client cope?

8. What responsibilities does the counselor have to address the campus environment, if indeed it is hostile and invalidating to students of color?

9. Martin did not seem to fit either in college nor within his cultural community. How may he be challenging the status quo in both these vastly different worlds?

10. Martin and the therapist shared similar sociodemographic characteristics: male and of Latino descent. How might these traits affect the therapeutic process?

11. How may Latino culture affect masculine and feminine roles?

12. How do you think a female therapist would impact Martin's behavior in the therapy environment?

Brief Analysis of the Case

◆ *Rapport and relationship building.* Martin's presentation can pose an interesting dilemma for therapists. Perceiving his behavior as a lack of interest in therapy, particularly during the first sessions, was a source of anxiety and concern for the therapist. In essence, a service is being offered but appears to be unwanted or unappreciated. Given Martin's cultural background, it is helpful to understand the next point. The concept of *personalismo*, that people and interpersonal relationships are more important than institutional rules and regulations, often makes the task orientation of the therapist inappropriate to the establishment of rapport in a relationship. Many Latino clients seek who are you as the therapist (an authentic person) rather than your role as a helping professional. In building rapport, talking about ordinary events and things (chitchat) can be a conduit to earn client trust. Many therapists, however, perceive such small talk as frivolous and not part of therapy. Yet in Latino and many other cultures, this form of interaction is central to building a working relationship. Thus, the objective therapist–client relationship can act as a barrier to effective multicultural relationships.

- *Trust and mistrust in counseling.* Research indicates that Latino clients prefer an interactive approach that includes self-disclosure on the part of the therapist and that rapport building is essential. As in the case of Martin, his experiences with institutions and authority figures have not been positive ones. He may approach the therapist thinking, "Before I can trust you and share my intimate thoughts and feelings, I need to know where you are coming from. Can you be trusted? What makes you any different than my professors, classmates, and administrators who have made decisions or judgments to my detriment? Before I self-disclose, I want to know where you are coming from." Ironically, such a dynamic means in many respects that helping professionals must self-disclose first in order to establish trust with their clients. In traditional therapy training, however, we have been taught that therapists should not self-disclose and that doing so is a taboo. Inevitably, clients will present challenges to you and judge your credibility based on how open and honest you appear. Counselors and therapists need to be skilled in using therapeutic self-disclosures in working with clients of color.

- *Individual versus systemic approaches.* Under traditional therapeutic models, the focus is primarily on the individual. There is an assumption that the problem generally resides in the individual, and change is directed at the attitudes, beliefs, and behaviors of the client. Although addressing these issues within the person is important, larger systemic issues are equally important. Additionally, simply acknowledging larger systemic issues in the therapy room is not enough. At what point and for which issues do we address and/or actively intervene at the systemic level? Martin was feeling that whenever he talked to others about his situation, all solutions or feedback focused on changing or "adapting" him into his environment. There may be an inherent risk of blaming the victim when in actuality the problems the client encounters are systemic in nature (prejudice/discrimination; a campus environment that is hostile and invalidating to students of color; lack of sensitivity of faculty, staff, and students to diversity issues, etc.) and not due to some inherent individual dysfunction. Disfranchised communities, particularly people of color, fear that they will be forced to assimilate and acculturate, thereby losing their sense of integrity. Although it is important to increase coping skills with clients, simply adjusting the client to the environment without regard for the pathological aspects of the campus climate, for example, may result in cultural oppressions. Balancing individual with systemic change is a great challenge to therapists.

• *Communication styles.* We are aware of the ethical, legal, and therapeutic issues related to touch and other forms of communicating with a client. A major breakthrough happened when I responded to Martin in a way that was familiar and warm to him. This type of handshake or greeting is a common way of communicating among many Chicano and African American communities—akin to hugging, kissing on the cheek, or bowing in other cultures. Yet traditional therapy may discourage such forms of communication. For Martin, however, this was appropriate, culturally acceptable, and sensitive. Yet little information or discussion is provided regarding culturally relevant behaviors or practices (rituals) that differ from traditional ways of greeting one another. High- and low-context style of communication may differ across racial and/or ethnic groups. The Euro-American style of communication usually engages in a low-context, straight and direct style of communication. Latinos and African Americans are said to have a preference for high-context levels of communication. What is being verbally said is just as important as nonverbal communication. Martin and I were speaking to one another in silence. In essence, the first four sessions were done in multiculturally congruent way, and the next sessions were done in a more traditional Western therapeutic approach.

• *Intersection of Latino culture and masculinity.* We can see that Martin was struggling with gender roles in his community of origin. Having good grades was a challenge to his masculinity or expected gender roles. Interestingly, it is not so for both genders. Women in his community found his good grades to be a positive attribute. We can also see a shift in this value once he entered college. We also wonder what Martin's father meant by not crying in front of others. Would doing so be a sign of weakness? And would this weakness make Martin vulnerable? We know that Mexican Americans are patriarchal systemically, but the father also evidenced some gender role and masculinity trait flexibility. In college, Martin seemed to face a different gender expectation—the expectation of the stereotyped, angry, violent brown male. Such was evident to him in his everyday interactions with his college environment.

Recommended Resources

Books and/or Articles

Acuna, R. (1995). *Anything but Mexican. Chicanos in contemporary Los Angeles.* London, England: Verso.

Duran, E., & Duran, B. (1995). *Native American postcolonial psychology.* Albany, NY: State University of New York Press.

Katz, J. (2006). *The macho paradox: Why Some men hurt women and how all men can help.* Naperville, IL: Source Books.

Martinez, J. L., and Mendoza, R. (1984). *Chicano psychology* (2nd ed.). New York, NY: Academic Press.

Noriega, C. A., Avila, E. R., Davalos, K. M., Sandoval, C., & Torres-Perez, R. (2010). *The Chicano studies reader: An anthology of Aztlan, 1970–2010* (Vol. 2). Berkeley, CA: UCLA Chicano Studies Research Center Publications.

Parham, T. A., White, J. L., & Ajamu, A. (1999). *The psychology of Blacks: An African centered perspective* (3rd ed.). Englewood Cliffs, NJ: Prentice Hall.

Piedra, L. M., Schiffner, T. A., & Reynaga-Abiko, G. (2011). Investing in the future: Expanding educational opportunities for first-generation Latino college students. In L. P. Buki & L. M. Piedra (Eds.), *Creating Infrastructures for Latino Mental Health* (pp. 117-137). New York, NY: Springer.

Ruiz, A. (1981). Cultural and historical perspectives in counseling Hispanics. In D. W. Sue (Ed.), *Counseling the culturally different: Theory & practice* (pp. 343-362). New York, NY: Wiley.

Villaruel, F. A., Carlo, G., Grau-Contreas, J. M., Azmitia, M., Cabrera, N. J., & Chahin, T. J. (2009). *Handbook of U.S. Latino psychology: Developmental and community-based perspectives.* Beverly Hills, CA: Sage.

Novels

Marquez, G. G. (2005). *Memories of my melancholy whores.* New York, NY: Knopf.

Villaseñor, E. V. (1992). *Rain of gold.* New York, NY: Delta Books.

Videos

Coppola, F. F., et al. (Executive producers), & Nava, G. (Director). (2004). *My family* [Motion picture]. United States: New Line Motion Pictures Video.

Greenfield-Sanders (Director and Producer). (2011). *Latino list* [Documentary]. United States:. HBO Entertainment.

Levin, M. (Director). (1994). *Gang war: Bangin' in Little Rock* [Documentary]. United States:. HBO Entertainment.

Netter, G., Zucker, D., & Zucker, J. (Producers), & Arau, A. (Director). (1995). *A walk in the clouds* [Motion picture]. United States: 20th Century Fox.

Nicolaides, S. (Producer), & Singleton, J. (Director). (1991). *Boyz n the hood* [Motion picture]. United States: Columbia Pictures.

Sandoval, C., & Miller, P. (Directors). (2009). *A class apart: A Mexican American civil rights story*. United States: American Experience.

13

Clinical Applications With Transgender Individuals

Anita R. Hund and Jane E. Reid

JUST A "PHASE"? THE STORY OF LESLIE

The cases in this chapter are composites from the practices of two therapists. Any resemblance to one actual person is coincidental.

Case Description

Leslie was a Mexican American, 19-year-old, transgender individual who identified as genderqueer[1] and a lesbian. Leslie was female assigned at birth; however, Leslie identified more strongly, but not completely, with a male identity. In a previous therapy, Leslie had always had the feeling that the therapist was encouraging Leslie to choose an identity. However, Leslie had the feeling that neither "male" nor "female" felt consistent. When asked, Leslie reported preferring gender-neutral pronouns, "ze/hir," which

---

[1] A list of terms used to indicate information about a transgender person's identity is presented in the section titled "Brief Analysis of the Case."

ze learned about by avidly searching the Internet. The therapist knew that gendered pronouns (he/his/him; she/hers/her) are particularly problematic for individuals who do not identify clearly within the gender dichotomy, and there have been efforts to create gender-neutral pronouns. The system preferred by this client is ze/hir/hirs/hirself. "Hir" is pronounced "here."

Leslie worked hard to establish an identity throughout adolescence in an effort to find a social group that helped hir feel a sense of belonging. Hir efforts resulted in different periods, including religious and "emo" periods. Ze spent significant amount of energy, in retrospect, attempting to fit in and trying to find an outer appearance that felt like it fit for hir. Once leaving hir childhood home, Leslie fell into a deep depression until ze came out as lesbian. While this process of coming out helped hir to feel more authentic in terms of hir intimate relationships, ze continued to feel something missing. Admitting hir sexual orientation to hirself provided hir with the space and clarity to consider questions of gender identity. Leslie felt certain about the desire for breast removal surgery and hysterectomy prior to attending therapy; ze felt less certain about wanting hormones. Leslie was unsure of how to make decisions about which physical interventions would help hir feel consistent and whole.

Leslie had a somewhat muted affect and often sat as far away from the therapist as possible. However, ze never missed or arrived late for a session, and expressed positive feelings about the therapy. Although Leslie has friends, ze rarely accessed other people when in need. This tendency was clearest during a root canal with unexpected complications. Despite physical needs and emotional distress, ze had considerable difficulty accessing support from anyone, including the therapist. In general, Leslie tended to perform at a very high level academically and appeared to others to be "well put together," even though ze was often anxious or depressed inside. It seemed difficult for hir to let others know when ze struggled. Prior to hir experience with the root canal, Leslie imagined that breast reduction surgery and hysterectomy would be easy and the recovery uneventful. Ze minimized any feelings about hir family's ambivalence around supporting hir financially or practically around the surgery. Leslie was very unnerved by the emotional impact of hir root canal; ze had not expected the need for recovery or support afterward. Ze was unable to make sense of hir reactions. The therapist reflected the ways in which Leslie expected hirself to do everything alone and began wondering with hir about what accessing support is like for hir.

Throughout these discussions, Leslie began to wonder if hir distress about hir reaction to the root canal was related to the realization of what it would be like to have surgery with little support.

Leslie's parents had hir when they were older. Ze reported ongoing struggles with them while growing up based on some cultural gaps exacerbated by their age; ze described them as very "traditionally Mexican" and Catholic. Ze decided to come out to hir family because having an honest relationship with them was important to hir. They struggled at first, which Leslie expected based on their Catholic and traditionally Mexican values. Following coming out to hir parents, Leslie requested a conversation between the therapist and Leslie's older sister. Leslie's sister was very opposed to surgery and expressed concern that Leslie was unpredictable and went through numerous "phases" throughout adolescence. The therapist became concerned about whether she should be supporting the transition. Although the therapist had not experienced Leslie in these ways, the conversation left her uneasy and worried that she had "missed something."

Reflection and Discussion Questions

1. Leslie describes a gender identity that does not fit neatly into either male or female. How might you approach conceptualizing hir identity issues?

2. How might Leslie's interpersonal dynamics and difficulty admitting the need for assistance and support be related to hir experience with navigating hir gender identity and expression?

3. What would the experience be like for you of using Leslie's preferred pronouns? How do you understand the importance of this to Leslie?

4. How would you proceed in therapy with Leslie as ze makes decisions about the options to pursue in hir transition? How might you support Leslie in transition, considering some of hir interpersonal dynamics? How would you support hir in light of intolerance in society?

5. How might you approach the conversation with Leslie's sister? Additionally, how might you make sense of the therapist's uneasiness, and how do you think the therapist should approach the issue with Leslie in session? What are some possible reasons for the difference between the sister's and the therapist's reactions to Leslie?

6. How do other cultural and identity issues interact to impact Leslie's experiences? What cultural strengths could be harnessed in the service of the work?

Brief Analysis of the Case

The case of Leslie presents a number of areas where a therapist could misdiagnose, mislead, or misunderstand transgender clients. Next are some key points to attend to related to identity and diagnosis.

• When clients are getting to know a therapist, they may be acutely attuned to cues signaling either safety and understanding or hostility and invalidation. Therefore, a multiculturally competent therapist maintains a strong knowledge base around language. This task is one of ongoing professional development because language is always shifting, and transgender individuals often come in with a wealth of information they obtained from poring over Internet resources in an effort to learn more about their identity in a cisgender society. Additionally, language that is useful or affirming for one client can be unhelpful and offensive to another. Listening carefully to the client's language and cultivating an open discussion about language can help therapist and client develop a mutual language that creates a climate of safety and self-understanding. A good example of this was Leslie's preference for gender-neutral pronouns, and the therapist's acceptance of this system. A number of terms used to indicate information about a transgender person's identity are outlined here.

> *Transgender:* A category including a variety of people experiencing incongruence with their assigned gender, including but not limited to transsexual people.
>
> *Transsexual* person: One who experiences strong incongruence with the societally assigned gender who may make body alterations though medical means.
>
> *Cisgender* person: One whose gender identity and gender expression align with the assigned sex at birth. The importance of this word lies in the intention to not identify one type of gender identity as normal, therefore pathologizing others.
>
> *Genderqueer:* An increasingly popular identity often used by people who feel their gender identities do not fit easily into a male/female binary.

Male-assigned or *female-assigned* person: Someone who was assumed to be male or female, respectively, at birth.

Transman or *FTM* (female to male): An individual who was female-assigned transitioning to perceived male.

Transwoman or *MTF* (male to female): An individual who was male-assigned transitioning to perceived female.

• To further create safety, therapists need to observe and challenge their biases toward a gender dichotomy, whether it is by normalizing a cisgender identity or by encouraging a complete transition to another gender. In this work, it is important to appreciate the different paths people may take in terms of physical transition. In work with Leslie, it may be tempting to encourage hir to settle on a gender and possibly accompanying procedures, as hir previous therapist did. These efforts would serve to make the therapist comfortable rather than to help Leslie. Additionally, they would replicate society's efforts to dictate hir identity.

• Therapists should avoid a "gatekeeper" role. Historically, medical providers required that transgender individuals receive letters from treating therapists verifying a period of treatment and readiness for the transition, a practice that many continue today. The question for therapy should not be deciding whether clients are really transgender but instead helping them carefully consider questions of what will help them feel grounded, comfortable, and actualized (Vanderburgh, 2011). Additionally, it can be important to encourage clients to base their decisions on accurate information by providing referrals to medical and other professionals. Information from the Internet can be very helpful; however, it may not always be accurate. The pressures around the supposed gatekeeper role in addition to discomfort around Leslie's rejection of the gender dichotomy impacted the therapist in the last case. The therapist responded by bringing Leslie's sister's concerns to the client. During conversations with Leslie, it seemed more likely that ze thought carefully, but privately, about certain decisions. To hir sister, the announcement might feel surprising and unpredictable. Leslie's history of keeping hir thoughts about hir identity quiet even to hirself has been a reasonable adaptation to transphobia. Additionally, hir sister interpreted hir "phases" in high school as a sign of pathology and a reason to discredit Leslie. However, Leslie's efforts to find an identity that fit for hir can be understood as efforts to make sense of underlying knowledge that hir assigned identity was not correct. A positive approach to the conversation with Leslie's sister required the therapist to be open to herself about her own biases and her fears.

- Cultural factors informed Leslie's experience; it is important to consider the ways in which traditional Mexican, Catholic values may make hir experience with hir family difficult. However, it is equally important to consider the ways in which the value of *familismo*—putting the needs of the family as a group over those of the individual—is a cultural asset that may provide hir family with the resolve to work through a difficult issue. It was important that the therapist accept the significance of communicating with a family member and understand that the intervention with the sister could be very helpful for Leslie if executed sensitively. Leslie is not just an individual but an individual situated in hir family and culture. Additionally, it is important to note that cisgender normative values pervade the cultures of all racial/ethnic groups.

- When considering Leslie's interpersonal style and hir disconnection from hir needs and emotions, it is important to consider the impact of growing up transgender in a society that normalizes a cisgender identity. When a person's sense of gender contradicts that which has been ascribed to the person, it is difficult to be true to self while living up to others' expectations. Additionally, the lack of accurate mirroring makes it difficult for people to understand themselves. Leslie worked very hard during hir life to find an identity that felt true while also pleasing others. These efforts required significant suppression of hir needs and emotions. Additionally, Leslie had a sense that ze could not rely on others. An obvious result would be depression and dissociation from one's needs, body, and emotions (Vanderburgh, 2011). Therapeutic approaches that empower Leslie to identify and acknowledge these things can be helpful. However, this work must be done at a careful pace, recognizing that Leslie may not be able to acknowledge certain things until ze is ready to face the consequences. For example, it was important that Leslie come to the realization that surgery may be difficult for hir on hir own. Facing the fact that ze needs hir family's support for the surgery but may not be able to get it may leave hir with uncomfortable feelings of anger toward hir family and anxiety about asking others for support. Therapists can expect that a client's ways of coping, pathological or healthy, will impact the decision-making process around and experience with transition. Leslie's interpersonal style and difficulty accepting hir needs will likely impact hir transition, making it difficult for hir to access necessary support. Therefore, an important part of the work may be helping Leslie make realistic plans around the transition process.

AN INCOMPLETE EXPERIENCE: THE STORY OF ALICE

Case Description

This case involves work with a second-generation Korean American woman in her early 20s who sought treatment for assistance with forming relationships. Alice was male assigned and had transitioned several months before beginning treatment. Alice had undertaken hormone replacement therapy and was considering surgery at some point in the future. She had already taken care of many of the institutional matters: changing her Social Security card and her driver's license.

Alice was out to her family. Her family was confused and distressed by her transition. While her father seemed angry and resentful, other family members seemed to be making a good effort in reckoning with the changes and the "loss" of their brother, son, and so on (from their point of view). Alice was appreciative that they were trying but felt sad and tense when she visited her family. She wished for more even though she did not really expect it. She felt that some of her family's difficulties stemmed from their adherence to their fundamentalist Christian religion. Alice experienced helpful mentors at work and elsewhere who had made her institutional interactions tolerable.

She described herself as a bit of a loner. She was often lonely and wished to have friends and a partner. She was shy and tentative with others. In the early sessions with the therapist, she was funny but also edgy and prickly: She was easy to like, but it was hard to express it to her, as she seemed closed off. Alice felt isolated; she yearned for contact and help from other transgender individuals. The therapist encouraged her to join a support group for transgender people; however, Alice was fearful of these situations because she imagined that most of the participants would be "freaks." She acknowledged that some of her feelings were related to her difficulty feeling positively about herself as transgender.

She spent several hours each day online, often playing video games and sometimes visiting online social sites. She had been very depressed before her transition; once she began, her symptoms lessened, only to return. She longed to have a family. She described a sense of at long last having things in order with her gender but of then having a sense of "now what?" with the rest of it: Her discomfort with her birth-assigned gender had felt like an impediment to forming friendships, finding a partner, and engaging with the world in an authentic and meaningful way. Now that the impediment had been removed, Alice wondered how to go about realizing these other desires and goals.

After several appointments, the therapist disclosed she was pregnant. Alice called after that session to cancel her next session; she stated that she wished to end the work due to financial considerations.

Reflection and Discussion Questions

1. What may have accounted for Alice's precipitous ending of therapy? More specifically, how may the therapist's personal circumstances have impacted the client? How might the therapist have handled things differently?

2. The case references the sense on the part of Alice's family that they have suffered a loss and that things have changed. In what ways might this formulation—that Alice's transition precipitated losses—be similar to or different from Alice's experience of this time?

3. How can Alice's experience of coming out help us to understand her relational experiences with her family? How might this inform our understanding of Alice's presenting concerns?

4. Alice describes a tension between her family's religion and her gender identity. What might be helpful to Alice in addressing this tension? Are there other culturally salient matters? If so, how would you begin to talk with Alice about these matters?

5. Alice expressed some fear and revulsion at the thought of associating with other transgender people; how would you address this and work with Alice around this?

6. How might you conceptualize her original depression? How might this be impacted by issues related to gender identity? What does the reappearance of her depression during the transition indicate?

Brief Analysis of the Case

• This case was not an obvious success. The therapist understood Alice's departure as a signal of some problem with the treatment. When clients leave early, therapists do not always know why. Some possibilities in this case include that the fee had been a burden to Alice, but she did not feel able to say so and test out the possibilities of a reduced fee. Alternatively, Alice may have been disrupted by the therapist's pregnancy. Alice has experienced disruptions in many other relationships. Perhaps the prospect of the therapist's leave of absence soon was too much for Alice to manage. Or it may be that the pregnancy highlighted something that Alice imagines the therapist has (a partner or family) that Alice wants but does not yet know how to have. Or it may highlight some gender tension about the differences between the bodies of these two women. Or there may be some other feature of the work or something the therapist said that Alice could not tolerate that caused the work to end. Even though ongoing events did not allow any of these hypotheses to be confirmed or disconfirmed, it is worth noting just some of the possible meanings.

• This case also suggests another important feature of work with transgender clients: Clients come to therapy for many things that have little to do with their gender. This client wanted to focus on themes of intimacy and relationships. These issues cannot be fully understood without attention to Alice's experiences with gender and being known or unknown by others, but these concerns are not themselves the focus of the treatment.

• Transgender individuals are not immune to society's messages about gender and often struggle with *internalized transphobia*, as evident in Alice's avoidance of other transgenders in support groups. These feelings can emerge in clients' feelings about their bodies as they transition and can intensify the social isolation many transgender people feel. Although this client yearns for connection with people who understand her, she is ambivalent about being associated with other "freaks." Working to understand her feelings while also helping her develop empathy and appreciation for herself and other transgender people became an important aspect of the work.

• Some transgender individuals will present with a history of mental health issues. Many people experience a lessening or disappearance of symptoms when they come to an internal acceptance of their gender identity and/or begin their transition, much like this client. Many people often find that their mental health issues return, as Alice's depression did, once they experience some difficulties related to the physical and social transition. A therapist should be cautious about interpreting this to mean that the transition is not healthy for the client or that the client is not fit for surgery. It is important to consider the fact that Alice's depression emerged as her transition began to impact her social relationships and ways she was perceived by society. It seems possible that her depression was related to the stress from prejudice and discrimination, being read incorrectly by others, fear of transphobia, and her family's reaction. Thus, conceptualization of transgender individuals' symptoms must include an understanding of the influence of the external environment(s) on the internal experiences (mood, sense of self, for example) of the individuals. Including societal impact in one's conceptualization of the presenting concern does not necessarily mean this will be the focus of treatment.

Recommended Resources

Books and/or Articles

Brill, S., & Pepper, R. (2008). *The transgender child: A handbook for families and professionals.* San Francisco, CA: Cleis Press.

Feinberg, L. (1997). *Transgender warriors: Making history from Joan of Arc to Dennis Rodman.* Boston, MA: Beacon Press.

Krieger, I. (2011). *Helping your transgender teen: A guide for parents.* New Haven, CT: Genderwise Press.

Lev, A. (2004). *Transgender emergence: Therapeutic guidelines for working with gender variant clients and their families.* New York, NY: Haworth Clinical Practice Press.

World Professional Association for Transgender Health. (2012). *Standards of care for the health of transsexual, transgender, and gender nonconforming people* (7th version). Retrieved from http://www.wpath.org/documents/SOC%20V7%2003-17-12.pdf

Videos

Busch, T., Brokaw, C., & Pilcher, L. D. (Producers), & Anderson, J. (Director). (2003). *Normal* [Motion picture]. United States: HBO Films.

Cram, B., & Schermerhorn, C. (Producers/Directors). (1997). *You don't know Dick:* Courageous Hearts of Transsexual Men [Motion picture]. United States: Berkeley Media, LLC.

Scotta, C. (Producer), & Berliner, A. (Director). (1999). *Ma vie en rose (My life in pink)* [Motion picture]. (1999). Belgium: Haut et Court.

Smothers, T. (Producer), & Simmons, J. (Director). (2005). *TransGeneration* [Television miniseries]. United States: New Video Group.

Vachon, K., & Kolodner, E. (Producers), & Pierce, K. (Director). (1999). *Boys don't cry* [Motion picture]. United States: Fox Searchlight Pictures.

Exercises

Bornstein, K. (1998). *My gender workbook: How to become a real man, a real woman, the real you, or something entirely different.* New York, NY: Routledge.

Fiction and Nonfictional Readings

Bornstein, K. (1994). *Gender outlaw: On men, women and the rest of us.* New York, NY: Routledge.

Feinberg, L. (1993). *Stone butch blues: A novel.* Ithaca, NY: Firebrand Books.

Green, J. (2004). *Becoming a visible man.* Nashville, TN: Vanderbilt University Press.

McCloskey, D. N. (1999). *Crossing: A memoir.* Chicago, IL: University of Chicago Press.

Websites/Blogs

National Center for Transgender Equality: http://transequality.org

World Professional Association for Transgender Health: http://www.wpath.org

REFERENCE

Vanderburgh, R. (2011). *Transition and beyond: Observations on gender identity* (2nd ed.). Portland, OR: Author. Available from http://www.transtherapist.com

14

Clinical Applications in Sexual Orientation

Douglas C. Haldeman

NO HOME IN THE WORLD: THE STORY OF TONY

Case Description

Tony is a 23-year-old African American gay man who presented for psychotherapy with a variety of issues affecting his professional and personal life. At the center of his concerns is the experience of feeling the effects of racism in the gay community and homophobia in his community of color. He was raised by a single mother in a small Southern city and reports having felt like an "outsider from the very beginning." By this he means that due to his light skin tone, stereotypically effeminate mannerisms, and lack of interest in sports, Tony was pegged as a "funny boy," bullied and criticized by peers and extended family members alike. As a child, Tony was highly intelligent but not academically motivated. Like many bullied gay kids, he skipped school with some frequency. Nevertheless, he was able to get a music scholarship to a college in a big city in the Northeast and moved away from his family home immediately after high school.

Tony sees himself in a dead-end job at a big financial institution, seemingly unable to complete the last five credits he needs to get his bachelor's degree. He seems to have little sense of what he wants to ultimately do professionally. He reports feeling depressed, stating that most nights he goes home, smokes marijuana, and watches television. Few friends inhabit his social world, but his primary confidantes seem to be heterosexual women. When Tony does socialize with other gay men, it is typically at a bar, where he feels marginalized as an African American man in a predominantly White gay culture. He reports feeling "invisible" among other gay men owing to racism in the gay community, and notes with some bitterness that the privilege and status among gay men of his age cohort, whom he refers to as "skinny White bitches," is still accorded to Whites first.

At the same time, Tony feels little connection to his family of origin or community of color, owing to the treatment he received growing up. Tony states that he is viewed with suspicion by other gay men of color, which he attributes to his light skin ("I'm not Black enough for them"). In return, he is wary of other Black gay men, whom he describes as "too Jesusy."

As a thin, White (albeit older) gay man, I wondered aloud how the therapeutic relationship would be affected by our racial dynamic. Over time, it became clear that my validating Tony's observations about racism among White gay men was in and of itself useful. For the first time, he reported, a White man was acknowledging the reality of his experience. He ultimately completed his bachelor's degree and went on to a corporate position that he found challenging and interesting. Tony purchased his first home and began a more proactive social life. Although he remained distant from his family of origin, Tony slowly created a "family of choice," including, ironically, the boyfriend he thought was out of reach: a tall, White model for a local retailer.

Reflection and Discussion Questions

1. What are the historical elements of Tony's "shame core," and how would you help him to address them? What role might his guilt and shame play in his depression and social withdrawal?

2. How can a White therapist integrate racial disparities as a useful aspect of the therapeutic relationship with a gay man of color?

3. What might the therapist consider in addressing Tony's sexual health?

4. How can therapy influence Tony's seeming lack of motivation in addressing professional and personal issues?

5. To what extent does substance abuse play a role in Tony's depression and social withdrawal?
6. How might Tony develop social relationships with other gay men of color? How does Tony connect with a predominantly White gay community?
7. What strategies might be most useful in empowering Tony to move from a victim mentality to that of a survivor?

Brief Analysis of the Case

Tony shares concerns common to many gay men of color: namely, there is a lack of connection with the predominantly White gay community and a sense of rejection or marginalization from his community of origin. This is understandable, given the difficulty many cultures of color have with individuals who are attracted to the same sex as well as the racism evident in the gay community. Not feeling at home in either place, to say nothing of the dominant heterocentric White culture, Tony feels isolated and unmotivated. Some of the next points are key in addressing Tony's depression and encouraging his proactive growth.

• The role of insidious trauma in Tony's history is a key element of his depression. Acknowledging the residual pain from early life of having been labeled a "sissy boy" with no safe refuge at school or home is powerful in and of itself but also mirrors his current life, in which he feels that there is nowhere to turn.

• As a result, Tony engages in self-destructive behaviors (excessive use of marijuana and alcohol) that need to be addressed. It is not just a matter of working to reduce or eliminate the abuse of chemicals: Good health behaviors (exercise, reasonable diet, and sleep regulation) need to be installed in the repertoire. In Tony's case, starting an exercise program was helpful in improving his mood and increasing his motivation level.

• According to the Centers for Disease Control and Prevention, the highest risk group for new HIV infections is young gay men of color. The reasons for this are not defined, but it is speculated that men in this group feel marginalized and will put their health at risk in order to have sexual or romantic connections with other men. In Tony's case, his normal desire to develop sexual and romantic relationships led to his engaging in unprotected sex on several occasions. This dangerous tendency was addressed in therapy and ultimately understood to be a function of his negative self-concept.

• All of these issues affected Tony's self-concept, which was very negative at the outset. Although a very fit and attractive young man, Tony saw himself as undesirable and unlikely to find a boyfriend. He carried the scars of a youth in which he was bullied and marginalized by his own peer group and family. Tony was reluctant to socialize, particularly with men whom he regarded as "out of his league." Slowly, as his trauma was acknowledged and his frustration with the gay community validated, Tony was able to focus on proactive behaviors. Standing at the intersection of racism and sexual prejudice is difficult, to say the least. Nonetheless, Tony gradually was able to access his strengths (health, intellect, social competence) in identifying those behaviors that are under his control. The result was a more satisfying professional and personal life. He did start to develop friendships with other African American gay men, which was important to him.

• A key factor in Tony's recovery was the shift in experiencing his own masculinity. Having been made to feel inferior in early life and feeling disconnected from the gay community created in Tony a sense of being "less than" a "real man." It was important to deconstruct his internalized feeling of inadequacy by challenging the attitudes Tony had internalized from a homo-negative family and peer group. As a result, Tony came to create a sense of being a man on his own terms, not the internalized messages from a hostile cultural environment.

These observations condense several years of work with Tony. To his credit, he was able to accomplish a great deal, owing to his own heretofore untapped capacity for positive action, fostered by an unconditionally supportive therapeutic relationship.

Recommended Resources

Books and/or Articles

American Psychological Association. (2012). Guidelines for psychological practice with lesbian, gay and bisexual clients. *American Psychologist, 67*(1), 10–42.

Cole, E. (2009). Intersectionality and research in psychology. *American Psychologist, 64,* 170–180.

Greene, B. (2007). Delivering ethical psychological services to lesbian, gay and bisexual clients. In K. J. Bieschke, R. M. Perez, & K. A. DeBord (Eds.), *Handbook of counseling and psychotherapy with lesbian, gay and bisexual clients* (2nd ed., pp. 181–199). Washington, DC: APA Books.

Nettles, R., & Balter, R. (Eds.). (2012). *Multiple minority identities: Applications for practice, research and training.* New York, NY: Springer.

Ortiz, F. (2009). Spirituality and psychotherapy: A gay Latino client. In M. Gallardo & B. McNeill (Eds.), *Intersections of multiple identities* (pp. 137–173). New York, NY: Routledge.

Fiction Reading

Baldwin, J. (1956). *Giovanni's room.* New York, NY: Dial Press.

Boykin, K. (2012). *For colored boys who have considered suicide when the rainbow is still not enough.* New York, NY: Magnus Press.

Riggs, M. (1991). In E. Hemphill (Ed.), *Brother to brother: Collected writings of black gay men* (pp. 189–205 and 253–257). Los Angeles, CA: Alyson Press.

Videos

Freeman, B. (Producer), & Riggs, M. (Director). (2008). *Tongues untied* [Motion picture]. United States: Frameline.

Carlson, J. (Producer & director), & Haldeman, D. (2008). *Working with gay male clients: A young man of color* [DVD]. Washington, DC: APA Videos.

MISSION IMPOSSIBLE: THE STORY OF BETH

The conflict between sexual orientation and religion has been well documented and can sometimes be the source of other symptomatic concerns. The next case looks at one aspect of this conflict, in particular resolving the harm done in attempts to change sexual orientation in the service of religious doctrine. This case highlights the particular vulnerability of persons in homonegative religious and familial environments who have a history of abuse.

Case Description

Beth, age 42, is employed as a nursing administrator at a private hospital. Since early childhood, she has belonged to a nondenominational charismatic Christian church. Her spiritual life has involved weekly church attendance, talking in tongues, and what she describes as "unconscious spells of religious ecstasy." She has been married for 20 years, and the couple has two teenage children. Beth reports that her marriage has been very unsatisfactory, having been physically and sexually abused by her alcoholic husband for much of their time together. However, when consulting her pastor about leaving her husband, Beth has consistently been advised to "submit to the will of God" and that she must obey her husband. She states that she has always experienced same-sex desires but never acted on them. Still, after years of abuse at the hands of her husband, she reports having longed for the touch of another woman.

Beth met a woman two years ago at a professional conference. This woman, an out lesbian, developed a romantic relationship with Beth, and the two fell in love. Beth reported having felt conflicted about the relationship from the start, given that she had never had sex outside her martial relationship, much less with another woman. Nevertheless, Beth characterized her new same-sex relationship as nothing short of a revelation, because she felt so loved and cared for by her female partner. Beth did not disclose the relationship to her husband but did discuss it with her pastor. Predictably, her pastor responded with outrage, telling her that she was a "homosexual adultress" and that she would be damned if she did not end the relationship and change her same-sex feelings.

In an effort to be compliant, Beth attempted to cut off the relationship with her lover (Ellen) but was never able to stay away from her for very long, so in love was she. On one such hiatus from the relationship with Ellen, Beth's guilt compelled her to seek consultation with her pastor to "cure" her of her homosexual desires. These meetings, which primarily involved prayer and threats on the part of the pastor, were unsuccessful. Finally, Beth was forced to lie down on the church altar while the pastor and several congregants screamed at her in an effort to "exorcise the evil homosexual demon." As the ritual became more bizarre, some of the participants flogged her with straw and consumed carbonated beverages in order to belch on her, which was said to be an effort to exorcise her evil lesbian demons.

Abusive and strange as it was, this ritual was the turning point for Beth, who decided once and for all that the religious environment in which she had been living was both wrong and dangerous. She left her husband and her church and moved in with Ellen. Beth reports being very happy with the relationship. She presents for therapy struggling with residual guilt as well as posttraumatic reactions following her treatment at the hands of her former pastor. Beth also seeks to redefine herself at age 42: Does the fact that she is in a same-sex relationship mean that she is a lesbian? What, if anything, will she do to replace her former church home? How does she adapt to a brand-new social network? These are some of the questions on Beth's agenda as she begins psychotherapy to heal some of the trauma of a sexist socioreligious world as well as the reverberations of failed reparative therapy.

Reflection and Discussion Questions

1. What happens in sexual orientation change efforts (SOCE) that could be traumatizing?
2. What is involved therapeutically in addressing the potential issues stemming from SOCE?
3. Beth has decided to separate herself from her husband and her former religious tradition but expresses guilt at leaving her children and the loss of her former church. What are the implications for treatment?
4. What is the role of guilt and shame in Beth's affective discomfort?
5. What can be helpful in addressing Beth's general history of abuse and oppression, particularly with respect to her self-concept?
6. How do we distinguish the related concepts of sexual orientation and sexual identity?

Brief Analysis of the Case

• This case of recovery from SOCE is interesting because of the odd methods (even for SOCE) used on a subject who is vulnerable by virtue of her religious belief system, her years in an abusive marriage, and her trust in a crazy and abusive clergyman. Nonetheless, owing in large part to the support of a committed same-sex partner, Beth comes to the realization that there is nothing inherently sinful or evil about her relationship with Ellen. She comes to therapy ready to deal with the effect of the oppressive forces in her life (abusive husband, institutional proscriptions against same-sex attraction, threats of eternal hellfire), and works hard in treatment to rescript her view of herself in a loving same-sex relationship.

• After months of unsuccessful prayer and a bizarre and humiliating ritual, it became clear to Beth that it was impossible—and unnecessary—for her to change her same-sex attractions. She continued to struggle with guilt (having failed SOCE) for a time but was, as a health care professional, persuaded by data that indicate there is no scientific basis for the efficacy or safety of SOCE. Reality testing in therapy helped Beth deal with her situational guilt. Additionally, Beth's case required a general focus on recovery from physical and sexual trauma at the hands of her husband. Like many survivors, she continued to experience free-floating anxiety, variations in mood, and finally anger. Normalizing these feelings and encouraging her to take whatever she defined as corrective action (in this case, divorcing her husband) moved Beth toward healing in this complex area.

◆ The consequences of SOCE can be extreme for many: chronic depression and sometimes suicidality, disrupted intimate relationships, poor self-esteem, and a sense of inadequacy as a woman or man. The recovery from these painful issues has to do with providing education and an alternative perspective that is compatible with the individual's life. It is as if the therapist helps the client by engaging the prefrontal cortex to develop a different, more positive script about same-sex attraction and relationships. This script is then rehearsed cognitively as well as behaviorally activated (sex-positive exercises, same-sex socialization) so that the midbrain, where the shame and guilt are living, is successfully neutralized.

◆ SOCE survivors, almost all of whom come from conservative religious backgrounds, who are unfamiliar with the cultural norms or even resources available in the gay community sometimes need support for navigating a terrain that is foreign at best and unwelcoming at worst. Therapists cannot be expected to know everything about lesbian, gay, bisexual, and transgender communities in their areas but should have some basic familiarity with how to provide appropriate guidance and education to clients seeking inclusion.

◆ Some survivors of SOCE reject religion or spiritual practice altogether; this is, in fact, probably the norm. But some, such as Beth, seek an alternative spiritual practice for healing. To this end, she took up "compassion meditation" (applied to self and others) as well as participation in a large organization of lesbians that sponsors pagan gatherings and rituals.

◆ *Sexual orientation* and *sexual identity*, while related terms, have distinct meanings. Sexual orientation is determined by the gender to which an individual experiences sexual arousal and attraction. Sexual identity is a construct of personal analysis, generally based on sexual orientation, gender identity (sense of being male or female), and sometimes social factors. Does the fact of Beth's relationship with Ellen make her a lesbian? Only if she says so. Everyone has the authority over their own sexual identity, whatever their sexual orientation may be.

Recommended Resources

Books and/or Articles

American Psychological Association. (2009). *Appropriate therapeutic responses to sexual orientation*. Washington, DC: APA Books.

Besen, W. (2003). *Anything but straight*. New York, NY: Harrington Park Press.

Drescher, J., & Zucker, K. (Eds.). *Ex-gay research*. New York, NY: Harrington Park Press.

Haldeman, D. (1994). The practice and ethics of sexual orientation conversion therapy. *Journal of Consulting and Clinical Psychology*, 62, 221–227.

Haldeman, D. (2004). When sexual and religious orientation collide: Considerations in working with conflicted same-sex attracted male clients. *Counseling Psychologist*, 32, 691–715.

Shidlo, A., Schroeder, M., & Drescher, J. (Eds.). (2002). *Sexual conversion therapy: Ethical, clinical and research perspectives*. New York, NY: Haworth Press.

Videos

Hussung, B. (Producer), & Canino-Hussung, M., & Hussung, B. (Directors). (2008). *Chasing the devil: Inside the ex-gay movement* [Documentary]. United States: Coqui Zen Entertainment.

Racster, C., Hamsher, H., Allen, C., Grant, R., & Light, J. (Producers), & Cary, R. (Director). (2007). *Save me* [Motion picture]. United States: First Run Features.

Websites/Blogs

Wilson, C. (2012). *Gay conversion therapy devastated my family*. Retrieved from http://www.huffingtonpost.com/chana-wilson/gay-conversion-therapy_b_1625274.html

15

Clinical Applications With People in Poverty

Debbie-Ann Chambers, Lucinda Bratini, and Laura Smith

THE WHITE PICKET FENCE LIFE:
THE STORY OF MARISOL

Case Description

Marisol was a 19-year-old, heterosexual, Latina female in her freshman year at a predominantly White university in the south-central United States. She appeared somewhat older than her stated age and was dressed in fashionable clothing with neatly coiffed, long, straight hair. She presented to the university counseling center with suicidal ideation after the breakup of a five-month-long romantic relationship. However, her affect was restricted, betraying no evidence of depressed feelings. Dr. Josefina Montalvo, a young Latina psychologist in her first year of working at the university counseling center, was assigned to work with her.

Marisol's chief complaint in the initial session was the loss of her romantic relationship. Marisol tearfully reported that she was at fault for the breakup, as her boyfriend walked off after she had angrily lashed out at him for rejecting her. Dr. Montalvo wondered whether the breakup had possibly triggered deep and old wounds of loss and rejection. Marisol expressed deep guilt and shame about her display of anger to her boyfriend. Dr. Montalvo's belief was that the experience of these emotions had likely overwhelmed Marisol and triggered her suicidal ideation. Her first concern, however, was to assess Marisol's level of risk for suicide and facilitate safety planning. During the assessment, Dr. Montalvo was struck by Marisol's restricted affect and the way in which she minimized the importance of her emotional concerns. At the same time, Marisol's minimizations helped her to stave off intent to commit suicide.

In their initial meetings, Marisol shared her history with depression, persistent isolation, and suicidal ideation and attempts. Marisol explained that she had sought treatment for her depression previously. Her psychiatric history included two hospitalizations associated with suicide attempts and deliberate self-harm, the first taking place when she was 16 years old. During her second hospitalization, at 18 years old, Marisol was diagnosed with borderline personality disorder at which point her mother reprimanded her harshly for being "weak-minded."

Marisol expressed feelings of anger toward her mother, describing her as a "bad parent"; she rejected her only daughter by sending Marisol to live with her grandmother after the first hospitalization. At the same time, she "understood" her mother's decision to send her to live with her grandmother. Marisol believed that her mother had "enough" on her plate and so could not also care for a daughter with a mental illness. Her grandmother, in contrast, had cared for more than 25 foster children in the past 10 years, so her mother saw her grandmother as someone who could deal with problem behavior. Marisol then reported in a low, hushed voice that her grandmother's fostering of children was not due to a love for children but because the funding she received as a foster parent provided her with the financial means to care for her own four children.

Whenever Dr. Montalvo validated the complex feelings associated with these experiences, Marisol quickly moved to a new topic. She attributed her continued struggle with depression to the fact that treatment had not and could not help her. As a result she no longer sought a "cure" for her depression. She had grown to see her symptoms as something she was "doomed" to have to live with for the rest of her life.

In subsequent sessions, Dr. Montalvo explored Marisol's developmental history and its influence on her experience with depression. Recollections of her childhood were not often expressed, but when they were they conveyed her family's struggle with poverty. Marisol grew up and continued to live in one of the poorest communities in the south-central United States. She was the only child of a single immigrant mother whose financial struggles led to numerous evictions, blackouts due to unpaid electric bills, and limited health care or child care. Marisol's mother also worked as an overnight security guard. For that reason, Marisol was often left unattended or with relatives or family friends. By the time Marisol was 7 years old, she had learned to care for herself by walking home from school alone and cooking her own meals. Beginning at the age of 9, Marisol was repeatedly sexually abused by a family friend. Marisol revealed this information to her mother, who responded by angrily calling her a liar. It was around this time that Marisol began engaging in deliberate self-harm behavior by cutting.

As Marisol described her experiences, she reported having intense feelings of anger toward her mother yet her affect remained restricted. In one particular session, Dr. Montalvo attempted to join Marisol's anger, empathizing with how painful this must have been for her and how hard it is to talk with her about these experiences. Dr. Montalvo wondered aloud about secondary feelings of hurt and pain related to the rejection and neglect she experienced from her mother, the pressure of having to care for herself at such a young age, and the dangers she encountered as result. Marisol, instead of being comforted by Dr. Montalvo's joining, became irritated. She responded by stating that it was useless to sit with or explore her feelings. She further said that what she wanted was to do was to learn skills to better communicate with her romantic partners. By the end of this session, Marisol had become distant and requested to end the session early.

It was after this session that Dr. Montalvo recognized she had dominated their sessions with her interpretations of Marisol's depression. Dr. Montalvo realized that she failed to co-construct treatment goals with Marisol. In the session that followed, she invited Marisol to discuss her reactions to their work thus far. Marisol was not hesitant to share that she felt misunderstood. She spoke of feeing perceived as unfortunate, poor, and neglected and that, like her previous White therapists, Dr. Montalvo associated her with people from "the ghetto."

Marisol was adamant that she was not like other people from the ghetto and spoke with confidence of her experiences as a high-achieving student. She had been bused to middle school and high school in an affluent middle-class community about an hour outside of the city. She proudly emphasized the clothing and shoes that her mother managed to buy her so that she looked as much like the other kids as possible. Her mother also relaxed her hair for this purpose. "She taught me to always fit in like that," she said, adding "I'm really middle class—we just live near the hood." At this point, it struck Dr. Montalvo that she had not explored with Marisol what it was like for her to be in a predominantly White school or how she felt about working with a Latina therapist. Marisol briefly talked about her current struggle making friends but denied the importance of race to her struggle.

After several months of therapy, when entering her second year in college, Marisol established a "sort of" romantic relationship with a male classmate. She had developed an acquaintance with a popular, academically accomplished White student named Matthew. She described the bright future she could enjoy with this young man, specifying the neighborhood they could live in, the house they could own, and the trips they could take together. When discussing Michael, she appeared much brighter and happier than Dr. Montalvo had ever seen her. She also disclosed that she had always wished to have biracial children. Dr. Montalvo was struck with how enthusiastic she appeared while discussing what Marisol called her "white picket fence life."

Over subsequent sessions, it appeared that the young man was not interested in a relationship with Marisol, avoided her, rejected her advances, and distanced himself from the group of friends they shared. Marisol suggested that she was at fault for his distancing; she pathologized her interpersonal style by attributing his rejection to her lack of self-control and her inability to behave like "a lady" in his presence. Marisol wondered whether she was good enough for this young man, whether she spoke well enough, dressed well enough, or acted well enough for him. In one session, Dr. Montalvo shared with Marisol her own feeling of sadness with how hard it must be for Marisol to constantly feel at fault, "It's like you're always doing something wrong, and like you always have to change." Marisol seemed deflated and quietly reiterated that she was "at fault." She shared that she could not imagine it being any different. This was the first time Marisol openly expressed vulnerable feelings without jumping to the next topic. They spent much of the session sitting in silence as they considered where this negative self-image could have come from.

Marisol continued to struggle to identify the roots of her experiences. She did not want to blame others for her faults or weaknesses, and she began to present as guarded and withdrawn. She seemed tense and avoided eye contact, and she shared that she felt hopeless when she thought of lack of progress in her relationship with Matthew. He had continued to ignore her calls and attempts at connection. Dr. Montalvo empathized with her sadness and wondered what it was like to share these feelings with her, a Latina therapist. Marisol simply shrugged her shoulders and returned to talking about her dreams of a life with Matthew.

Dr. Montalvo was left wondering to herself about the meaning of this fantasy relationship with Matthew as well as the dynamics of their relationship. She recognized that the session in which she and Marisol processed their relationship and their shared identities had proved difficult for Marisol. Feeling stuck, Dr. Montalvo sought consultation from a peer supervision group at the counseling center. One of the senior clinicians, Dr. James, a White woman, listened to a description of the case and said, "I think you are overlooking one of the more obvious explanations. The client is borderline and has already had two hospitalizations. She seems to have pulled things together for a short time but is now becoming delusional and is showing signs of regression into a more decompensated state. Let's get this client set up with someone for an extended assessment, and then we can go from there."

Reflection and Discussion Questions

1. What is the role of poverty in the client's presenting problem?
2. How does the client's social class status directly and indirectly affect her presenting concern and her ability to heal from it?
3. Dr. Montalvo sensed that something was going on in her relationship with Marisol that was impacting their work. What do you think it might be?
4. What was the meaning of Marisol's self-reported middle-class identification?
5. Dr. James accurately made reference to Marisol's case history. What thoughts do you have about her recommendations?
6. Do you think the diagnosis of borderline personality disorder applies to Marisol? How can social class, race-ethnicity, and gender affect the diagnosis?
7. What meanings could be attributed to Marisol's fantasies about her new college acquaintance?

Brief Analysis of the Case

• As this case exemplifies, poverty can be revealed as an aspect of treatment in ways that are both direct and indirect. Marisol conveyed her family's struggles as she shared some of her family history. While she did not speak about their migration story, Latina/o immigration has been linked to various forms of sociopolitical oppression and economic hardship. At the same time, U.S ideals have propagated the "American Dream," leading to internalization of notions of class mobility. However, in the case of Marisol's family, the necessity of economic survival meant that her mother had to work numerous jobs, late nights, and long hours at minimum pay. The limited resources available to poor and working-class people have a direct impact on their daily experiences.

• The impact of poverty is heard in Marisol's story as well as in the process of therapy, which points to her experience and possible socialization in terms of emotional expression. hooks (1993) contended that in the context of oppression, emotional repression has become a strategy for survival. hooks examined the ways in which African American parents in the apartheid South had internalized the norms of their masters, represented not only in the methods used for punishment but also in practices of denying comfort, consolation, and a space to express vulnerable emotions. Similarly, Marisol's experience as a survivor of sexual abuse was denied and invalidated. Her attempts to make her sadness visible by engaging in self-harm behavior were also unacknowledged.

• Given her developmental experiences, Marisol learned to guard and protect her emotions from others. This self-protective strategy may be crucial for clients for whom emotional expression has meant lack of safety. In Marisol's case, not containing her emotions has resulted in severe consequences. Failing to recognize and understand oppression as a pathogenic agent, and so engaging in the practice of pathologizing individuals, may lead therapists to utilize psychotherapeutic tools that further oppress poor and working-class clients of color. As Belle and Doucet (2003) discussed, poverty and oppression must be addressed not only as contextual factors but as direct causes of emotional trauma.

• The impact of classism and poverty can be seen through Marisol's internalizations of the signs and symbols of the material life she dreams of, a life that is different from her own.

• Being poor and working class is not a topic openly discussed; nonetheless, Marisol expressed some of the cultural messages she had internalized about class. Her ideas of success and happiness included the dominant beliefs regarding economic privileges, ownership, and status. Internalized classism is also reflected in her denial of group membership and her anger and blame toward members of her working-class community.

• Another issue that arises in this case is the way that professionals recognize, understand, and speak about poverty and its sequelae. For Dr. James, the answers are obvious and tied to the use of diagnostic nomenclature. Certainly, the symptoms that resulted in Marisol's prior hospitalizations were real and serious, but to move too quickly toward conventional labels and assessment tools may be to overlook the impact of poverty—both physically and emotionally—in a client's life. Professionals must be aware as well as challenge the classist, racist, and patriarchal underpinnings of conventional diagnostic categories.

• Therapists, like people in every profession, wear their social class in sessions both literally and figuratively. When clients struggle with the meaning of class membership in their lives, therapists must be aware that the messages they convey about their own class status will likely impact the therapeutic relationship. Everything from our clothing to the bottle of purchased water on our desk may convey messages about class privilege. Few of us believe we hold negative views of working-class or poor people, yet, as Leondar-Wright (2005) pointed out, classist attitudes sometimes can be discerned in disdain for people who do not exercise, for people with Southern accents, or for country music fans.

Recommended Resources

Books and/or Articles

Bourdieu, P. (1984). *Distinction: A social critique of the judgment of taste.* Cambridge, MA: Harvard University Press.

Chalifoux, B. (1996). *Speaking up: White working class women in therapy.* In M. Hill & E. D. Rothblum (Eds.), *Classism and feminist therapy* (pp. 25–34). New York, NY: Harrington Park.

Gonzalez, J. (2001). *Harvest of empire: A history of Latinos in America.* New York, NY: Penguin Books.

hooks, b. (1994). *Outlaw culture: Resisting representations.* New York, NY: Routledge.

Smith, L. (2009). Enhancing training and practice in the context of poverty. *Training and Education in Professional Psychology, 3,* 84–93.

Smith, L., Chambers, D., & Bratini, L. (2009). When oppression is the pathogen: The participatory development of socially just mental health practice. *American Journal of Orthopsychiatry, 79,* 159–168.

Novels

Cruz, A. (2001). *Soledad.* New York, NY: Simon & Schuster.

Diaz, J. (2007). *The brief and wondrous life of Oscar Wao.* New York, NY: Riverhead Books Penguin.

Leblanc, A. N. (2003). *Random family: Love, drugs, trouble and coming of age in the Bronx.* New York, NY: Scribner.

Morrison, T. (1970). *The bluest eye.* New York, NY: Pocket Books.

REFERENCES

Belle, D., & Doucet, J. (2003). Poverty, inequality, and discrimination as sources of depression among U.S. women. *Psychology of Women Quarterly, 27,* 101–113.

hooks, b. (1993). *Sisters of the yam: Black women and self-recovery.* Cambridge, MA: South End Press.

Leondar-Wright, B. (2005). *Class matters.* Gabriola Island, Canada: New Society.

DO YOU HAVE EYES TO SEE ME?
THE STORY OF MICHELLE

Case Description

Michelle was a 37-year-old, employed, African American, single mother of two children. She was assigned to see Dr. Hall, an African American woman in her early 30s and a new psychologist in a community-based mental health clinic. Dr. Hall was Michelle's fourth therapist in the clinic over a span of years; Michelle's previous therapists all left for various reasons. Working with several therapists over the span of treatment was a commonplace occurrence in a clinic that struggled to meet the overwhelming needs of the surrounding community. Sometimes the graduate student trainees would leave at the end of their rotation; however, staff therapists also tended to leave after a year or two.

When Dr. Hall met Michelle, her client appeared depressed; she had a noticeable lack of energy and a defeated posture. In initial sessions, Michelle described a life of grinding poverty. She became homeless when she was 12 years old after her mother left her abusive father and fled across state with her three children. Michelle and her family then moved around to many shelters for several years before finally finding housing. During those years, Michelle took on the role of parent to her younger brothers because her mother needed to be away for long hours working in low-paying domestic jobs. Michelle said that she understood that her mother needed to leave her abusive father and needed to work very hard to support the family. However, Michelle also talked about missing the comforts of her rural, close-knit, Southern community, and described becoming stressed in her late teens as she witnessed her younger brothers become involved in neighborhood gangs.

Dr. Hall explored Michelle's developmental history and interpreted its role in Michelle's current depression. She worked with Michelle to introduce potential insights, such as the idea that her depression was related to unexpressed anger toward her parents, guilt regarding the circumstances of the siblings whom she had "coparented," and/or feeling the overwhelming burden of being the "good" child. To Dr. Hall, these insights represented progress in Michelle's therapy, yet Michelle was still visibly depressed and dejected in appearance. Dr. Hall considered to herself the many possibilities for Michelle's enduring depression, including secondary gain resistance.

Finally, in one session, Dr. Hall asked Michelle about her reactions to the treatment thus far. Michelle hesitantly responded that many therapists had already explored similar things with her. At this point, it dawned on Dr. Hall that she had not explored with Michelle what it was like for her to be in a clinic where she so often switched therapists. As she did so, Michelle began to open up about her life circumstances and how they had affected her freedom to make decisions. One decision that she could not make for herself, for example, was to enter therapy with a private practitioner. Michelle spoke about her inability to afford the life she wanted, the stresses of being a single mother, the constrictions of working for minimum wage in a retail store with little freedom to arrange her schedule as she needed, of not getting adequate child support, and the catch-22 of being denied some benefits because she made "too much money." Michelle described feeling invisible to others, as if she had fallen through a huge hole in the street that others were simply pretending was not there. Dr. Hall acknowledged to Michelle that it seemed that she too had ignored the hole that Michelle had fallen through and that possibly Michelle felt like Dr. Hall did not really see her.

After this point in the treatment, Michelle became increasingly open about her current life and, in one session, shared that after several years of fighting, she had eventually won child support, only to discover that the back support, which amounted to thousands of dollars, would be paid at a rate of less than $100 a month. Dr. Hall was visibly angry and began counting on her fingers how long getting the full amount owed would take. Michelle's affect lifted, and she laughed out loud as she said that this had been her exact reaction. Dr. Hall remarked on the false stereotypes of single mothers of color and told Michelle that she believed her story typified how classist society can be in their stereotypes. Michelle told Dr. Hall that she felt moved by her genuine expression of anger to Michelle's plight.

In subsequent sessions, Michelle revealed that she had felt like a bad mother for not being able to better provide for her children. Michelle said that her son's school had threatened to call the local child services bureau because her son was often late. Fearful of asking her boss for time off to take her children to school, Michelle had to rely on the help of a neighbor, who, in dealing with her own restricted schedule, brought Michelle's son to school late. Michelle also revealed that she had accrued a huge debt because of late rent payments and had been hopeful that the back child support would help with her debt. Dr. Hall assisted Michelle by investigating various case management and homelessness prevention programs. Although the search ultimately was unsuccessful, Michelle reported that she felt strengthened by Dr. Hall's support and got the courage to advocate for herself to her landlord to reduce her debt and buy herself extra time to pay the back rent. Michelle also advocated for herself at work. Although her boss did not give her the flexibility she needed, a coworker helped by filling in for the first 20 minutes of Michelle's shift so that she could take her child to school.

The issues of Michelle's past kept resurfacing in session. In one particular session, Michelle said that she was not sure whether the guilt she sometimes felt was due to a wish to be the "good" child, referring to one of Dr. Hall's insights from an earlier session. This was the first time Michelle had openly disagreed with a therapist. Michelle and Dr. Hall then wondered together where else this guilt could be coming from. Michelle described growing up in a church where sin and hell were often preached, especially around issues of sexuality. That session revealed the guilt that Michelle felt for being a mother out of wedlock and how she sometimes wondered whether her poverty and her children's father leaving her were punishment from God. Dr. Hall empathized with Michelle's deep feelings of guilt and shame.

In subsequent sessions, Dr. Hall actively worked to redress the issue of shame by acknowledging the pain of Michelle's shame and accepting her feelings, using their relationship to point out Michelle's strengths and working to increase Michelle's self-compassion by discussing the very real constraints of a life of poverty. In later sessions, she also wondered aloud about whether there were alternative religious messages that Michelle had ever come across to suggest that poverty was *not* a punishment from God. Michelle grappled with this for a while, but the question allowed her to be more open with others about her belief of God's punishment. This led to a friend suggesting literature to her about liberation theology, which posited a preferential option for the poor.

In the ensuing sessions, Michelle was more animated. Her posture grew more confident, she laughed occasionally, and she began to advocate for herself more, both in her job and in her personal life. She revealed that some of her former therapists had challenged her on not doing more with her life, with one therapist even asking her why she had passively allowed so many things to happen to her. Michelle had not felt encouraged to share her economic struggles, anticipating that she would be blamed just as she had blamed herself. Michelle timidly revealed to Dr. Hall a long-held dream to pursue a master's degree in education, with a specific focus of working with children in poverty. She told Dr. Hall that she had not been sure that she deserved to get a master's degree but that she now felt some permission to stop ignoring her dream. Michelle said that while she was fearful of not being accepted into a program, she no longer felt undeserving.

Reflection and Discussion Questions

1. What is the role of poverty in the client's presenting problem?
2. How does her social class status directly and indirectly affect her presenting concern and her ability to heal from it?
3. How did you think the social class differences between client and therapist may have initially manifested within the working alliance and affected the treatment?

4. What different ways can you think of by which the therapist could have addressed potential social class issues?

5. What do you think of the therapist's initial insights into the client's concerns?

6. What do you think of the therapist's disclosure of her own anger about the delay in the award of the client's child support?

7. The therapist raised the issue of stereotypes regarding single mothers of color. Where else do you see the operations of stereotyping, classism, and/or racism in this client's life?

8. How do issues of religion and social class seem to intersect and play out in this client's life?

9. How would you have reacted or responded to the client's disclosure of her guilt about being a single mother and her fear that her poverty was a punishment for that?

10. What do you think of the client's coming to feel more deserving of a master's degree? What might have helped contribute to this?

Brief Analysis of the Case

• This case highlights the impact of psychological service delivery options (or lack thereof) offered in poor communities. As a low-income woman, Michelle was fortunate in having access to the services of a community-based clinic. Nevertheless, the high turnover of therapists available there resulted in a revolving-door experience for clients like Michelle. This service configuration has the potential to reenact painful feelings of powerlessness in poor clients. It also means that poor clients are frequently subject to revolving-door treatment as clinicians leave to take better-paying jobs or graduate students complete practica and move on.

• Poverty impacts emotional well-being at material, emotional, and social levels—dimensions of life that are interrelated with each other. Clearly, when a client is homeless or in danger of homelessness, emotional well-being is compromised in a tangible way. Moreover, status as a person living in poverty brings with it great social stigma. Low-income people are shown to us via the media as ignorant, immoral, and dysfunctional; poor children have already internalized these images of their families and communities. The resulting experience of social exclusion and marginalization that poor people face has the potential to impact their sense of worth and agency in the same way that any other form of internalized oppression can.

◆ As deeply as poverty pervades people's social and interpersonal experiences, a person is never *only* poor. In other words, poverty (and, correspondingly, class privilege) always exists at intersections with other identities, which may be manifested within characteristic manifestations of classism, racism, sexism, and/or other forms of oppression.

◆ Through the experience of multiple oppressions such as classism, racism, and sexism, socially marginalized people become chronically disconnected by repeated experiences of invalidation. In this case, Michelle described feeling as if she had fallen through a hole in the street that others were pretending was not there. Such experiences can foster a sense of anger, shame, and a consequent hiding of the self. Part of the role of the therapist is to facilitate a mutually empathic and genuine relationship in which the client can feel encouraged to voice his or her disavowed experiences and feelings.

Recommended Resources

Books and/or Articles

Belle, D., & Doucet, J. (2003). Poverty, inequality and discrimination as sources of depression among women. *Psychology of Women Quarterly, 27,* 101–113.

Ehrenreich, B. (2001). *Nickel and dimed: On (not) getting by in America.* New York, NY: Henry Holt.

Hays, S. (2003). *Flat broke with children: Women in the age of welfare reform.* Oxford, England: Oxford University Press.

hooks, b. (2000). *Where we stand: Class matters.* New York, NY: Routledge.

Jordan, J. V. (2000). The role of mutual empathy in relational/cultural therapy. *Journal of Clinical Psychology, 56,* 1005–1016.

Jordan, J. V. (2010). *Relational-cultural therapy.* Washington, DC: American Psychological Association Press.

Smith, L. (2010). *Psychology, poverty, and the end of social exclusion: Putting our practice to work.* New York, NY: Teachers College Press.

Walker, M., & Rosen, W. B. (Eds.). (2004). *How connections heal: Stories from relational-cultural therapy.* New York, NY: Guilford Press.

16

Clinical Applications With Persons With Disabilities

Rhoda Olkin

WHY DIDN'T YOU TELL ME YOU WERE IN A WHEELCHAIR? THE STORY OF JOLEEN

Case Description

Joleen is a 22-year-old African American woman, currently finishing her first year of community college. Four years ago Joleen was in a car accident which injured her spine at the T12 level. She was in the hospital, transferred to a rehabilitation facility for about five months, then moved back with her parents. Prior to her accident she had been living with a boyfriend, but he broke up with her after her accident. Now she lives with her parents near campus and is able to wheel to school. In the rehabilitation facility, she felt abused by one of the staff members. For example, he would leave her on the toilet and go take his coffee break, sometimes not returning for half an hour. If she complained, he would get surly, serve her meal last after all the other patients got fed, or forget her pain medication.

Money from the insurance of the driver who hit her car paid for a wheelchair, and the state Department of Rehabilitation was paying for community college. Her father made changes to the home as best he could to make it more wheelchair accessible. However, Joleen cannot use the restroom independently because it is too small, nor can she leave the apartment by herself because she needs assistance with the front door and the lock due to more limited arm strength and finger dexterity.

Joleen contacted a counselor because she felt overwhelmed, ambivalent about her dependence on her parents, and frustrated in creating her own life. She has a new boyfriend, whom she met at college. He is African American, and his mother has diabetes. Several members of his extended family have various disabilities, and a cousin used a wheelchair after a gunshot wound. He was attracted to Joleen because she asked questions in class and liked to discuss ideas. They dated for several months before wanting to become sexual, but since sexuality required some planning, privacy, and a comfortable place, they have difficulty finding space for themselves. Joleen's parents like the boyfriend, but Joleen feels unable to ask them to give the young couple privacy to have sex, and when she asked them if her boyfriend could "spend the night," they said no. Thus, Joleen and her boyfriend want to make a plan to live together, but there are numerous practical limitations. Her mother voices many concerns about Joleen living away from home, and Joleen has a hard time telling which fears are realistic, which fears she shares, and which fears are just her mother's worries: "Her voice is in my head, you know?"

When Joleen arrived for her first session, the Asian male therapist was clearly startled to see her in a wheelchair. He was flustered as Joleen maneuvered her wheelchair from the waiting room into his office, and it immediately became clear he would have to rearrange several chairs, a small table, and a lamp to allow her to enter the room. He immediately blurted out, "Oh, you didn't tell me you were in a wheelchair!" to which Joleen replied, "I didn't tell you I was African American either. Is this a problem?" The therapist realized he was out of line and apologized, which is probably why Joleen stayed for the session. He did not know to ask Joleen whether she wanted to transfer to a chair (she did not), so he moved all the chairs out of the way, allowing Joleen to position her wheelchair so she faced his seat. He started the session asking Joleen why she was "wheelchair bound" (the term used by the disability community is *wheelchair user*) and when she said she had a T12-level injury, he asked her what that meant. Thus, the first few minutes of therapy were spent with Joleen educating the therapist about levels of injury and what they meant in terms of functional impairments. The therapist further compounded his error by asking if the boyfriend also had a disability, implying that an able-bodied man would not be interested in a woman with spinal cord injury (SCI).

Based on vocabulary and grade history, Joleen would seem to be above-average intelligence. However, she is struggling in some of her current classes and has trouble concentrating on homework. She has numerous interests, including politics and current events, movies, and music. She played basketball prior to her accident, but since then is less interested in watching sports. She is not clinically depressed but does seem despondent and hopeless about her ability to change her living situation. Also, she wonders why her boyfriend is attracted to her, if this is related to his mother's arthritis and diabetes and the fact that he often took care of her, and if this is "normal and healthy" for a relationship. When the two of them are out and about together, most people assume her boyfriend is her caregiver. Staff persons often ask him about her ("What would she like for lunch?") so that she feels invisible. At first he was intrigued by how stigma attached to disability outweighed stereotypes about Black men, but more recently he gets impatient and directs people to talk to Joleen directly. Joleen appreciates how he manages the stigma of disability by proxy and believes this bodes well for their future together. However, she is aware of all that her parents do for her and wonders if he is truly ready to take this on.

Reflection and Discussion Questions

1. How much knowledge and information do you have about spinal cord injuries? As a therapist, if you worked with Joleen and had little information about this medical condition, what would you do?

2. What qualifications or experiences do you have in working with people with disabilities? Are you comfortable in their presence? If not, what could you do to become more comfortable?

3. If you were to anticipate the types of psychological issues most likely to be raised by a person with an SCI, what would they be? What impressions, beliefs, attitudes, and stereotypes do you hold about people

who use wheelchairs? Do these beliefs, attitudes, and stereotypes differ for other types of disabilities, such as blindness or deafness?

4. Given Joleen's age, ethnicity, and disability, is it appropriate for her to be living at home? Do you assume she will want to work toward greater independence?

5. Suppose Joleen cancels her fourth session at the last minute because of a breakdown of assistive technology. Would you charge her for the session? What might you say at the beginning of the next session?

6. What assumptions do you make about Joleen's boyfriend and his attraction to a woman in a wheelchair? Do you wonder if something is wrong with him, and why he is attracted to Joleen?

7. Suppose Joleen and her partner inquired about their sexual relationship and ability to obtain enjoyment. What advice would you give the couple regarding sexual techniques for a person with an SCI? What assumptions do you make about Joleen's sexuality? Are these based on ethnicity, gender, or disability? Which is more paramount to you as you think about sexuality?

8. When Joleen is "despondent and hopeless," do you mirror those feelings, and likewise feel that her future is hopeless? What possible life do you imagine for Joleen? Does this picture change if she were White? Japanese American? Mexican American?

Brief Analysis of the Case

• *Is your office accessible?* The answer to this is not a simple yes or no and differs for various disabilities (e.g., physical, visual, hearing). Areas to be assessed include handicapped parking, proximity to public transportation, the entrance to the building (ramp and automatic door opener), restroom, elevator, and finally your own office. Joleen is under no obligation to tell you about her disability prior to the first session and is within her rights to expect your office to be accessible. It is the responsibility of therapists to familiarize themselves with what accessibility means.

• *Do your homework.* It is not reasonable to expect Joleen to educate the therapist about SCIs. Do some reading as soon as you know about the injury. Almost everyone with an SCI knows the level of the injury (e.g., T3, C4) and whether the lesion is complete or partial; learning this information about the client in an early session will give you an idea of his or her functional impairments. Later you can learn more specialized information first from reading, then from the client (e.g., pain, sexual functioning, bowel programs). There is the possibility of an undiagnosed traumatic brain injury (TBI) related to the accident that caused the SCI that was overlooked in the immediate medical emergency. Cerebral swelling may have prevented assessment, and a TBI may not have manifested itself until after discharge. Consider simple assessments regarding cognitive abilities. Posttraumatic stress disorder is more frequent post-SCI than had been realized but should not be assumed to be present—the person may have no memory of the trauma. Time since injury is an important factor because the adjustment process for SCI is very intense for the first few years. Living and aging with an SCI often brings new decrements in functioning or new medical problems. Wheelchair users are more susceptible to pneumonia, decubitus ulcers, and bladder infections.

• *Abuse.* As a woman with a significant disability, Joleen is susceptible to various sources of abuse, which, if present, is likely to endure for a longer period than would be the case for a woman without a disability. The abuse might take disability-specific forms, and the SCI may make leaving an abusive situation harder, due to dependence on daily physical assistance.

• *Models of disability.* The therapist should become familiar with the three major models of disability (the moral, medical, and social models), adopt a disability-affirmative stance, and be open to the model of the client. A mismatch in models, language, and approach could cause a rupture in the therapy.

• *Assistive technology.* It is important for the therapist not to stare, or to conspicuously avoid staring, but to see the person, not the wheelchair, as primary. Never mention that you know someone in a chair, unless it is you personally or your parent. Offer to shake hands, as people with disabilities report the reluctance of others to touch them. Clients using electric wheelchairs may shift position of the wheelchair during sessions, which will make a slight whirring noise that should not become a distraction. Joleen may have more last-minute cancelations than nondisabled clients due to the unpredictability of assistive technology and paratransit systems.

• *Multiple identities.* Joleen's identity as female, African American, and disabled has to be considered synergistically. She is likely to have a harder time gaining employment than either men with disabilities or White women with disabilities. Education will increase her chances for employment so helping support her continuation in community college is paramount. Persons with disabilities who are employed are more likely to marry, less likely to live below the poverty line, and less likely to be institutionalized. If Joleen lives in a predominantly African American community in a city or suburb, she is likely to be farther from a rehabilitation hospital and other services, have fewer public transportation options, and live in an environment that has fewer curb cuts, accessible housing, and other environmental accommodations. Positive factors associated with being African American come from within the community, such as involvement of the extended family for assistance, more access to informal systems of social support, and involvement in strong community-minded religious institutions.

♦ *Prioritizing goals.* It is possible that just getting to therapy requires a fair amount of time and effort, and Joleen may need assistance getting to the appointment, requiring that she find someone each week to help her. Since she is highly likely to be living on government assistance, the number of sessions may have to be curtailed due to limited funds. Therefore, therapy should not be considered to be open-ended but short term and focused. Clinical depression is a possible presenting problem, but it is not a necessary stage of adjustment to disability and if present should be treated as aggressively as any depression. Joleen may be experiencing numerous daily microaggressions, both from other people and from the built environment, so she may need more emphasis on stress inoculation and coping with these daily events. Since the effects of SCI are encompassing and affect almost every aspect of life, setting concrete goals is helpful. Joleen's parents may be traumatized by almost losing their daughter and by her injury; family therapy could help sort out realistic fears and hence establish realistic goals. The upper limits on independence are more likely to be imposed by limited financial resources and fears than by the disability per se.

♦ *Putting it all together.* Disability-affirmative therapy is a guide to help therapists conceptualize clients with disabilities; it relies on a template of eight client issues to understand so that the therapist can develop a case formulation that neither overemphasizes nor underestimates the role of disability. Overall, Joleen is a client more like, than unlike, other clients in that she will have her own goals, her individual history, her quirks and quiddities, and her unique personality. Disability may run through these aspects of her, but they do not solely define her.

Recommended Resources

Books and/or Articles

Bruyere, S., & O'Keefe, J. (Eds.). (1994). *Implications of the Americans With Disabilities Act for psychology*. New York, NY: Springer.

Flanagan, S., Zaretsky, H., & Moroz, A. (Eds.). (2010). *Medical aspects of disability* (4th ed.). New York, NY: Springer.

Mayo Clinic. (2009). *The Mayo Clinic guide to living with a spinal cord injury: Moving ahead with your life*. New York, NY: Demos Medical.

Olkin, R. (1999). *What psychotherapists should know about disability*. New York, NY: Guilford Press.

Olkin, R. (2008). Disability-affirmative therapy and case formulation: A template for understanding disability in a clinical context. *Counseling & Human Development, 39*(8), 1–20.

Sullivan, C. (2008). *Brain injury survival kit: 365 tips, tools and tricks to deal with cognitive function loss*. New York, NY: Demos Medical.

Readings on Spinal Cord Injury

Barker, R. N., Kendall, M. D., Amsters, D. I., Pershouse, K. J., Haines, T. P., & Kuipers, P. (2009). The relationship between quality of life and disability across the lifespan for people with spinal cord injury. *Spinal Cord, 47*, 149–155.

Goldman, R. L., Radnitz, C. L., & McGrath, R. E. (2008). Posttraumatic stress disorder and major depression in veterans with spinal cord injury. *Rehabilitation Psychology, 53*(2), 162–170.

Hatcher, M. B., Whitaker, C., & Karl, A. (2009). What predicts posttraumatic stress following spinal cord injury? *British Journal of Health Psychology, 14*, 541–561.

Kreuter, M., Taft, C., Siosteen, A., & Biering-Sorensen, F. (2011). Women's sexual functioning and sex life after spinal cord injury. *Spinal Cord, 49*, 154–160.

Lequerica, A. H., Forchheimer, M., Albright, K., Tate, D., Duggan, C. H., & Rahman, R. (2010). Stress appraisal in women with spinal cord injury: Supplementary findings through mixed methods. *International Journal of Stress Management, 17*(3), 259–275.

Migliorini, C., Tonge, B., & Taleporos, G. (2008). Spinal cord injury and mental health. *Australian and New Zealand Journal of Psychiatry, 42*, 309–314.

Nosek, M. A., Hughes, R. B., Taylor, H. B., & Taylor, P. (2006). Disability, psychosocial, and demographic characteristics of abused women with physical disabilities. *Violence Against Women, 12*(9), 838–850.

Olkin, R. (2004). Disability and depression. In S. L. Welner & F. Haseltine (Eds.), *Welner's guide to the care of women with disabilities* (pp. 279–300). Philadelphia, PA: Lippincott Williams & Wilkins.

Sipski, M. L., & Alexander, C. J. (Eds.). (1997). *Sexual function in people with disability and chronic illness: A health professional's guide.* Gaithersburg, MD: Aspen.

Readings on Ethnicity and Disability

Asbury, C. A., Walker, S., Belgrave, F. Z., Maholmes, V., & Green, L. (1994). Psychosocial, cultural, and accessibility factors associated with participation of African-Americans in rehabilitation. *Rehabilitation Psychology, 39*(2), 113–121.

Belgrave, F. Z., Davis, A., & Vajda, J. (1994). An examination of social support source, types, and satisfaction among African-Americans and Caucasians with disabilities. *Journal of Social Behavior and Personality, 9*(5), 307–320.

Hernandez, B., McCullough, S., Balcazar, F., & Keys, C. (1997). Accessibility of public accommodations in three ethnic minority communities. *Journal of Disability Policy Studies, 19*(2), 80–85.

Olkin, R. (2006). Persons of color with disabilities. In M. Constantine (Ed.), *Clinical practice with people of color: A guide to becoming culturally competent* (pp. 162–179). New York, NY: Teacher's College Press.

Smith, D. L., & Alston, R. J. (2009). The relationship of race and disability to life satisfaction in the United States. *Journal of Rehabilitation, 75*(1), 3–9.

Videos

Mitchell, D., & Snyder, S. (Directors). (1997). *Vital signs: Crip culture talks back* [DVD]. United States: Fanlight Productions.

Olkin, R. (2005). *Disability-affirmative therapy: A beginner's guide (with instructor's manual)* [DVD]. Alexandria, VA: Alexander Street Press (formerly Emicrotraining; video #460).

Assessments/Inventories

De Groot, S., van der Woude, L. H. V., Niezen, A., Smit, C. A. J., & Post, M. W. M. (2010). Evaluation of the physical activity scale for individuals with physical disabilities in people with spinal cord injury. *Spinal Cord*, *48*, 542–547.

Novels and Fictional/Nonfictional Readings

McBride, J. (2012). *Tale of two gimps: Such is life.* N.p.: Author.

Neville, J. B. (2012). *How I roll: Life, love and work after a spinal cord injury.* Doylestown, PA: Platform Press.

Reese, L. (2012). *Spinal cord injury: My life beyond the outhouse: The first two years.* N.p.: Author.

THERE IS NOTHING WRONG WITH YOU A JOB CANNOT FIX: THE STORY OF GEORGE

Case Description

George is a 32-year-old White male who was born with cerebral palsy (CP). CP has a wide range of effects. George walks with a very pronounced bilateral limp, his arms tend to jerk spasmodically, and he drools. He has a learning disability but above-average IQ. His speech is labored and difficult to understand. Sometimes he tries a different word, or to spell a word, when someone does not understand him. Due to his age, he attended school since the 1975 passage of the Education for All Handicapped Children Act (now called Individuals with Disabilities Education Act). In the first grade, he was placed in special education with children with autism and intellectual disabilities. His mother fought to place him in a regular classroom and prevailed by second grade, but George knew that others assumed he was "slow."

Throughout school he received services to help with carrying his books, feeding, and writing. In middle and high school, he was in the "resource room" for part of the day because he needed to dictate his homework. He chafed at once again being with the "slow kids" in the resource room. He had one friend who sometimes hung out with him, but usually he was alone with his aide. In college, he lived in a dorm all four years and continued to have some assistance at school, such as note takers, transportation on campus, and writers/typists. In large classes, instructors might not be able to connect his written work with the person, and he would get good grades. However, in smaller seminars where he was called on to participate, his grades were considerably lower. He felt that this was partly because others had trouble understanding him and would pretend they did when they really did not and partly because of prejudice, the assumption that someone who looked and moved and spoke like he did must not be very intelligent. Nonetheless, George graduated with a 3.5 grade point average from a top-tier university. He then received a master's degree in journalism, finishing six years ago. Since then he has not been able to find a job. George lived at home with his mother through graduate school but now lives alone.

George is very lonely and quite depressed. He is mostly alone in his studio apartment. His main social activity is to go to a bar on the corner where they know him well and where the bartender is not shy about saying, "What did you say?" or "Could you repeat that?" Because this is his social outlet, he drinks two to five beers or glasses of wine about five nights a week. He looks for work daily and applies for any job that involves writing or journalism but never gets past the phone call or interview. When he has someone else make the calls for him (e.g., his mother or a friend), the reaction is often even worse from the prospective employer, as they imagine someone so disabled he cannot talk on the phone.

George's mother decided that George should move out when he finished graduate school. She was dating a man she subsequently married and wanted time alone with this man. She found an apartment for George and arranged for movers. She was clear about her feelings that he needed to be more independent from her and that it was "finally her turn." (George's father left shortly after his birth when his CP was diagnosed, telling the mother, "I didn't sign on for this." She relayed this story to George often in his childhood.)

George had never been in a romantic relationship and tended to develop crushes on the few women in his sphere, such as his attendants or his previous group therapist. He had kissed one woman in college, and she had pulled away, saying kissing him was "like kissing a slab of wet liver." George was humiliated by this and hadn't tried to kiss anyone since.

George's mother called to make the initial appointment, explaining to the therapist that it would be hard to understand George's speech. She attended the first session as well but made it plain she didn't want to attend more sessions, that George had to work on things on his own, that he could take the two buses or call paratransit to get to therapy. The therapist's impression was that she was dumping George on the therapist so she could make a getaway.

George carries a backpack because he can't get a wallet out of his pocket, and he exerts a lot of energy when he walks. He often has body odor, as if he had been working out. When he gets up from the chair in therapy, he splays his lower limbs out, drops to the floor on his knees, turns toward the chair, and hefts himself to a standing position. The therapist, a relatively young, female, able-bodied, predoctoral trainee, was eager to show that she was okay with disability, but her discomfort could be seen in small acts. She was embarrassed to ask him to repeat more than once something she did not understand. She never remarked on his body odor, although clearly this would be an issue in any job interview. She plunged into a description of the social model of disability, telling George that there was nothing wrong with him a job could not fix. George's response was to say, "I don't want any of that victim shit," which puzzled the therapist—she was only trying to say that it was society's problem, not George's. She was relentlessly upbeat and full of ideas for George to try, even if they had not worked in the past (e.g., his counselor at the Department of Vocational Rehabilitation no longer sent him on job interviews). She assumed his depression was normative for someone with a significant disability, and hence she encouraged his expression of negative emotions, which only further discouraged him.

Reflection and Discussion Questions

1. Given that George has a significant disability, what are the odds of him having experienced sexual or physical abuse? Who would be most likely to have abused him? What might have been the reaction of others if he told someone about any abuse?

2. According to George, the Department of Vocational Rehabilitation had given up on him, and his assigned counselor did not return his calls. Is this a problem? Does the therapist have a role in addressing this? If so, what might that be?

3. Do you, as the therapist, feel discouraged about the roadblocks facing George? Do you believe he can/will get a job? What might make that more likely? What role does therapy play?

4. Getting to therapy is physically labor intensive (two buses and walking several blocks) or unreliable (paratransit). How might this be handled in the therapy? What alternatives might there be?

5. When you think about the "good enough" mother, what does this include for the mother of a child with a significant disability? What are some essential topics of conversation you would want her to have had with George? How might she convey her attitude toward his disability? What do you think of the story she told George about why the father had left?

6. What are your personal reactions to the physical descriptions of George? Does this image evoke discomfort in you? What could you do to become more comfortable?

7. Do you know anyone similar to George? What was that relationship, and how does it affect your views of George?

8. Was it a mistake for the therapist not to comment on George's body odor? Would commenting be experienced as judgmental or as failing to understand disability issues?

Brief Analysis of the Case

• *Abuse.* George is 2.1 times more likely to have been abused as a child, either sexually or physically or both. Additionally, there were people who were in his life because of his disability who were in positions to harm him, such as the driver of the special bus he rode to school, his aides, his attendants (who helped him with activities of daily living during college, such as bathing, eating, grocery shopping, preparing meals). If George told anyone about the abuse, he was more likely to be disbelieved, as there is a misconception that no one would harm a child with a disability. Any police or child protective services sent to investigate could be likely to see George as asexual. Further, they might not see George as a good witness, given the difficulties understanding his speech.

• *Systemic problems.* There are many supposed support services for people with disabilities. Often these systems become part of the problem. For example, paratransit requires a two-hour window to pick up a person before an appointment and another two-hour window after the appointment. Thus, a 50-minute therapy session could stretch to five hours, most of the time spent waiting for paratransit to arrive (if it does—paratransit is notorious for failure to arrive). The Department of Vocational Rehabilitation is always un-derfinanced and is mandated to cover particular priorities, which shift from time to time. Therefore, cases that do not successfully close (i.e., result in a job) are seen as a drain on the system and get pushed aside. Although the placement rate in jobs is consistently higher for White men with disabilities than for African American men or women with disabilities, George's speech involvement will be a deterrent to employment. There is a stable hierarchy of acceptability of disabilities, and CP is in the lower 20%.

• *Romance.* In terms of romance, the things that make any man attrac-tive will apply to George as well. Although in general women accept a wider range of characteristics (compared to males), George's disability has several features that are likely to seem unattractive to others. His awkward and jerky body movements, drooling, and slurred speech are likely deterrents to finding a partner. Furthermore, persons with disabilities who work are more likely to socialize and to get married than are those not in the workforce, so George's unemployment can have negative repercussions on his social and romantic life. Because of his limited interactions with women, he has not developed social skills in dating. He tends to get crushes on the few females in his circle; this will be important for the young female therapist to keep in mind, as he may develop a romantic attachment to her. How she handles this will be a critical incident in the therapy.

• *Family issues.* In general, the family factors that promote resilience in children apply to children with disabilities as well. But children with dis-abilities are much more likely than nondisabled children to live alone with a single mother and to live in families that have incomes below the poverty line. George's mother seems to feel she was abandoned by her husband be-cause of George's disability, which could have implications for her feelings toward her son. What is "good enough" mothering for a nondisabled child may not suffice for a child with significant disabilities. Being a single parent is hard enough, but with the additional tasks related to George's disability she had even more to handle (e.g., attending individualized education plan meetings, possibly battling with the school to get George needed services, increased medical appointments, obtaining and maintaining durable medi-cal equipment, finding community resources). Having a child with a dis-ability may have affected her ability to socialize and to date. Therefore, when George went to college, she may have experienced a newfound sense of free-dom that she is reluctant to relinquish. Since she remarried, she may want to focus on her new partner relationship. Unfortunately, she has moved away from George at a time when he still needs considerable assistance and before he has any other support structures in place. Therapy will have to consider whether, and how and when, George's mother (and perhaps her new husband) will be included in treatment.

• *Countertransference.* Mental health professionals are not immune to the ubiquitous negative messages about disability in society, nor are they especially enlightened about disability. Only about 11% of programs accredited by the American Psychological Association have any specialized coursework in disability, and that course is likely to focus on one of only three topics (e.g., intellectual disabilities, autism, or learning disabilities) rather than on the general sociopolitical aspects of disability. The therapist's initial reactions to George's appearance, demeanor, movements, and speech are as likely to be as negative as anyone's and may be betrayed in small ways. For example, she might not shake George's hand when first greeting him, she may be too quick to help him with the door, she may be overly cheerful, or she may finish his sentences incorrectly. Studies on prejudice suggest that someone who believes she is not prejudiced might have even more unconsciously negative behaviors than someone who knows she is prejudiced. Having supervision from someone well versed in disability issues is critical, and video-recordings of sessions will be important in excavating the subtle signs of discomfort.

Recommended Resources

Books and/or Articles

Blotzer, M. A., & Ruth R. (Eds.). *Sometimes you just want to feel like a human being: Empowering psychotherapy with persons with disabilities.* Baltimore, MD: Paul Brookes.

Murray, M. (2011). *Always carry two straws in your pocket.* Raleigh, NC: Lulu.

Olkin, R. (1999). *What psychotherapists should know about disability.* New York, NY: Guilford Press.

Stanton, M. (2012). *Understanding cerebral palsy: A guide for parents and professionals.* London, England: Jessica Kingsley.

Videos

Blue, J. (Writer). (2009). *Comedy Central* presents: *Stand-up* season 13, Episode 21, "Josh Blue" [Television]. United States: Comedy Central.

Hadary, S. H. (Producer), & Hadary, S. H., & Whiteford, W. A. (Directors). (1999). *King Gimp: A documentary* [Documentary]. United States: Video Press.

Olkin, R. (2005). *Disability-affirmative therapy: A beginner's guide (with instructor's manual)*. Alexandria, VA: Alexander Street Press (formerly Emicrotraining; video #460).

Fiction Reading

McBryde Johnson, H. (2006). *Accidents of nature*. New York, NY: Henry Holt.

17

Clinical Applications With Older Adults

Kelly O'Shea Carney and Derald Wing Sue

THE CHALLENGES OF CAREGIVING: THE STORY OF SARAH

Case Description

I immediately liked Sarah when I met her. She was 75 years old and had a great sense of humor. She was a very down to earth and often said that she looked forward to our therapy sessions. She clearly benefited from the support she received within the sessions, and I enjoyed getting to know her. Sarah's strength and determination reminded me of my grandmother, and the natural affinity between us helped to immediately establish good rapport.

When Sarah first came to my private practice, she was caring for her husband with Alzheimer's in their home. She presented with clear signs of depression and anxiety related to the demands of her caregiving responsibilities. She was frequently tearful while talking about her husband and his many needs and described herself as tired, overwhelmed, anxious, and deeply saddened by the changes in her husband. Sarah described her husband as very confused, resulting in the need for her to provide lots of hands-on care and support, such as supervising his daily activities, dressing, bathing, and assisting him in the bathroom. In addition, she was responsible for all their home management and maintenance tasks. Sarah reported that sometimes her husband would become angry and difficult to manage, and at those times she felt angry too. These situations frightened Sarah because she understood that her husband could not help what he was doing, but she also felt helpless and overwhelmed in those moments. Sarah was not sleeping well because her husband did not sleep well and often wandered the house at night. She would get out of bed when he was up so that she could observe his activities and make sure he did not leave the house or do something that could harm him.

Within our sessions, we discussed the option of placing her husband in a nursing home, but Sarah felt it was her duty to care for her husband at home for as long as she possibly could. Sarah described herself as a devout Catholic and was very involved in her church. Her church community was a wonderful support to her and offered respite in the form of help with meals and regular home visits. In spite of these periodic visits from her church family, Sarah described feeling alone and isolated. Her day revolved around her husband, and she was unable to engage in the activities she used to enjoy or visit with her friends uninterrupted.

Sarah had some health problems of her own. She was morbidly obese and had a number of cardiovascular issues, such as high blood pressure, high cholesterol, and peripheral vascular disease. Often I noticed that she was out of breath as a result of her walk from the parking lot. Her legs also appeared very swollen and red at times, making it painful for Sarah to walk. Sarah reported that she saw her physician regularly and that her health was stable. Although we talked about the importance of self-care, Sarah maintained that she did not have time to watch what she ate or exercise because her husband required her constant attention. On the rare occasions when he was sleeping or occupied, Sarah was grateful for the opportunity to get off her feet and watch TV as a diversion.

Sarah was the mother of two adult children, both of whom lived locally and were involved and supportive. She also had seven grandchildren whom she was connected to and very proud of, ranging from 10 to 23 years old. In fact, she said that her eldest granddaughter was about my age and also interested in psychology. Sarah was retired librarian and was very well read. She had researched her husband's dementia and seemed knowledgeable about his disease process but often seemed surprisingly unaware of and unconcerned about the potential impact of her own health issues.

Sarah reported that she had been in counseling before on at least three other occasions. In the past, she had sought counseling for help with depression, which she described as an issue she had struggled with on and off since she was in her 30s. Sometimes the therapy helped, and other times it did not. In addition to the counseling, Sarah had been on and off medications for depression and anxiety over the course of her life. When I met her, Sarah was taking a selective serotonin reuptake inhibitor antidepressant to manage her sadness, anxiety, and poor sleep. Sarah also revealed that on at least one occasion she and her husband had sought marital therapy. She described their marriage as intermittently "rocky" due to the fact that her husband had been a heavy drinker when he was younger. Later in life, he had become sober, and Sarah described those years as the happiest in her marriage.

Sarah was my client for over a year. Sometimes she came weekly, and other times I would not see her for a couple months. On at least two occasions, she forgot that we had appointments scheduled and I had to call her to reschedule. We primarily talked about her caregiving struggles, focusing on coping strategies, but we also discussed the dynamics within her family. Sarah struggled with the fact that her children wanted to take care of her, which was a change in roles that she did not like. She also talked about her struggle to lose weight and the ways that her age and health changes made it difficult for her to do all she wanted to do for her husband.

Sadly, my work with Sarah ended very abruptly. She had a heart attack, and her family moved her to an assisted living home, along with her husband. A few months later, I heard that she had passed away. It makes me sad that I did not have the chance to say good-bye to Sarah, and sometimes I wonder if I could have done more for her. She was such a nice person and faced so many struggles later in life. It is no surprise that she was depressed when you think about all the difficulties she had to face.

Reflection and Discussion Questions

1. What are the primary diagnostic issues presented in Sarah's case? What tools might be used to develop an accurate diagnostic conceptualization of this client?

2. What are the central clinical issues that you would have focused on in working with a patient like Sarah? What would you identify as the goals of therapy for this client?

3. What are the key family issues that might have been addressed with Sarah? How might these issues have been effectively addressed?

4. Identify the primary ways in which this therapist may have been influenced by stereotypes related to aging. How might the therapeutic process and outcomes have been different if the therapist were more aware of those stereotypes?

5. What strategies would you suggest for dealing directly with the diversity issues that arose between this client and her therapist? How did the age difference between the therapist and the client affect the therapist's view of this woman and her conceptualization of the clinical issues?

6. What opportunities and/or obligations does this case present for interdisciplinary collaboration? What steps might you take to ensure that Sarah's care was coordinated with other key caregivers?

7. What support systems existed for this client? How might you have helped to mobilize those supports? Do you consider mobilization of supports an appropriate role for a therapist to play?

8. What were the benefits of this therapeutic process for the client? What ways could you imagine that would have created greater benefit for the client?

9. What opportunities does this case present for helping the client address issues of loss? What strategies might you use for addressing those issues of loss with the client?

10. How might this therapist cope effectively with the issues of loss raised by this patient's death? How might fear of anticipated loss have influenced the clinical relationship between this patient and her therapist?

Brief Analysis of the Case

• The assessment of older adult clients should always be comprehensive in nature, taking into account not only traditional mental health factors but also physical health, cognition, and daily function. The brief medical history of this client suggests that there were important medical issues present as well as the possibility of some cognitive changes that the therapist could have explored.

• Individuals with multiple cardiovascular risk factors are at risk for the development of cognitive changes. As a result, cognitive screening should be included in the initial assessment of older adults. However, it is important to utilize tools for the assessment of cognitive function that have been normed for older adults. Several good brief cognitive screening tools can be utilized to identify the presence of cognitive deficits.

+ When working with older adults, collaboration with the primary care physician can be critical to supporting the client's well-being. In fact, many insurers, including Medicare, require documented communication between primary care and behavioral health providers. Although the client may decline to allow the sharing of information between providers, the underlying medical conditions that commonly develop as people age contribute to the importance of an integrated approach to care.

+ Caring for an individual with dementia is considered to be one of the most demanding forms of caregiving. Caregivers of individuals with dementia are considered to be at high risk for chronic illness, depression, and premature death. Providing these caregivers with emotional support, linkages to support services, and respite from caregiving is essential to maintaining the caregiver's health and well-being. When working with older adults, it is important to be familiar with the local supports and services available to them to facilitate linkage to the appropriate services.

+ Depression and forgetfulness are *not* natural consequences of aging. However, this is a common misconception among health care providers and the general public. As a result of this misconception, depression and early signs of cognitive dysfunction are often overlooked and undertreated among older adults. In this client, there is a reported history of depression requiring treatment, suggesting a higher risk for significant depression in the context of increased life stress, such as caregiving.

+ Anxiety is more prevalent among older adults than depression. Moreover, anxiety is a commonly identified symptom by older adults who are depressed. Because anxiolytic medications can have many adverse side effects in older adults, antidepressants with anxiolytic effects typically are used to treat both anxiety and depression in older adults.

+ Younger professionals working with older adults are often faced with transference and countertransference issues related to the age difference. It is important to identify and work with these issues to ensure that they do not interfere with accurate conceptualization of the client and effective intervention. For example, in this case, the therapist's association between this client and her grandmother may have made her less likely to challenge issues that the client preferred to avoid, such as addressing her own physical health needs.

◆ Older adults often struggle with the shifting roles within their families, just as their adult children may struggle with how to appropriately support their aging parents as their health and function change. Family sessions with older adults and their adult children can be an effective intervention to open channels of communication and build consensus about roles, responsibilities, and a plan of action to support the older adult.

Recommended Resources

Books and/or Articles

American Psychological Association. (2004). Guidelines for psychological practice with older adults. *American Psychologist, 59(4)*, 236–260.

American Psychological Association, Task Force to Update the Guidelines for the Evaluation of Dementia and Age-Related Cognitive Decline. (2011, August 15). *Guidelines for the evaluation of dementia and age-related cognitive change.* Retrieved from http://www.apa.org/pi/aging/resources/dementia-guidelines.pdf

Knight, B., Karel, M., Hinrichsen, G., Qualls, S., & Duffy, M. (2009). Pikes Peak model for training in professional geropsychology. *American Psychologist, 64*(3), 205–214.

Snyder, P., Jackson, C., Petersen, R., Khachaturian, A., Kaye, J., Albert, M., & Weintraub, S. (2011). Assessment of cognition in mild cognitive impairment: A comparative study. *Alzheimer's & Dementia, 7*, 338–355.

Unutzer, J., Schoenbaum, M., Katon, W., Fan, M., Pincus, H., Hogan, D., & Taylor, J. (2009). Healthcare costs associated with depression in medically ill fee-for-service Medicare participants. *Journal of the American Geriatric Society, 57*, 506–510.

Videos

Harris, L., & Johnson, M. (Producers), & Cassavetes, N. (Director). (2004). *The notebook* [Motion picture]. United States: New Line Cinema.

Hoffman, J. (Producer). (2009) The Alzheimer's Project [Motion Picture]. United States: Home Box Office.

NIH (Producer). (2004) The Forgetting [Documentary]. United States: Twin Cities Public Television.

Assessments/Inventories

Council of Professional Geropsychology Training Programs. (2008). Pikes Peak Geropsychology Knowledge and Skill Assessment Tool, Version 1.3. Retrieved from http://www.copgtp.org/uploads/documents/Pikes_Peak_Evaluetion_Tool.pdf

Nassredine, Z. *Montreal Cognitive Assessment.* Retrieved from www.mocatest.org

Nasreddine, Z. S., Rossetti, H., Phillips, N., et al. (2012). Normative data for the Montreal Cognitive Assessment (MoCA) in a population-based sample. *Neurology, 78, 765.*

Websites/Blogs

Alzheimer's Association Caregiver Center: http://www.alz.org/care/overview.asp

American Psychological Association Caregiver Briefcase: http://www.apa.org/pi/about/publications/caregivers/index.aspx

National Family Caregivers Association: http://caregiveraction.org

Nonfictional Readings

Mace, N., & Rabins, P. (2011). *The 36-hour day: A family guide to caring for people who have Alzheimer disease, related dementias, and memory loss.* Baltimore, MD: Johns Hopkins University Press.

Sheehy, G. (2011). *Passages in caregiving.* New York, NY: Harper.

I'M NOT CRAZY: THE STORY OF MR. CHANG

Case Description

Mr. Henry Chang is a first-generation 85-year-old recently widowed Chinese American gentleman who presented to his physician, Dr. Schulman, with complaints of poor digestion, loss of appetite, headaches, difficulty sleeping, and general malaise. His medical history is largely unremarkable except for diagnoses of gastroesophogeal reflex disease (GERD), a right knee replacement in 2005, and osteoarthritis. He currently takes Prilosec for his GERD and naproxen twice a day for his arthritis. The patient's health problems were often exaggerated by his forgetfulness in regularly taking his medication. He informed Dr. Schulman that he used to be very socially active with many friends but that things had changed and he no longer found joy in life. Mr. Chang's family physician, who practices within an integrated outpatient care unit, requested a brief psychological evaluation immediately following his office visit with Mr. Chang as a means of ruling out any contributing mental health issues. The patient, however, failed to show twice for scheduled appointments with the psychologist.

Mr. Chang did show for his third scheduled appointment but only with great urging from Dr. Schulman. He was seen by a young White female psychologist, Dr. Martin, who reported great difficulty in establishing rapport with the client. Mr. Chang seemed uncooperative and guarded and was somewhat reticent and reserved in the interview, offering minimal but polite responses to questions. According to Dr. Martin, he became very "defensive" when the topic of his mental state was discussed. Dr. Martin felt that the formality of the doctor–patient relationship might be creating a barrier between her and the client, so she tried to place Mr. Chang at ease with "small talk" about his family relationships and by addressing him by his first name, "Henry." She even encouraged Mr. Chang to call her by her first name, "Emily," rather than "Dr. Martin." She tried to explore Mr. Chang's family relationships, the impact of the recent death of his wife, and his resistance to exploring his feelings. These, she believed, were responsible for his depression. Throughout the interview, Mr. Chang denied any emotional difficulties, stated he was not lonely or depressed, and became increasingly agitated and resistant to answering questions. Whenever Dr. Martin pressed him for feelings associated with his increasing age, death of his wife, and feelings of isolation, Mr. Chang seemed to withdraw more and more. When the session ended, the therapist recommended to Mr. Chang that he make another appointment, but he stated he would "think about it." In relating her impression to the treating physician, Dr. Martin described Mr. Chang as "obstinate," "inflexible," "passive-aggressive," and "resistant to psychological treatment." She concluded that Mr. Chang would not benefit from therapy and that at his advanced years, it would be best to allow him to live the remainder of his life as he desired.

Although Mr. Chang never returned to see the psychologist, he did continue to show for his regular medical appointments with Dr. Schulman. It was at one of these sessions that he confessed to the doctor about "feeling poorly," being constantly tired, and needing medication to address his stomach pain and improve his energy level. When asked about questions related to his mood, Mr. Chang admitted to feeling sad and hopeless but denied being depressed. He did miss his wife and found their home too large to maintain. Indeed, he used only the bedroom and den; he seldom made use of the kitchen, living room, and the rest of the house. He noted that his arthritis and increased loss of balance made cooking his own meals and going to the bathroom at night difficult. He had fallen on two previous occasions when he lost his balance in the bathtub. His two sons who lived in different parts of the country wanted him to move into an assisted living situation, but he had so far refused. His daughter who was married with two younger children had offered to have her father move into their spare room, but Mr. Chang said he did not want to burden her family.

Because Dr. Schulman did not feel comfortable giving advice to his patient, he again encouraged Mr. Chang to make an appointment with Dr. Martin and to discuss ways that might improve his outlook and to consider alternative living situations. At this suggestion, Mr. Chang loudly proclaimed that he was not "crazy," he would not see a "shrink," and denied any mental health problems. He stated that he preferred to speak with Dr. Schulman, who as an older man nearing retirement himself seemed to understand his situation better. Dr. Schulman, however, indicated he was not qualified to provide the type of assisted living advice required and that his role was a medical one. From his perspective, Mr. Chang was in relatively good health and his continual somatic complaints were greatly exaggerated and/or due to normal aging. Rather than refer Mr. Chang back to the psychologist, Dr. Schulman recommended a social worker who could help "explore ways" in dealing with his current living situation. Dr. Schulman assured Mr. Chang that he would continue to be available for treating him medically. This reassurance seemed to elicit a positive response from Mr. Chang, who agreed to see the social worker.

The social worker, a much older woman than Dr. Martin, explained her role at the clinic as a problem solver, reassured Mr. Chang that they would work together to address his living situation and would work closely with his physician to address health-related issues. She did not initially explore his emotive state but confined her questions and comments toward practical matters related to Mr. Chang's medical problems, living situation, ways to remember taking his medication, and interest in how he spent his spare time. The social worker often shared her own thoughts and observations associated with her own aging parents, the physical changes they experienced, the loss of close friends and family, and their feelings of frustration and emotional turmoil they underwent. Mr. Chang would listen intently and seemed to enjoy providing insights about the social worker's parents. Indeed, at times, it appeared that the conversations about the social worker's elderly parents served as an indirect means of talking about Mr. Chang's own feelings of frustration, loneliness, and depression.

Throughout their interactions, the social worker always addressed her client as "Mr. Chang" and presented advice or suggestions tentatively. She would always ask Mr. Chang for his perspective and encouraged him to tell her whether her ideas seemed practical and whether he had suggestions as well. She treated Mr. Chang with a great deal of respect and often punctuated their discussions by asking for his advice. This approach seemed to open the gateways to Mr. Chang's desire to talk and share his apprehensions, feelings, and family concerns. The following information came to light during the three brief sessions spent together.

Mr. Chang had been married to his wife for nearly 60 years before she died from an unexpected heart attack nine months earlier. He had owned three fairly successful grocery stores that allowed him to put all three of his children through college without the need for loans. The loss of his wife and the infrequency of visits from his sons and daughter left him feeling isolated and lonely. He did not blame them for their lack of visits because they had families of their own and lived on the East Coast, while he lived in San Francisco. Yet he yearned to see them more often and talked about his grandchildren with great pride and affection. His isolation was compounded by friends and relatives who themselves began to pass away until he no longer had a support network or social life. He was able to cope with these losses as long as his wife was alive, but her death left him feeling that "I have no one anymore." He described how joy, happiness, and his lust for life had disappeared. He had stopped attending the local Protestant church, where he and his wife were once very active. They had always enjoyed their monthly trips to South Lake Tahoe, where they took the inexpensive San Francisco Chinatown buses with friends. They often stayed at the casinos and had a great time engaging in "small-time" gambling with slot machines, enjoyed dining at buffets with their friends, and took in a show or two.

When asked about his history of substance use, Mr. Chang indicated that he has "a few" drinks—Seagram's Seven on the rocks—before and during dinner. He clearly stated that this has been his routine for many years and challenged the perception that there was anything wrong with his past drinking. When the social worker agreed that there was nothing wrong with his social drinking, Mr. Chang admitted that lately, however, he found himself drinking increasingly heavy amounts during the evening hours when he felt most lonely. He emphasized that his increased drinking was a recent phenomenon but that it was a concern of his. Mr. Chang also reports that he regularly took Motrin PM to address insomnia. He attributed his inability to sleep as due to "old age." But he did admit to lying in bed and constantly ruminating about how hopeless his situation was and looked forward to joining his wife. When asked whether he had ever thought about taking his own life, Mr. Chang stated, "Of course not! I'm not crazy. I would never take one of my guns and shoot myself." Upon questioning by the social worker about his guns, Mr. Chang indicated that they had been used for protection in his grocery stores but he now kept them in his home.

Reflection and Discussion Questions

1. Clinically, what do you believe is happening to Mr. Chang? Does he have a mental disorder? If so, what would be your diagnosis? What are the contributing factors? If not, how would you explain and make sense of his psychological state?

2. How do you make sense of Mr. Chang's adamant assertion that he was not "crazy" and would not see a "shrink"? In what ways may Asian culture and being of advanced age explain some of Mr. Chang's reactions to this implication? If you were a therapist, how would you respond to Mr. Chang's reactions in a culturally sensitive manner?

3. Mr. Chang seemed to respond poorly to Dr. Martin but seemed to be more disclosing to both his personal physician and social worker. Why do you believe this to be the case? Are there clues provided in the characteristics and behaviors of Dr. Schulman and the social worker that can help you in your therapeutic approach to Mr. Chang?

4. In what ways can race, gender, and age affect the therapeutic relationship between Mr. Chang and Drs. Schulman and Martin and the social worker? How does traditional Asian culture perceive these sociodemographic variables?

5. Would the advanced age of older clients affect your outlook, goals, and therapeutic treatment of clients? For example, Mr. Chang is 85 years old and nearing the end of his life. He might have only 5 to

10 more years of life left. If he were at risk for suicide, how concerned would you be in comparison to seeing a client in their 30s or 40s?

6. Would you have concerns about Mr. Chang's safety, given the facts and information provided? Why or why not? Given the information specified, would you say that Mr. Chang was at risk for suicide? What specific aspects of the case would lead you to this conclusion?

7. To what extent might age-related health problems be playing a role in Mr. Chang's deteriorating function? How would you assess the relative contribution of normal age-related changes, pain, and illness in Mr. Chang? How might these changes interact with Mr. Chang's social and cultural perceptions of his changing health?

8. What social supports and services might be engaged to assist Mr. Chang? He seems to have minimal social support, few close friends, and is relatively isolated from his two sons and daughter. What role might you play in mobilizing those supports?

9. To what extent might the use of over-the-counter medications and alcohol be playing a role in Mr. Chang's mood and function?

10. In our society, it is often said that as one ages, one's social status and worth in our culture diminishes. However, in other societies, such as the Chinese, increasing age is often correlated with higher status, prestige, and wisdom. How might this be affecting Mr. Chang?

Brief Analysis of the Case

• Older adults, particularly those of the current 80-plus-year-old cohort, tend to have limited knowledge and understanding of mental health issues. Many of these individuals consider any mental health matter to be highly stigmatizing and may be limited in their ability to verbalize their issues and concerns in psychological terms. Further, it is important to consider Asian perspectives associated with mental disorders as well. Among traditional Chinese, often a clear distinction is not made between mental health and physical health. Both are intertwined. Seeking help means going to a "real doctor" rather than a mental health provider. Furthermore, shame and disgrace are often associated with "mental illness." Directly admitting to psychological problems (depression, anxiety, etc.) is very difficult because it is a sign of weakness and reflects poorly on the family. Many traditional Asians are more likely to present their psychological disorders via somatic complaints and seek help from their physician.

• Statistics support the fact that older adult males, age 85 and higher, are at higher risk for suicide than any other demographic group. There are, of course, racial/ethnic differences that a health provider would benefit from knowing. For example, older adult White males are three times more likely to commit suicide than their African American, Latino, and Hispanic counterparts. But contrary to the belief that Asian Americans have low rates of suicide, studies suggest that suicide among Asian older women is much higher than among their White female counterparts. Regardless of the client's race/ethnicity, however, suicide in the latter years must be a strong consideration for the health provider. It is important that a suicide lethality assessment be made in light of the many correlates of suicide found to be present with Mr. Chang: elderly male, recently widowed, abusing alcohol, feelings of hopelessness, lack of social support, isolation from family, and access to lethal means for suicide (guns). Other important findings are these: 75% of older adults who commit suicide visited their primary care physician within a month of their suicide; 20% of older adults who commit suicide visited their physician on the same day they killed themselves. It is incumbent upon mental health providers to be thoroughly knowledgeable and conversant with the correlates of suicide.

• How might understanding the data shared above affect the therapist's work with an older client? Dr. Martin seems to be overlooking the warning signs associated with Mr. Chang's potential for suicide. For example, she seems to believe he is not a good candidate for "therapy" and that, at his advanced age, he should be allowed to live it as he desired. Behind this statement may lay a bias that is reflected in her work with older and younger clients. Would she be as cavalier if the client was a teenager versus someone older like Mr. Chang? Is there a reflection of values here that needs to be explicitly stated? Would you as a therapist act differently with a potential suicidal young adult than with an older one? What ethical, legal, and clinical values guide your answers?

• Many of the guidelines developed for working with older adults are weak in their understanding of cultural differences among Asian Americans, African Americans, Latino/Hispanic Americans, and Native Americans from that of their White counterparts. This is even reflected in the terms used to describe the older population. In the United States, we use the term *older adult* rather than *elder*, which is perceived negatively. Yet most people of color prefer the term *elder* because it is a sign of respect, prestige, and wisdom. Acknowledging Mr. Chang as an elder is a great honor, as advancing age confers increased respect and status in Asian culture. Contrast that with our youth-oriented society, where older people are often assigned decreased status and value. How might this information affect work with Mr. Chang?

- It is important to note the contrasting styles of Dr. Martin and that of the social worker. The social worker seems to have been able to establish a better working relationship with Mr. Chang than the psychologist. Why? To address this question, we need to look at both cultural factors that may influence the therapeutic relationship and sociodemographic differences between the provider and client.

  - Three major differences are especially important in Asian culture: age differences, gender differences, and racial/cultural differences. Mr. Chang is much older than Dr. Martin, he is a man in a relationship with a woman, and he is Chinese. In traditional Chinese culture, age is a powerful determinant of stature and influence. Younger individuals are expected to be respectful toward their elders and to play the role of student who learns from the wiser person. Chinese culture is also a patriarchal culture that values males over females, as reflected in women's more subservient relationship to men. We are not advocating these as values that must be accepted by the therapist but merely point out that age, gender, and race have a powerful effect on the working relationship. For Mr. Chang to be seen by a young, female White psychologist presents role reversals and interpersonal dilemmas that may strike at his pride and self-esteem. Dr. Martin does not appear to be aware of the cultural ramifications of her age, gender, and race on Mr. Chang. The issue, therefore, is how a therapist would overcome these potential therapeutic barriers.

  - The social worker, who is slightly older, female, and White, seemed to have greater success with Mr. Chang. As a social worker, her approach focused more on pragmatic problem solving related to his environment and social supports, which can be a more comfortable focus for elders in general and with Asian elders in particular. In addition, the social worker seemed to recognize the impact that age, gender, and cultural difference played in her interactions with Mr. Chang and appropriately altered her approach to him as a result. One might surmise that Mr. Chang did not find Dr. Martin credible (due to her lack of cultural sensitivity) but respected the work of the social worker because she seemed to understand the cultural differences and responded accordingly. Unlike Dr. Martin, who addressed the client as "Henry," the social worker never used his first name but called him "Mr. Chang." In Asian culture, the apparent formal means of addressing an elder shows respect. The social worker treated Mr. Chang in a manner that allowed him to feel respected, that his knowledge and own perceptions were important and legitimate, and confined her initial work with him to very practical and applied matters. For example, framing depression and other mental health problems as a physical illness and providing education related to its causes and treatment can be a helpful way of reducing stigma for older adults. Often the concept of medical illness is more comfortable and familiar to elders, so education that frames the issue in terms of the physical causes and effects is often better received than more psychological explanations of symptoms.

◆ It is very important for health care providers to be cognizant and knowledgeable about how aging affects the physical and psychological development and life experiences of older persons. Substance abuse is becoming an increasingly prevalent problem among older adults. Among the older cohorts of older adults, misuse of over-the-counter medications and alcohol is more common. Among younger cohorts of older adults, particularly baby boomers, illicit drug use is increasingly common. As people age, normal age-related changes in metabolic function alter the way that medications, alcohol, and other substances are metabolized by the body. As a result, intoxication can occur with fewer drinks, and medication interactions and side effects become more common, placing aging individuals at greater risk of adverse outcomes.

◆ There are many clues in the case of Mr. Chang that point to therapeutic goals in his life circumstance. First, it is important to address his current living situation. Ordinarily, an assisted living situation might ensure his safety (falls and emergency situations) and provide him once again with a social support network (decrease isolation). He is financially well off, so economics would not be a barrier. Another possibility is taking up the offer of his daughter to stay with him. Although he feels a burden, most elderly Asian parents expect and prefer to spend their later years with family. This would have to be carefully explored with Mr. Chang and his daughter, perhaps with the assistance of the social worker. Second, lessening his social isolation, especially as he seems to have been a very socially active person in the past, would be a primary goal. Could his church be enlisted to help in this regard? Would any of the congregants be able to help Mr. Chang be an active parishioner once again? What about senior centers? Third, family appears very important to Mr. Chang. Although his two sons and daughters live across the country, can they in some way alter responsibility for visits or even invite their father to rotate staying with them for brief periods of time? As a therapist, what other suggestions might you make in working with Mr. Chang?

Recommended Resources

Books and/or Articles

American Psychological Association. (2009). *Multicultural competency in geropsychology. A report of the APA Committee on Aging and its Working Group on multicultural competency in geropsychology.* Retrieved from http://www.apa.org/pi/aging/programs/pipeline/multicultural-competency.pdf

American Psychological Association, Presidential Task Force on Integrated Health Care for an Aging Population. (2008). *Blueprint for change: Achieving integrated health care for an aging population.* Retrieved from http://www.apa.org/pi/aging/programs/integrated/integrated-healthcare-report.pdf

Arnold, M. (2008). Polypharmacy and older adults: A role for psychology and psychologists. *Professional Psychology, Research and Practice, 39*(3), 283–289.

Centers for Disease Control and Prevention and National Association of Chronic Disease Directors. (2009). *The state of mental health and aging in America. Issue Brief 2: Addressing depression in older adults: Selected evidence-based programs.* Atlanta, GA: National Association of Chronic Disease Directors.

Conwell, Y., & Pearson, J. L. (2002). Suicidal behaviors in older adults, theme issue. *American Journal of Geriatric Psychiatry, 10*(4), 359–361.

Hinrichsen, G. A. (2008). Interpersonal psychotherapy as a treatment for depression in later life. *Professional Psychology: Research and Practice, 39*(3), 306–312.

Schuman, I., Schneider, A., Kantert, C., Lowe, B., & Linda, K. (2012). Physicians, attitudes, diagnostic processes and barriers regarding depression diagnosis in primary care: A systematic review of qualitative studies. *Family Practice, 29,* 255–263.

Skultety, K. M., & Zeiss, A. (2006). The treatment of depression in older adults in the primary care setting: An evidence-based review. *Health Psychology, 25,* 665–674.

Sue, D. W., & Sue, D. (2012). *Counseling the culturally diverse: Theory and practice.* Hoboken, NJ: Wiley.

Videos

National Institute of Health Senior Health. *One woman's experience with dementia.* Available at http://nihseniorhealth.gov/depression/faq/video/depression1_na.html?intro=yes

Assessments/Inventories

Kroenke, K., Spitzer, R., and Williams, J. (2001) Validity of a Brief Depression Severity Measure. *Journal of General Internal Medicine, 16*(9): 606–613.

Yesavage, J. A. (1988). Geriatric Depression Scale. *Psychopharmacology Bulletin, 24,* 709–711.

Websites/Blogs

American Psychological Association, Depression and Suicide in Older Adults Resource Guide: http://www.apa.org/pi/aging/resources/guides/depression.aspx

National Institute of Health: Senior Health—Depression: http://nihseniorhealth.gov/depression/research/01.html

National Institute of Mental Health: Older Adults Depression and Suicide Fact Sheet: http://www.nimh.nih.gov/health/publications/older-adults-depression-and-suicide-facts-fact-sheet/index.shtml

Positive Aging Resource Center: Older Adult Emotional Health: www.positiveaging.org

Substance Abuse and Mental Health Services Administration, Office of Applied Studies. Older Adults: Substance Abuse and Mental Health Problems: http://www.oas.samhsa.gov/aging.cfm

Fiction Reading

Gruen, S. (2006). *Water for elephants.* Chapel Hill, NC: Algonquin Books.

Author Index

Subject Index